# LANCASHIRE CLOCKS
# AND
# CLOCKMAKERS

## BRIAN LOOMES

DAVID & CHARLES
NEWTON ABBOT LONDON
NORTH POMFRET (VT) VANCOUVER

*By the same author*

THE WHITE DIAL CLOCK

WESTMORLAND CLOCKS AND CLOCKMAKERS

YORKSHIRE CLOCKMAKERS

ISBN 0 7153 6917 2

Library of Congress Catalog Card Number 74-20457

Set in 11 on 13pt Baskerville and printed in Great Britain by Latimer Trend & Company Ltd Plymouth for David & Charles (Holdings) Limited South Devon House  Newton Abbot  Devon

Published in the United States of America by David & Charles Inc North Pomfret  Vermont 05053  USA

Published in Canada by Douglas David & Charles Limited 132 Philip Avenue  North Vancouver  BC

# CONTENTS

# LIST OF ILLUSTRATIONS

PLATES

4

*Page*

Photographs not otherwise acknowledged are from the author's collection

### LINE DRAWINGS

# PREFACE

Lancashire is one of the most important counties in the history of provincial British horology, and one of the least appreciated. The late A. J. Hawkes made an interesting contribution to the subject in *The Clockmakers and Watchmakers of Wigan*, a book which today is very hard to come by. The late J. L. Hobbs recorded his observations on the clockmakers of North Lonsdale, and some of these were published in the Transactions of the Cumberland & Westmorland Antiquarian & Archaeological Society (1935–9). His friend and colleague, J. Melville, helped me locate certain other of his notes which were never published. The late F. Buckley recorded horological items from early Liverpool directories and newspapers, and his manuscript notes on these are preserved at the Guildhall, London. But no one has apparently attempted a systematic recording of the makers of the whole county, which seems to me a good reason to try to do so. Hence this book.

Numerous friends and correspondents have assisted and it would not be right to omit mention of some of these. Most of the Lancashire museums were helpful in supplying lists of their local clocks and watches, and L. A. Burman and O. N. F. Fairclough of the Liverpool Museum were especially helpful. R. Sharpe-France, Archivist of the Lancashire Record Office, kindly gave permission for me to quote extracts from certain inventories, which give vital insight into the background. The Archives Department of Westminster City Libraries have given permission for me to quote from the records of Gillows of Lancaster and to use an illustration from the estimate books in their possession.

My grateful thanks are due to my colleague, Peter Nutt, for once more assisting with the research, and to Roger Trunkfield for similar help; to my friends Brian Morison and David Barker for help and encouragement; to E. L. Edwardes and E. J. Tyler for their patience and courtesy; to Wilfred Spencer for most interesting details about his clockmaking ancestors; to Alan Treherne, Dr John Penfold, Chris Bailey, L. F. Miller, H. E. G. Roberts, M. J. Gandy, R. A. Garnett—who all assisted in various ways. Most of all I must thank my dear wife, who suffered it all.

# INTRODUCTION

This book attempts to summarise all the reliable information I have been able to assemble concerning Lancashire clockmakers. Watchmakers have also been included. Whilst the two trades were usually separate, it is often difficult to know from a directory entry which trade a particular man followed (unless examples of his work are known). Therefore it is not always possible to separate the two trades in a work of this type. A clockmaker often sold watches, and vice versa, but a man who made one seldom made the other.

Watchmaking was a specialist craft on its own, so whilst watchmakers are included in the lists, this book does not claim to be a work on watchmaking, and it has proved impossible to include men engaged in the many specialist facets of the watch part-making system. Not only were they far too numerous, but a man who made watch hands, for instance, did not sign his work and therefore to record his name is pointless. An indication of the depth of that specialisation may be seen in the occasional very early mention of it which I have included. As early as 1640 William Topping specialised as a watchspring maker; William Winstanley was another working in 1675; William Laithwaite was a watch-case maker in 1710, and others are mentioned where they seemed sufficiently early to be noteworthy.

That the book must be incomplete I am well aware. New names will come to light as time goes by, but it seems better to make available what is known than to delay for twenty years in order to claim greater completeness. I have included only data which I have been able to confirm personally or which come from a reliable source. The standard lists contain many errors, and there seems to me to be no merit in perpetuating these.

8

The period covered is from the beginnings of domestic clockmaking in the late seventeenth century up to 1860, which period should be long enough to include any real maker of Lancashire clocks. Those sold after 1860 were almost all imported clocks. Close on 2,500 names are listed.

A few words about the sources of the information may help the reader in his use of it. Firstly names have been noted down over the years from actual clocks and watches, along with an estimate of the period or date, if known. Secondly data have been gathered from old records of many kinds, which assist in establishing positive dates of a maker's life. A third source has been directories, though the precise addresses given in some of these can be seen to be unreliable by the variations in successive issues. The dates given should not be taken to indicate any finality except where dates of birth and death are known.

The designations of clockmaker and watchmaker are used only where there is good reason to specify. Where not specified the man comes under the general trade term of a clock and watchmaker. The great majority were watchmakers; many of them probably worked anonymously for a master.

Many entries contain details of marriages or baptisms of children. Since a tradesman could not usually afford to marry until his apprenticeship was ended, and since he often did so as soon as that time came, marriage entries are frequently a very useful guide to the period when a man began to work on his own. Names of wives are given, when known, to help distinguish a man from others of the same name.

The text material is intended as a guide largely for the beginner (or for those not familiar with Lancashire clocks), and it is hoped that this together with the biographical data should enable him to establish the period of his clock.

Books have already been published on clockmaking in several districts of Britain—Cornwall, Devon, Somerset, Leicestershire, Suffolk, Yorkshire, Westmorland, as well as Wales and Scotland (see Bibliography). The regional variations and fashions to emerge from these county works are fascinating, and illustrate that the country's clockmaking skills and activities did not begin and end in London, as some older books would have us believe. To those whose only knowledge of northern clocks has come from London-based books, which saw Lancashire clocks as the elephantine buffoons of the clock world, I hope this book may help redress the balance. To those interested in the overall national picture of clockmaking, it is hoped this book may provide a few more pieces of the puzzle. To those interested in local history it may give a further means of insight. But my foremost aim is to help the owner of a Lancashire clock to identify its maker and period, and to answer some of the questions which beset the beginner and which some of the more technical books take for granted as common knowledge. A brief Glossary explains the specialist meaning of a few terms which may not be familiar to every reader.

# I

# THE CLOCKMAKERS

Admirable as the skills of the earlier clockmakers unquestionably were, it is important that we should get them into perspective. For a blacksmith it is a far cry from making horseshoes and agricultural hardware to developing a craft which produces finely finished clocks. It was said of Thomas Tompion, the Bedfordshire blacksmith who became a famous London watchmaker (we Northerners have been known to simulate ignorance as to who Tompion was): 'The great Tompion had never make (sic) watches, had he not first made hobnails.' There may be truth in this, but we must guard against the inference that the Tompions of this world progressed from making cartwheels to clockwheels by sheer excellence of manual dexterity and a 'true' eye.

A clockmaker, gifted as he may have been, was just as reliant on the tools at his disposal as on his skills, and it is not always fully realised what an extensive supply of tools he had available even from early times. For instance, the newcomer to clocks is often most deeply impressed by the clockmaker's skill at cutting symmetrically toothed wheels—which in fact he did by machine! The wheel-cutting engine was supposedly invented by Robert Hooke about 1670, though we know that more primitive forms of tooth-spacing devices existed long before this. The wheel-cutter enabled the selected number of teeth to be cut evenly around the wheel perimeter. Though the wheels still required finishing by hand, the 'engine' performed the measuring and spacing so often wrongly regarded as breathtaking miracles of handiwork.

Other highly specialised tools were developed for many of the

11

individual processes of clockmaking, and, more to the point, a very important centre for the making of these tools was Lancashire. This specialised trade in tools for watch- and clockmaking, and also part-making, grew to the point where, by the late eighteenth century, Lancashire supplied much of Europe with these materials. The tool and supplies catalogues, which survive today from that period, show what an enormous range of equipment was available. Catalogues exist from John Wyke of Liverpool (about 1770), Peter Stubs of Warrington (about 1800), and James and Thomas Jones of Prescot (early 1800s). Peter Stubs charged £12 for his cheapest wheel-cutting engine, £14 14s for the largest size; entries in his despatch books over one week in 1812 show shipments of items to Sheffield, Grantham, Birmingham, Chester, Norwich, Coventry, Lincoln and Keighley.

Stubs was first and foremost a file-maker. Files at that time were far more important than we might realise from their place in our modern world. Today machine processes have taken over where in the past hundreds of different types of files were used by all manner of tradesmen, not metal-workers alone. Stubs files became so famous for their high quality that other file-makers, notably in Sheffield, ultimately forged the PS monogram on their own products to try to steal some of the Stubs market. Later Stubs supplied other tools, including clock- and watchmaking tools and parts, and sold them even to Birmingham, London and Coventry, the great clock- and watchmaking centres.

Thomas Hatton, the famous London watchmaker, could already write in 1773: 'The tools made in Lancashire are the best executed.' By 1830 even Birmingham had to admit the superiority of Warring-ton tools. Pinion wire, brass corner-spandrel castings, pillars, wheel-blanks—almost any ready-made clock parts could be bought in by the later eighteenth century, with just the hand-finishing work to be be done. With watches, part-making was even more specialised, and many hundreds, even thousands, of people worked at making small component watch parts such as hands, cocks, springs, pillars, verges, and dozens of other items, supplied to the 'watchmakers' who in fact were largely assemblers and retailers.

We now glance briefly at the evidence of just how well-equipped the early clockmakers were. From wills and inventories of the goods they left, we can see not only the extent of the tools they had but the relative values placed on them. The inventory of the goods of Thomas Bridge of Bolton, clockmaker, taken at his death on 28 February 1717(-18), amounts to £17 6s 6d—the total of his worldly possessions including his stock-in-trade and work tools. It is significant that the most valuable item by far was 'the Ingen—£4.0s.0d.' (ie the 'engine'—wheel-cutting engine). Additionally he possessed a 'grett lath' (large lathe) and a smaller one; 'sandbox and flasks'— presumably for casting his own brass; a weighbeam; four pairs of vices (£1 4s), two turn benches; two pairs of hand vices; files; screw-plates (for making his own screws); two pairs of 'balows' (bellows); a steady and two stocks; four hammers; five pairs of forging tongs; a 'nail tool' (nailmaking tool); and 'other worke twoles' (tools). Such a man was a self-contained factory unit. All he needed were metal supplies. For comparison it is interesting to note that he also possessed a case of pistols valued at 10s. His wheel-cutting engine was as valuable as *eight* pairs of pistols!

Most interesting also is a number of old clocks he had—not new clocks that he was making, but 'iron belonging to two ould Church Clocks 4s.0d.', and 'one second-hand clock £1.5s.0d.'. It is debatable whether the latter term means a clock with a seconds hand or a second-hand clock, but probably the latter, as a new eight-day clock with seconds hand would have been worth about £4, and even a thirty-hour one would have been over £2.

The inventory of Peter Aspinall of Wigan, 'spurrier' (spur-maker) and clockmaker, dying in 1677, listed files, hammers and suchlike blacksmithing tools in his shop—his workshop, of course, not a retail shop. Thomas Clarke of Ashton-under-Lyne, clockmaker, who died in 1712, had his own forge too, and left 'one engine' (£1 10s), many files, forging tools, vices, lathe, six hammers, '2 paire of compasses, 2 paire of dividers, 3 paire of plyers, 2 scrapers and a ffroster' (a froster may well have been a matting tool, used to get the roughened texture for a dial centre), saws, hand shears and other tools, and amusingly one mousetrap! John Wright of Whalley, clock-maker, died in 1755; his engine was valued at £1 5s 6d and was the

13

most valuable single item in his workshop out of a total value of tools and furnishings of £12.

Joseph Pryor of Liverpool, a well-to-do master watchmaker, died in 1720, leaving in addition to his personal effects (such as one silver-hilted sword at 15s and one coat of arms in the lobby at 2s), watchmakers' tools to the value of 10s. He was in his 70s then and no doubt 'retired', hence the small stock of tools. George Taylor of Liverpool, watchmaker, who died in 1722, left a more realistic set of tools valued at £11 6s 7d—and an 8d lanthorn to work by. Thomas Smoult of Lancaster, watchmaker, died in 1749 leaving watchmakers' 'implements' to the value of £10.

That the working tools often formed a substantial proportion of the value of a man's total effects is especially apparent amongst the less wealthy tradesmen, where their value is proportionately very high. The picture sometimes conjured up of these men producing masterpieces in metal almost with their bare hands is erroneous. This is not to decry the considerable skills such men possessed in the use of their tools, but just to get the picture into perspective a little. Given the raw materials, they possessed the means of working them.

Whilst examining inventories, let us consider briefly what stocks of watches and clocks a maker might have on hand. The answer in most cases is very little. A clockmaker would normally make a clock to order, rather than make up stocks ahead of his requirements to sell from a retail shop. For most men the 'shop' they had was their *work*shop. One or two did have retail shops, but these were rather jewellers, silversmiths, hardwaremen, in other words shopkeepers who also worked at their own branch of the trade.

Thomas Smoult of Lancaster, who died in 1749, was a shopkeeper as well as a working watchmaker. His inventory shows sales stock of silver plate, gold rings, old plate, jeweller's work, etc. The only clock he had was a longcase clock for his own use in the kitchen. John Brewer of Rochdale was a hardwareman and working clockmaker. He died in 1720. His inventory lists a whole variety of items typical of the stock of such a dealer, including powderhorns, whips, frying-pans, horn buttons, horn and ivory combs, razors, spurs, buckles, rules, curtain rings, candlesticks, smoothing irons, joiners' tools, hundreds of thousands of nails, even coffin handles, but not a single clock in stock, though he did make (or supply) them. George Taylor of Liverpool (died 1722) had just one clock and case of his own, value £5. Joseph Pryor (died 1720) also had one clock and case (£4 10s) of his own, and 'two spring clocks' (bracket clocks) valued at £14, much higher in value than the longcase clock. We can deduce from what we know of contemporary prices that the longcase clocks which Taylor and Pryor owned were both 8-day ones, 30-hour ones being about half of the stated value. Pryor also had 'a parcel of watches, movements and cases' at £16.

Thomas Clarke of Windle (died 1726) had 'part of a clock, a watch and tools' at £2. James Barton of Ormskirk, died 1715, left two clocks at £3 10s the two. Thomas Clarke of Ashton-under-Lyne died in 1712 leaving a spring clock 'part work'd and part unworked', £1 7s, and another new clock almost finished at the same figure. These examples illustrate sufficiently that only a very small stock was carried, and that mostly in clocks in the process of being made. The varying prices are difficult to correlate since one does not know how reliable was the valuation made by the appraisers.

Another interesting feature shown in these inventories is one hinted at earlier, that these men often seem to have had stocks of *old* clocks and *old* parts. James Whittaker of Middleton (1720), 'two old clocks—£1.4s.0d.'. Thomas Bridge of Bolton (1717), 'iron belonging to two ould church clocks 4s.0d.'. Thomas Clarke of Ashton-under-Lyne (1712), '12 pound of old iron 1s.0d.', and 'cast work and in odd brass 7s.6d.'. John Wright of Whalley (1755), 'all old and new brass 12s.6d.'. Even with a watchmaker (Joseph Pryor, 1720) we see: old iron 120lb, 10s; old lead 120lb, 7s 6d. George Taylor the watchmaker (1722) had pewter by weight to the value of £4 2s and brass to the value of 3s 4d.

What is showing up is the tremendous wastage of old-fashioned, badly worn or broken clocks which would frequently be turned in to the clockmaker in part-payment for a new clock. This could be one strong reason why examples of lantern clocks from this area are almost non-existent today. Being old-fashioned, such clocks would have been turned in for their value as scrap, the brass melted down

15

and re-cast by the clockmaker. This is especially important when we consider that such a trade-in could reduce the new cost of say £2 10s for a 30-hour longcase clock (without case) by about £1. The old steel or iron might well have been traded in by the clockmaker to set off against new iron parts from his supplier. This set-off would be considerable, when we think of the brass and steel in an old 8-day clock, where the weights alone can weigh 28lb. When John Wignall of Ormskirk supplied a new 8-day clock and case in 1804 for £7 14s, he allowed £1 1s for an old clock taken in part-exchange.

A clockmaker would usually begin his training by being apprenticed. Usually the period was seven years and we generally assume this to have taken place at the age of fourteen, so that a man would be free from his training at the age of twenty-one. Sometimes, however, children were apprenticed as early as twelve years of age, and there is little doubt that on occasions the apprenticeship system was seen by the master as a way of obtaining cheap labour and by the parents as an opportunity of lessening the burden on their household expenses, since the child usually had free food and lodgings in the master's house as part of his wages. However the premium payable to a master for taking an apprentice could be as high as £30.

The Lancashire background is different from that of most counties because of the very high concentration in the Liverpool–Prescot–Warrington area of labour engaged in the making of tools, parts and finished watches, and to a lesser degree of clocks. To indicate where part-making ends and assembly begins is far from simple. Most part-makers worked under the outwork system, working in their own homes rather than in the employer's factory. Raw materials or unfinished parts would be delivered to them perhaps weekly, and finished goods would be collected at the same time. Payment was made on the amount of work done—by piecework.

The outworker might work largely for one master. Alternatively, as he was really a freelance worker, he might be producing for more than one master at a time. Similarly he himself, in busy times, might employ assistants or sub-contract work. In practice workers often had to borrow money from the masters ahead of their production rates: this meant that they would be permanently in debt to the master,

16

which debt they could hope to reduce only very slowly, and before it was cleared no doubt some minor setback, such as a spell of illness, would oblige them to ask for a further advance. It is often said that this situation suited the masters very well, since the outworkers' indebtedness meant that they were more or less tied exclusively to a master. The line between prosperity and starvation was a thin one for many such Lancashire outworkers. Many of them however had a small-holding or ran a small farm, which at least provided them with food.

Our concern in this book is with clockmaking rather than the making of parts or tools. The making of watch parts was a particularly specialised and complex business and we cannot attempt to study that here. It is important however for us to appreciate this background since the majority of the very large numbers of workers in the clock and watch industry in Lancashire were outworkers engaged in watch part-making. Hence statistics, which at first sight might suggest that Lancashire clockmakers outnumbered those of any other county, can be recognised as very misleading. For instance the 1831 census showed 1,114 clockmakers in Lancashire, 449 in Yorkshire. In 1851, Lancashire had 3,165, Yorkshire 835. Yet Yorkshire was a much larger clock-selling county than Lancashire in terms of retailing of clocks—simply because of its larger population. Compared with the 3,165 Lancashire workers in the 1851 census, the 1851 directory lists only 450 (excluding part-makers). The difference of course lies in the fact that the 450 were masters and the remainder (the vast majority) were probably outworkers making watch parts. These latter came under many specialised categories, which included watch-balance makers, barrel makers, bolt makers, casemakers, spring makers, cleaners, cock makers, finishers, frame finishers, fuzee finishers, hand makers, pillar makers, wheel makers and so on, in all twenty-four different subdivisions of watch-part making.

After 1851 the huge numbers in this trade began to reduce slowly, on account of increasing competition from imported items. Lancashire supplied much of the trade in England (including London) and abroad both with watch parts and tools, but in assessing Lancashire's position with regard to retail clock*selling*, we must discount these specialist component makers.

B                                                                        17

It is an interesting reflection that when the average person sees a clock, he bases his estimation of it on the dial and the case. These are the very items in which most clockmakers took little or no part. Dials were made by engravers or dial painters, and cases by case-makers. Clockmakers with better taste or wealthier customers ordered from the better suppliers. When the admirer says: 'What a beautiful clock. Old so-and-so must have been a good maker,' what he really means is: 'Old so-and-so must have had the good sense and finance to use a capable dial engraver and a good casemaker.'

From the early eighteenth century the clockmaker became increasingly a finisher and assembler of parts produced by specialist suppliers, rather than an actual maker of parts. This applies most strongly to the more famous makers, London ones too. The more famous the maker, the less likely it is that he would spend time working with a file; instead he would entrust such 'menial' tasks to his journeymen. The master's role was to decide, influenced of course by his customers, what type of clock to make, and the resulting clock was created from his own discriminating judgement; its components may have come from several different workshops. Perhaps such a craftsman can be considered successful when he has prospered enough to afford to employ others to perform this craftwork for him, under his supervision.

Even from early times clockmakers had available to them quite an extensive literature on horology and mathematics. The planning of an apparently complex clock of great ingenuity was a considerably easier task than might first seem to be the case. From the early days of his apprenticeship a clockmaker would make notes and working diagrams, so that once he had seen a clock with a certain type of unusual layout, making one along similar lines was simplified by reference to his notes. The making may still have required great skill; but we must recognise that the man with the skills to construct a complex clock need not necessarily have been a brilliant 'inventor' too.

Clockmakers were often very competent at their trade. Some were superb craftsmen. Some were botchers and bunglers—oh yes! We are often apt to forget this side and conclude with a too rosy picture

18

of thousands of talented and dedicated geniuses. Life in Lancashire was seldom like that. Poverty was never far away from the doors, even of clockmakers; clocks were amongst the first luxuries that people would forego during hard times. A man with no work to go to could manage very well without a clock to get him there!

In these conditions making another shilling was at times more important than adding a few more artistic flourishes. Some men failed. Some left the trade or took on secondary occupations. John Simpson of Lancaster found a soldier's life more rewarding. The story of John Spencer III (told me by his descendant, Mr Wilfred Spencer) is an interesting illustration of this less publicised side. Initially a third-generation clockmaker, Spencer gradually backed out in favour of innkeeping, from which he presumably found it easier to make a living; we must remember that this is the time when cheaper foreign clocks began to flood into Britain. Some very un-flattering comments were made concerning his abilities when in 1833 an examination was held concerning his farm at Birchenlee, near Colne, which he had sold. He was then trying to claim that he thought the sale had been only a mortgaging and that he had been cheated on account of his simple-mindedness. In fact he seems to have been rather a rogue. In the words of one witness, a stonemason, Spencer 'was not considered anything of a genius, but had abilities sufficient to learn the clock dressing business from his father. Spencer was rather slow at the business, but seemed tolerably well acquainted how to put a clock together. On one occasion . . . he found Spencer engaged in putting a clock together. That the clock was an eight-day repeater and struck wrong. That Spencer looked at the back to try to discover the reason, that on seeing him in search of something he (witness) asked him what he was looking for. Spencer replied that the clock always struck 12 and he (Spencer) could not find out the cause, and that the clock was of a different construction to those he (Spencer) had been accustomed to. That he told Spencer the clock wanted a spring, and he (witness) put his finger to the place, and then it would strike. Spencer said he had nothing that would answer for a spring, however at the request of the owner's wife, he (witness) put in the spring.'

19

It is interesting that a clockmaker who could be shown his job by a stonemason, even one familiar with clocks, could still be said to be able to make clocks 'tolerably well'. John Spencer fortunately was not typical, and many Lancashire clockmakers were craftsmen of the highest order. However it is through these interesting glimpses into their lives, which we get only on rare occasions, that we see them more clearly. James Taylor of Ashton-under-Lyne, who on his death in 1813 at the age of 89 left 15 children, 103 grandchildren and 61 great-grandchildren, appears to have been almost as productive of offspring as of clocks. When we picture Stephen Simpson's shop in Church Street, Preston, with its automated ram above the doorway striking the hours on a bell with its horns night and day, we might be permitted to wonder whether the neighbours regarded 'the Tup's Clock' and the ingenuity of its maker as a blessing or a curse.

# 2

# THE CLOCKS

In this chapter we will consider briefly two aspects of Lancashire clocks: firstly a few elementary stylistic features, which should help the beginner fix the period of his clock; secondly any unusual or distinctive characteristics in which Lancashire clocks differ from those of other counties.

Let us begin with a few points about lantern clocks. Surviving lantern clocks of known Lancashire make are so exceedingly rare that the beginner may be forgiven if he does not know what one looks like. In most other northern counties they are equally, or almost equally, rare; yet books by southern authors seem to be unaware of this fact. I do not know of a single surviving example, though one assumes that some do survive. (One by John Livesey of Bolton is recorded, said to be about 1700, though I do not know its whereabouts.)

Surviving domestic clocks of any sort are very rare in Lancashire before 1700. This is partly because the pre-1700 clock-owning population was quite small, so few clocks were made here at this time. Of those made before 1700 very many were later traded in, their scrap value set against the cost of a new clock. As already shown, there is widespread evidence in inventories of this trading in of old or worn-out items. Wastage was therefore very high amongst clocks which at this time were far from numerous anyway. To a lesser degree the same applies to clocks from 1700 to 1750, though wastage here was not quite so severe. It does not in any case altogether explain the almost total absence of lantern clocks.

In Lancashire we are concerned really only with domestic clocks

21

after 1660, as pre-1660 (pre-pendulum that is) examples would be very few indeed. I use the general date of 1660, although it is now widely accepted (on the evidence of Ahasuerus Fromanteel's advertisement) that 1658 was the year of the introduction of the pendulum to this country. In fact it is not impossible that pendulum clocks were made shortly before 1658.

In the South, lantern clocks of pre-1660 style and origins continued to be made along modified principles to accept the new pendulum, but within a few years the introduction of the long pendulum rendered the lantern form, with its vulnerably exposed ropes, weights and pendulum, a none-too-practical proposition in an everyday household setting. In Lancashire the absence of this pre-1660 tradition meant that there was not the same 'school' there to modify, and true pendulum clocks of longcase form were much more likely to be introduced as a complete concept from the start. Hence in this area the 30-hour *plate-framed* pendulum clock *with case* became the standard cheaper type of clock almost from its invention, whilst in the South the even cheaper lantern clock lingered, though obsolescent, into the mid-eighteenth century; its development there into the posted-framed or 'birdcage' type of 30-hour clock was hardly seen in the North.

Apart from the fact that its pendulum, weights and ropes were sensibly enclosed in a case, the northern 30-hour longcase clock of the late seventeenth century was almost always a far more costly item than its southern contemporary, the lantern clock. Both types could be bought for about £2 10s (in 1700), but the additional cost of a case would put up the total price of the cased clock by a further £1 or so. We northerners find it puzzling if not distressing to read glowing descriptions of the virtues of the anachronistic southern lantern clock of this period in the same books which decry as unworthy of attention the 30-hour country longcase clock, the more so since whilst the lantern clock was already dying out the 30-hour longcase was just beginning to blossom into a form which lasted for almost two centuries more.

The 8-day clock was a much more costly item than either the lantern or the 30-hour clock, being almost twice the price of the latter. Hence it was much scarcer in Lancashire in this early period. The earliest Lancashire clocks we might expect to come across would be of the type illustrated on page 33 (*left*). This one is by James Whittaker. They would have a 9- or 10-inch-square brass dial (this one in fact is 9 inches) and would probably be of 30-hour duration, as this is. James Whittaker worked at Middleton near Manchester, where he died in 1720. No place-name appears on the dial, despite the fact that it was legally compulsory for all clockmakers to put their name and abode on their clocks. The omission is not uncommon in Lancashire, as elsewhere in the North, and is especially common amongst clockmakers from a small town or village (as Middleton then was), the name of which would be unknown twenty miles away. Characteristics which help identify clocks of this age are small dial size, all-over engraved dial centre, twin-cherub corner spandrels, calendar (when present) shown through a square or circular box above the VI.

This clock of course is a single-hander, telling time to the nearest quarter-hour, each quarter-hour division being marked off on the inner edge of the chapter ring. Two-handed clocks, such as we are accustomed to today, were also made at this time, both as 30-hour and 8-day clocks. A two-handed 30-hour clock, however, would be more common perhaps twenty years from this time, and at the period of the James Whittaker clock the one-hander would be the more common of the 30-hour type. Eight-day clocks were always two-handed.

The features indicated above were soon to change. Spandrels of one design seldom remain in fashion for more than twenty years. The twin-cherub style was probably the earliest in the county, followed by the 'mask' type as seen on page 51; several patterns of the mask type occur, mostly in the 1710–40 period. One pattern appearing in the 1750–60 period is known as the 'four seasons' spandrel, each cornerpiece being a figure illustrative of the season. A large cherub-head pattern also occurred in mid-century (quite different from the London cherub-head style). A design of an urn supported by two birds appeared about 1730–50 (page 51).

By 1700 (a little later on some 30-hour clocks), dials had dropped

23

the engraved centre, and this instead was 'matted' or 'frosted', ie given a roughened even surface rather like a sandpaper finish. Elaborate engraving had changed to complete plainness, sometimes with ringed turnings around the winding-holes (page 101)—though the engraved decoration around the winding-holes on page 51 is most unusual. The 'half-quarters' (halfway points between each quarter-hour) were often marked in the early years of the eighteenth century by an asterisk, fleur-de-lis or similar indicator, as can be seen on pages 51a and 51b. The reasons for the half-quarter markers are unknown, though recently-uncovered data suggest that the half-quarter of an hour was the smallest unit of time in general (conversational) use at that time. Minutes and seconds were of more interest to scientists and astronomers than to the average person, who would have made appointments by the quarter-hour or half-quarter-hour rather than by minutes.

The quarter-hour divisions, seen on the inner edge of the James Whittaker one-handed chapter ring, also appear on two-handed clocks during the early eighteenth century (pages 51 and 101). Then, about 1740, the quarter markers begin to be left off, whilst the half-hour markers remain.

The quarter-hour divisions, which might seem superfluous on two-handed clocks, were probably retained for this period of a generation or so to meet the needs of those who were unsophisticated in their familiarity with clocks and their need for fine divisions of time. In the late seventeenth century, or even in the early eighteenth, a clock bought into a household may well have been the first one that family had ever owned. By the second quarter of the eighteenth century a generation of potential purchasers familiar with clocks from birth had matured. For them the reading of time from a clock dial had become instinctive, and consequently the need to simplify a dial down to a single-handed reading had greatly diminished; by 1760 the single-handed markings on two-handed dials had disappeared. The two-handed clock dial catering for the younger or more sophisticated public was standard by mid-century.

However single-handers were still made as late as 1770, especially in rural areas for a less-sophisticated, older or poorer clientele—they were a little cheaper to make than two-handers. Single-handers are very unusual in Lancashire after 1770. In the South, one-handers persisted into the nineteenth century; but in the North as a whole they did not. The carved stone which John Spencer II of Colne placed over his door bearing the date 1760 also bears the design of a clock dial; this sign, by which his customers were to recognise a typical clock, shows a one-hander. An understanding of the reasons for, and period of, one-handed clocks is important as the beginner is often tempted to attribute to them a far greater age and scarcity than they merit.

Page 51a is illustrative of several other interesting features of this period. The dial is an arched one, yet the arch is a separate section added on to the square. The arched dial came into fashion about 1720. A clockmaker holding a stock of square dials was able to sell them as plain square ones or with added arch. A clock with a separate arch is often of this early period as later arched dials were usually made as a single sheet.

The arch of the Burgess clock has a calendar dial, which is very seldom in this position except during this early eighteenth-century period when makers were experimenting with uses for this new arched area. Long link arms were needed to operate a calendar dial in the arch, and it was far easier to position the calendar just above the VI numeral, which became almost the standard position for it by mid-century. The calendar date was normally shown through a square (sometimes circular) hole just above the VI until about 1760; then from about 1760 onwards by a mouth-type aperture (see pages 51 and 101); by 1770 a pointer indicator was often preferred as an option to the mouth aperture, as on page 119.

The brass moon dial (above the VI on the Burgess clock) is known as a 'Halifax moon', or halfpenny moon (it was popular in the Halifax area), and this type was normally positioned below the XII, occupying the space which a seconds dial might otherwise take. By mid-century the moon phases were more commonly shown on a painted disc in the arch (pages 101 and 119).

The dial by Standring of Bolton shows the next step along the path of stylistic development. This clock is unusual in having an extra

25

train of wheels to chime the quarter hours—known as a 'ting-tang' chime. It plays 'ting-tang' on two bells once at quarter-past, twice at half-past, three times at quarter to, and four times on the hour, followed by the hour-count which is struck on a third bell. Quarter-chiming clocks and musical clocks are very uncommon, though sometimes one finds an ordinary striking clock which was converted to a musical one in Victorian times. Such a converted clock is nothing more than a fake, although an old one perhaps. The Standring clock is quite original.

The dial style is reasonably typical of the mid-century, having a matted centre with just a small amount of engraving work, here being the motif of a lion and a unicorn.

In the arch is a motto: 'Time flies, pursue it man, for why, thy days are but a span.' Such reflections on the fleeting nature of time and man's transitory state were popular on Lancashire (and Yorkshire) brass-dial clocks of the later eighteenth century; one rhyme on a brass-dial clock of about 1790 by John Clifton of Liverpool reads: 'Time shews the way of life's decay.' The dial of the clock by Peter Fearnley of Wigan (page 101) bears the legend: 'Time is valuable. Tempus Fugit. The man is yet unborn who duly weighs an hour.'

By 1760 the matted dial centre has begun to give way to a new exuberance of engraving work. The engraving of the dial centre is now quite lavish, often expertly and beautifully done, but sometimes to the point where it can be difficult to make out the position of the hands. This is sometimes referred to as 'over-engraving'. The heavily engraved centre is sometimes criticised as a sign of late 'decadence' by those accustomed to London clocks, where the engraved centre was not used at this period, but of course engraved centres were normal on Midlands and northern clocks.

The dial of the Peter Fearnley clock has a centre with a superbly engraved design, but here the clockmaker has taken the most unusual step of going one stage further and actually cutting out the engraved pattern as a piece of fretwork of the highest calibre. The dial centre is then backed with red velvet giving a really striking appearance. This fretting of the dial centre is very unusual and the reader is unlikely to come across other instances of it.

26

The Peter Fearnley dial (page 101) has a centre seconds-hand, sometimes called a 'sweep' seconds-hand, and also has a centre date-hand. So four hands radiate from the centre—an interesting idea, but not such a practical one, as multiple hands make for poor legibility, and on an already elaborate dial centre this is not good design. Nevertheless it is a superb clock and many a collector would be delighted to own it. The clock is showing six minutes to two on the twenty-first day of the month.

The spandrels on the Fearnley clock are of large rococo design, the centre roughly resembling a question mark. This is a common pattern on Lancashire clocks between about 1760 and 1780, especially on 8-day clocks with painted moon dials in the arch, as here. The method of indicating minutes on dials by about 1770 has normally changed from the full minute band (as on page 51) to simpler dots, marked out more easily with a drill, as on page 119.

An interesting Lancashire practice, though not one confined purely to this county, was to give a 30-hour clock the appearance of a more costly 8-day one by providing it with dummy winding-squares. Visitors seeing the dial would think the clock was more costly than it really was—an instance of eighteenth-century snobbery.

Sometimes sham winding-squares were marked out just by the engraving on the dial. Sometimes actual holes were cut through and real winding-squares fixed, which of course could not turn but were simply attached by wire sprigs behind the dial. These appear on both brass and painted dial clocks, mostly in the later years of the eighteenth century. I have seen them on clocks by Thomas Williams of Preston, Stephen Simpson of Greta Bridge, and others. The dial by John Grundy of Whalley on page 119 is an example of a 30-hour clock looking like an 8-day one, as is that on page 51 by Browne of Liverpool.

The Grundy clock dates from about 1775. The spandrels are of a most unusual pattern and so do not help greatly in dating it. The engraving of the dial centre suggests that this is after 1760, when this type of engraving became popular—as with the Fearnley clock, though Grundy's engraving is neither as elaborate nor as finely executed. There is another similarity in the dial: the minutes are marked

27

by dots, not by a double engraved band. Dots were quicker, easier, cheaper. When the painted dial was introduced, about 1770, this is the type of minute marking they always used, and it seems possible that the makers of brass-dial clocks copied the idea of dotted minutes from the painted dial. It is a useful tip, almost always applicable, that dotted minutes on a brass-dial clock date it as post-1770. This applies in Lancashire, though perhaps not nationally.

The calendar dial above the VI has a pointer, rather than the earlier aperture system. A calendar pointer, as here, is also normally a sign of a post-1770 clock. (The centre date-pointer of the Fearnley clock is of a different type and not included in this generalisation.)

Hands on brass-dial clocks have so far always been made of steel, and the clocks illustrated show typical examples. The straight minute hands of the Burgess, Browne and Standring clocks develop into a serpentine shape by about 1760–70, as on clocks by Grundy and Fearnley. Brass would be used, for example, for the date-hand on the Fearnley dial purely to help distinguish it from the time-hands. So far, we may notice, hands do not match, the hour-hand being quite different in shape from the minute-hand.

Simple 30-hour clocks of the Grundy type still retain the old locking-wheel striking system, the count-wheel being positioned outside the plates at the back of the movement. Some books unintentionally give the impression that because this was the oldest striking system, clocks which have it must be early ones. In fact 30-hour clocks almost always have locking-plate (or count-wheel, another name for the same thing) striking, even as late as 1860.

The painted dial, which appeared shortly after 1770, consisted of an iron dial sheet covered with a hard layer of fine white paint and then overpainted with coloured or gilt painted decorations in the corners and in the arch. Whilst there were a few makers of painted dials in the North, the great majority of Lancashire clockmakers bought them from Birmingham, the main manufacturing centre. The clockmaker himself did not make painted dials, but for some years he did continue to make his own movements, just as he had made them for brass-dial clocks. It is not true that because painted dials came from a 'factory' the movements behind them must also

28

have been factory-made. In the late eighteenth and early nineteenth centuries movements were still made, or at the very least still finished and assembled, by the clockmaker himself. The presence of an iron fixing bracket (called a falseplate) behind some (mainly early) 8-day painted dials is often an indication of a hand-made movement. By the 1840s complete clocks (dials with movements) could be bought wholesale by the 'clockmaker', who by this time was more a retailer and servicer. Of course there was no need for a false-plate on such later factory-supplied clocks. The falseplate was sold with the dial to help the clockmaker fit his individually made move-ment to the dial.

In most northern counties the painted dial had become so popular by 1785 that brass-dial clocks were very much in the minority. In Lancashire there seems to have been a certain conservatism, in that the brass-dial clock was still common in the 1780s and 1790s, mainly now on the more imposing and costly 8-day arched-dial clocks. By 1800, however, very few brass-dial clocks were still being made, except for the regulator or semi-regulator type, which had a single-sheet brass dial, often circular in shape. The regulator was a time-piece (ie non-striking) made with special emphasis on precision, often for the clockmaker's own use, or for scientists, astronomers, etc, and usually of very plain appearance. Decoration was subordinated to performance, and many regulators have special types of escape-ment or pendulum for precision timekeeping.

Painted-dial clocks retain the type of numbering used on brass-dial ones in their early period, 1770 to 1800. Shortly after 1800, hour numbers begin to appear in Arabic characters, and when this hap-pens the 5 and 10 minute numerals are often omitted: minutes are marked only at 15, 30, 45 and 60. About 1830, Arabic hour numbers fall from favour and hours are now marked once more by Roman numbers, as they were before 1800, but with one major difference—minutes cease to be numbered at all. This variation in numbering style is a very helpful aid to dating painted-dial clocks, though other features must be taken into account too. (For a full treatment of this subject see my book *The White Dial Clock*.)

Early hands, as we have already seen, were made of steel, being

29

hand-cut and filed by the clockmaker, who made them to his own individual pattern whilst conforming to a strict general style. By 1800 steel hands of matching pattern have arrived, the minute-hand being now a longer and slimmer version of the hour-hand. By 1820 brass hands begin to appear, again of matching pattern, and these soon became standard on all longcase clocks from now on. In 1822 a customer of Isaac Simpson of Chorley specified when ordering a clock that it was to have 'steel fingers'—the implication is that by now brass hands, usually stamped out by machine, had become the normal type, but this customer particularly wanted the older type. In 1800 hands (of steel of course) cost 7d a pair; seconds-hands about 2d each. In the 1830s brass hands cost 8d a pair; seconds-hands 2½d each.

Some clockmakers catered for their wealthier clients by making bracket clocks, which though sometimes placed on wall brackets were more often intended for, and used as, table or mantle clocks. These were spring-driven, and were considerably more costly than longcase clocks—an average example costing about twice as much. Lancashire bracket clocks are not often seen today, and they were never popular in the way that longcase clocks were.

A few of the more skilful makers created clocks of an experimental or complicated nature. An astronomical and world-time dial clock exists by Barker of Wigan, an astrological clock showing sunrise and sunset times by John Clough of Manchester, and a world-time dial by John Spencer (II?). A clock of this sort presupposes a very wealthy customer. Whilst most country clockmakers might not have been capable of making such a clock, their lack of customers in this price market probably never gave them the chance to try. A country clockmaker was more likely to be asked to turn his talents to making clockwork roasting jacks than world-time dials, and indeed he often did make such jacks.

A port like Liverpool must necessarily have felt the influence of sea-traffic in several ways. This is reflected in the large number of watchmakers there who also made, or sold, marine chronometers— used in timekeeping at sea with special reference to navigation. Being more akin to watchmaking, chronometer making does not merit detailed discussion here, but its presence in the overall picture must be mentioned.

Sometimes a customer asked for his name to be lettered on a dial, and the spaces normally taken up by the numbers I to XII bear instead the letters of the man's name: this feature may occasionally be found on Lancashire clocks and watches. An example which comes to mind is one by John Fisher of Preston, where the first owner's name, Henry Watson, is engraved on the dial in place of hours, starting with H for VII and ending with N for V. It is perhaps more common on painted-dial clocks than on those with brass dials.

Clocks were imported from Europe and America in ever-increasing quantities in the second quarter of the nineteenth century. The directories of 1848–58 even list under a separate heading those who dealt in imported clocks. European and American clocks were made to stand on the mantlepiece or hang on the wall. They were much more compact than English longcase clocks and very much cheaper. The cheapest American clocks had wooden movements, but these suffered from damp on the long sea voyage. Chauncey Jerome of Bristol (USA) claimed to be the first to make the 30-hour wall clocks with brass movements, and shipped his first to Britain in 1842, housed in what was termed the 'O.G.' case, from the ogee-shaped moulding framing it. The directory of 1851 actually includes the Liverpool address of Jerome & Company, presumably a warehouse and office to handle this large-scale importing.

Native grandfather clocks survived into the 1850s and 1860s. Examples are recorded by several late makers, such as Henry Lee of Bolton and William Brown of Preston, neither of whom appear in directories till 1851. The same does not apply in the south of England, where by 1850 foreign clocks had ousted the longcase. In Lancashire (and Yorkshire) the fondness for them lingered on. Even so the grandfather clock was no longer a practical proposition, and by 1880, when American shelf clocks sold for as little as 2 dollars 35 cents (under £1), they were extinct.

I have not mentioned 'grandmother' clocks. This term is used to describe a small grandfather, though at what height one draws a line is debatable. A grandfather clock standing less than 6 feet high would be very unusual. The term 'grandmother' is generally used to refer to clocks standing about 5 feet or less. These fall into two categories. Most are 'modern' clocks made as miniature versions of eighteenth-century models. Really they are old, anachronistic reproductions made at the end of the last century or early in the present one and so 'out of period'. Some are beautifully made; most however are cheap and tasteless affairs housing German factory-made clocks. The second category are simply fakes, made up out of old bits and pieces, using such things as old lantern-clock chapter-rings, reproduction spandrels, and so on. The cases of the latter were (and still are) often made in a distressed manner to simulate wear and tear. Grandmother clocks have been in great demand for many years because they are easily accommodated in a modern home. I have never yet seen a genuine eighteenth-century one, though I have seen many fakes. I once examined some stock of a deceased clock restorer, whose outbuildings contained several such clocks with the most beautiful tiny cases—only half-finished!

*Page 33 (left)* Thirty-hour single-handed clock by James Whittaker of Middleton, c 1690. The time is marked off in quarter-hour units; *(right)* thirty-hour painted-dial cottage clock by Lawrence Shakeshaft of Preston, c 1790, badly in need of restoration. The calendar hand is missing but the matching steel hands are apparently original

*Page 34* (*left*) Eight-day clock by Burgess of Wigan c 1730, in oak with walnut crossbanding, height 6ft 11in, base restored; (*right*) thirty-hour clock by Joshua Browne of Liverpool c 1740, plain oak, 7ft 10in. Note pierced fret in hood to release sound of bell

# 3

# THE CASES

Early Lancashire clock cases in general conform with the pattern of casemaking throughout northern England. Later Lancashire cases often have distinctive characteristics, which enable them to be recognised as belonging to that county. In fact later Lancashire casework is perhaps more easily recognisable by its style than that of any other area.

Some books in the past have grouped together later case styles of several northern counties and called them, quite inaccurately, 'Yorkshire clocks'. Indeed one recently published book shows an illustration of such a 'Yorkshire' case, which in fact is as Lancashire as it could possibly be. In the North, of course, we know better, and nothing is more infuriating than for a Yorkshireman to see an illustration of a Lancashire case misdescribed as a Yorkshire one. The two are quite different. Even though in this sense the word 'Yorkshire' is intended to refer to the style rather than the county, it not only indicates the author's inability to distinguish the two, but it misleads the newcomer who does not know the difference. Certain Scottish cases of the early nineteenth century, especially of the circular-dial type, can look very much like some London cases of the same time. If I were to refer to such London cases as Scottish (whether in inverted commas or not), or vice versa, there would be outbursts of indignation from both directions.

Let us begin with the earlier period, when a clock case of a certain style would look no different whether built in Lancashire or any other provincial area of England. Marquetry cases, such as appear on London clocks in the later seventeenth century, seem to be extremely rare in Lancashire. So too do lacquer or japanned cases. This rarity may have been due to an absence of taste for these styles in the county, and even today many people might prefer the natural beauty of a wooden-surfaced case to the 'artificial' surface of lacquer. Perhaps more important the scarcity may have been due to the comparatively high cost of such cases. Some may no doubt have been taken to replace the cases of more valuable London clocks. The scarcity of late seventeenth-century walnut cases may be due to the same reasons, and perhaps also to this wood's being subject to woodworm attack.

However we must recognise too that clockmaking was not nearly as widespread an activity in these early years (late seventeenth and early eighteenth centuries) as it was after about 1760. The population was not only much smaller but much poorer. The number of households who would be willing to invest in such a luxury as a clock were few enough. Those who would run to a marquetry or walnut or lacquer clock were fewer, and of those that did, many might select one from London, where it might be supposed (correctly or otherwise) that they would obtain a more sophisticated article.

The early cases in Lancashire were mostly made of plain solid oak or of softwood, cases in the latter normally being painted at the time. Softwood cases were cheapest and least durable, being particularly prone to woodworm attack; hence many have perished. Surviving cases from the late seventeenth century are mainly oak, and there are not great numbers of them. They were mostly made to house 30-hour clocks, the commonest and cheapest type, probably with 9- or 10-inch-square brass dials. They had to be cheap, hence we must expect them to be plain and simple in design. Figure 1 shows the typical outline and proportion of late seventeenth-century cases of this type.

The main appeal today of such a case, apart from the interest of its very age, must be in its proportions and outline, its colour and patina, for there is little else about it—no fancy cabinet work or exotic woods, but absolute simplicity. It is low in height, perhaps ranging between 6 and 7 feet, usually just a little over 6 feet. It is slim, probably under 12 inches wide in the trunk. Its hood will almost

36

certainly slide forward, as with all later longcase clocks. Early London clocks had hoods which slid upwards, but this is not a practical system for cottage clocks and I doubt whether any Lancashire cases ever had it.

The hood pillars at this time would be plain or of the 'barley-sugar' twisted type, but would be attached to the hood door as three-quarter pillars and hence would swing open with the hood door. Heavily carved cases exist, some of which bear seventeenth-century dates: these are generally *not* of that period however, and we will discuss them further in due course.

The trunk would be long and slim, being perhaps twice as long as the base, even longer. The main trunk door would be of similar proportions, taking up almost all the available trunk space with just a framework of surround. This very long slim trunk and door is perhaps the most distinctive feature of early cases, often giving them an appealing sleekness. The door may well have a circular aperture cut into its lower area, into which is fitted a glass panel. This is known as a lenticle glass. As the brass pendulum bob is usually visible through it, its purpose was perhaps to enable one to see from across the room whether the clock was going, though unless one was deaf this would usually be obvious from the sound of the tick.

The long slender trunk door usually has a flat top at this time, and around the door perimeter might be a narrow beading or perhaps alternatively a thumbnail groove, known as an ovolo moulding, though one associates this more with the early years of the eighteenth century.

The clock may have stood on feet or on a plain wooden plinth (the diagram shows the latter): not on those little round 'bun' feet one sees on London clocks, but on a type of bracket foot, which was little more than a plinth with a shaped piece cut out of the centre at front and sides.

It is far from uncommon to find clocks with two front bracket-type feet and none at the back. This was done for the same reasons that some tables had three legs rather than four: partly it was an aid to stability on an uneven floor; partly it was cheaper in the making. The clock simply leaned against the wall. Often clocks were screwed

37

*Figures 1 and 2*
(*left*) Typical case outline of the end of the seventeenth century and beginning of the eighteenth, in oak or pine, standing about 6ft 3in, as made for a simple thirty-hour clock; (*right*) typical case outline of the late eighteenth century in mahogany, as made for a good eight-day clock with brass or painted dial, standing 8ft 3in

or nailed to the wall for extra stability: the numerous holes this has left in the backboard of many a case are often a puzzle to the owner today.

Most clock enthusiasts tend not to use the phraseology of the antique furniture dealers to describe periods. Whilst a piece of furniture might be described as 'Queen Anne' or 'Georgian', such terms are usually too vague for clocks. With practice one expects to be able to date a clock to within say ten years either way. It is usually possible to refer to a clock by its decade.

The case so far described has been the typical 30-hour clock case, its essential feature being cheapness and therefore simplicity of design and construction. With an 8-day clock, almost twice the price of a 30-hour one, the customer was likely to be a little less penny-pinching, and therefore the cabinet work might be expected to be a little more adventurous and a little more costly, even on infrequent occasions very luxurious.

An 8-day clock of a slightly later period is shown on page 34. This is basically an oak case but with crossbanding of curl walnut around the door of the hood and trunk and the (restored) base panel. Crossbanding, whilst it does have some constructional advantage, is very largely for show, for decoration rather than function. The trunk door is actually of chestnut, a wood similar in appearance and texture to oak, but here providing a slight variety of grain. This case, dating from about 1720–30 had an arched hood to take the 'new' shape of dial, just now becoming fashionable on the slightly more costly clock.

Where the square-dial clock sometimes had a pierced, fretted panel immediately above the hood door (pierced to let out the bell sound), this arched-dial clock has a painted panel of imitation fretting—a red-painted background with a gold-painted decorative 'fret'. This panel sometimes has a pierced (through) fret, sometimes has a blanked-out (blind) fret. Frets appear both on 30-hour and 8-day clocks with both square and arched dials; usually the more elaborate and time-consuming frets would be on the 8-day arched (costlier) cases. Not every case has such a fret of course, but many do.

Some clocks also have frets at the sides of the hood, occasionally

39

pierced ones to let the sound out, occasionally glass-panelled ones. The latter were probably to make the movement visible and would enable the owner of an 8-day clock to judge whether the clock needed winding by the amount of gut-line remaining on the barrel, without having to unlock the case door to inspect the position of the weights.

The case shown on page 34 has free-standing pillars to the hood, a slightly later style than the earlier three-quarter pillars attached to the hood door. It also has a shaped top to the trunk door, here a rather extreme shaping, which is also a sign of development in style. The trunk corners, square on the earlier clock for simplicity, now have a slight canted angle cut into them, giving just that little extra 'finish'. This is an indication of the gradual progression from the square-cornered trunk to one with a shaped corner, whether canted or quarter-round, an increasingly helpful pointer to period as the eighteenth century progresses.

Inside the hood doors of many clocks, attached to the lower door frame on the side opposite the hinges, is an interesting device. Sometimes it is a wooden latch, sometimes a metal L-shaped hook or staple, which passes through a cut-out hole in the inner framing. Originally such catches fastened from the inside by means of a sliding iron bolt or wooden turnbuckle or metal hook-latch. Once closed, the hood door could not be opened without withdrawing the bolt, and that was done by opening the trunk door and reaching one's hand up inside the hood. This was not merely a hood lock. It was also a safety catch, which, when fastened, prevented the entire hood from sliding forward accidentally or from being knocked off. The hood of the clock on page 34 has such a fastening device. The original bolt is now lost but the guides which held it can still be felt inside the case. People are often puzzled at seeing remnants of this type of device (sometimes no more than the hole remains), but that is all it was, just a safety catch. From the records of Gillows of Lancaster comes the following interesting item in 1771: 'for a iron bolt & stope to set on a clock case glass door [hood door] with 2 howers labour omitted when settled—10d.'

The most noticeable feature of casework from the point of view of development is the trunk door. We saw the start of a shaped top on page 34. Some door tops at this time have an arched centre, reflecting the dial shape. By mid-century all kinds of shapes develop, becoming progressively more elaborate and often reaching a point, as in the Fearnley and Grundy clock cases on pages 52 and 102. A style more common in Lancashire than in other neighbouring counties is one where the door top is a simple half-circle, as in Figure 2 which shows the Gillows line drawing. The door gradually becomes shorter in height and broader, as cases broaden generally towards the later eighteenth century. The increasing width of dials from about 11 inches in the 1750s to as much as 15 inches in the 1850s was the essential factor in increasing the case width.

Whilst cases grew broader they were relatively restricted in height. A maximum of 7 feet 6 inches was enough for most ceilings; not many would exceed 8 feet. This caused the proportions of cases to change. It is interesting to note that of twelve of Gillows' working drawings, the tallest clock was 8 feet 9 inches, the smallest 6 feet 4 inches and most were under 8 feet. Increasing width and fixed height cost the outline some of its earlier sleekness, and by mid-century this transition had begun.

As part of this stylistic development, the door gradually ceased to fill the whole length of the trunk; and the trunk in itself was now apparently, if not actually, shorter than before. A space was left both above and below the door, which therefore gradually became short and wide. This was at the time regarded as an improvement in design, though today not everyone shares that opinion. The space above and below the door was now 'spare', and was available for decoration, sometimes with blind frets in the 'Chippendale' manner, later with lines of fancy inlay, bandings or stringings. I use the term 'Chippendale' reluctantly, not for the purpose of reflecting on to Lancashire clock cases any of the prestige which that name today imparts, but because it is widely understood when describing this type of blind or applied fret. In reality Chippendale's designs did little more than help publicise styles that were already in use before the publication of his book, and such of his own adaptations of current styles as he did apply to clock cases reveal by their impracticability that he was unfamiliar with clocks; also, ranging as they do between 8 feet 4 inches and 9 feet 1 inch, they were too tall to be acceptable in Lancashire.

Whilst Lancashire casework of the late eighteenth and early nineteenth centuries developed in a way not dissimilar from that in other northern counties, it was very different from London casework. Cumberland and Westmorland casework in many ways is closely allied to that of Lancashire, much more so than for instance that of Yorkshire. However it is the strong contrast of Lancashire cases with those of London which has so distressed some writers in the past; being accustomed to the latter they were unprepared to understand this northern style. The degree by which Lancashire cases failed to resemble London ones was taken as a measure of their shortcomings, the London case as the norm which the northern case must have been trying to imitate. Some harsh criticisms of northcountry work were made by men who added insult to injury by calling Lancashire cases 'Yorkshire clocks'.

Lancashire cases never tried to resemble London ones. By the late eighteenth century the Lancashire case had developed an individual style. Good Lancashire cases not only equal but are often superior to those of other areas, in design, in choice of superb woods, especially of fine mahogany, and in first-class workmanship. In order to appreciate them we must first put out of our minds any thoughts of comparison with London cases, just as we could hardly begin to appreciate French carriage clocks by wondering why there is no cuckoo popping out at every hour. After all the Gillows cabinet-making concern went from Lancaster to London (not the reverse); then, it is not impossible that the swan-neck pediment, which appears occasionally on London cases, may have found its way there through influence from the northern counties, for it is not a native London feature. I do not mean to suggest that all Lancashire cases are outstandingly beautiful; naturally they are not. Some are ugly, but then that could be said of every area, London included.

Very fine 'Spanish' mahogany (from the Spanish West Indies) is found on Lancashire cases from a surprisingly early date. This is no doubt partly due to Liverpool's importance as a trading port with that part of the world. As early as 1744, for instance, Gillows sold three mahogany cases at £2 5s each for export *back* to the West Indies. A number of Gillows cases were made for sea captains, no doubt for export rather than personal use.

Let us consider some of the features of the cases illustrated, which can only stand as representative due to limited illustration space. The commonest hood top here is the swan-necked pediment, called at the time a 'scrolled pediment'—this is probably true of all northern counties. In Lancashire, however, this pediment has a distinctive difference, being a more complex moulding in cross-section, giving a deeper (sometimes heavier) overhang and often terminating in a carved rosette or whirl (at the time called a 'rose'). The rose was often gilded originally, now usually polished down to bare wood over the years. This was not a feature exclusive to Lancashire, but it was more common there than elsewhere. In most counties the brass disc terminals (called paterae) were more common. The shaped panels below the swan necks were often of wood, painted blue or red with gilt decorative work. Sometimes they were of glass, and these painted glass panels of simulated frets were especially popular in this county but not elsewhere, to the point that glass inset panels alone are very much a pointer to a clock case having a Lancashire origin.

On some Lancashire cases, often those intended to be more ostentatious, a box-like superstructure was built above the scrolled pediments, as on the Fearnley case (page 101). This provided a base for each of the two side finials and also a raised area for the centre finial. These finials themselves, often of wood, and the 'spandrel' areas of the hood were often gilded on this type of case. Again this feature, whilst not confined to Lancashire, is more common there than elsewhere. Obvious exceptions are such clockmakers as Thomas Lister junior of Halifax, Yorkshire, who seems to have often bought his more ostentatious cases from Lancashire.

A band running across the trunk top above the door commonly bears a blind (or applied) fret—see pages 52 and 101. Base panels frequently have canted corners, which on richer cases may also carry blind frets. Frets are not rare in other counties, but are more

43

common in Lancashire. The brickwork base, as on the Fearnley of Wigan clock (see page 52), is a characteristic very much confined to Lancashire, especially the Liverpool area; it is unusual to find it in other counties.

Some Lancashire cases, particularly those of Liverpool clocks, have double pillars to the hood, twin reeded front pillars which increase the hood width and add to the very ornate and sometimes over-fussy appearance. Square-section reeded pillars are typically Lancashire, especially where double pillars are used. The hood door is often ogee in shape of moulding used (s-shaped); hood doors of cases from most counties have a simple flat surface. Hood pillars commonly have turned and gilded wooden caps and bases—those from other counties more often have brass caps and bases.

The plain semi-circular doortop is another Lancashire feature, by no means unknown elsewhere but more common in this county. Figure 1, a clock case drawn from the records of Gillows of Lancaster, dates from 1787 and shows several of the features mentioned above.

Incidentally there is a slip in this drawing—can you spot it? I have already mentioned the fashion for shortening the trunk door, thus leaving a blank area below it. This could be used for decoration or simply boxed round with beading, as here. On Figure 1 you might notice that the door hinges are marked in the positions normal for a long-doored case. Evidently it was an afterthought in this particular instance to shorten the door and make a panel below, and the design book shows that the artist forgot to re-position his lower hinge, which can still be seen marked against the lower box panel. Of course these working designs were only meant as a rough guide to the cabinetmakers. This is interesting not only because it shows that these designers were fallible, but as an indication that this fashion is just beginning at this period, the change from long to short door being a last-minute refinement in this instance.

The trunk corners on most late eighteenth-century clock cases carry reeded quarter columns, as on the Fearnley clock (page 52). Occasionally one sees an alternative variation of what we would now call a Chippendale-style 'cluster-column'. This consists of three turned spindles joined at intervals, sometimes producing a bamboo-like effect. At the time these were termed 'Gothic quarter columns' or 'Gothic sticks' (Gillows records for 1787). Variations of these can be seen at the base of the Standring trunk columns (page 52). These triple-cluster columns are perhaps more common in Lancashire than out of it.

Most of the above remarks relate to later eighteenth-century town clocks. However the more common 30-hour country 'cottage' clock continued to be made, very little changed casewise from mid-century to the end of the century. Mahogany was used more often for the costlier cases we have just looked at in detail, and whilst mahogany cases might date from as early as 1740, most would be no earlier than 1760. Oak and deal cases on the other hand were made right through the eighteenth century and into the nineteenth. Page 102 shows a straightforward 'cottage' clock case in oak made about 1780. Such a case would cost only one-quarter as much, or even less, as one of the mahogany ones described earlier.

The famous firm of Gillows of Lancaster, cabinetmakers, was begun about 1695 by Robert Gillow and by 1770 had a branch in London, although their furniture was sold there before that date. Nicholas Goodison, in his monograph on *Gillows' Clock Cases*, quotes many extracts from the original records of the firm (this booklet is well worth the attention of anyone with a serious interest in the subject), but there must be much more to be uncovered from further research into some of the 180-odd volumes of Gillows manuscripts. The Gillows name today has an aura about it, just as the Chippendale name does. Its reputation, built up for finer pieces of furniture, tends to obscure the fact that Gillows made plain and simple softwood furniture too, for all cabinetmakers had to cater for the pockets of their ordinary customers, not purely for the wealthy. It is interesting to ponder for a moment on just who the Gillows customers were.

The normal assumption has been that the clockmaker ordered his cases from a cabinetmaker, such as Gillows, so that he could sell a complete clock. Examination of the Gillows records shows that not infrequently the reverse applied, and this is confirmed from another

45

direction, in that selling-prices of clocks from clockmakers often indicate that the clock was sold *without* the case. Gillows were in the habit of buying in clocks to sell with their cases, as complete jobs, and some clocks even bear their name on the dial. Some of their customers were clockmakers, but only a small minority. We know that Edward Cawson, Henry Bell and also Thomas Williams of Preston were clockmakers who bought Gillows cases. Most of the Gillows customers, however, have names which we cannot identify—were they other cabinetmakers, exporters, general merchants? Some must have been private customers, but very few it seems, since names that appear more than once (for clock cases), as many do, must have been traders of some sort. Much more research into this topic needs to be done.

We have still to discuss the tricky topic of carved cases, which many books malign as being either 'Victorian' copies or else plain cases carved in Victorian times. It has long been fashionable to put down all manner of dubious antiques to the unfortunate 'Victorians' —or else to describe them as 'Flemish'. It is however unquestionably true that some 'Victorians' did inflict grievous damage to furniture, even clock cases, by carving it, just as they saw it as an exercise in skill rather than vandalism to convert clocks to strike on gongs rather than bells, and to add a musical movement to a normal clock thereby making it into a 'musical clock'. However, clock enthusiasts who live in Lancashire will be well aware that carved oak cases do exist which come into neither of the categories mentioned: these are original, usually heavily carved, usually stained black, and usually oak. Mostly they seem to be of the period between 1770 and 1800 and contain brass-dial clocks of 'medium' quality. The style of this black oak carving has been described as seventeenth century, and occasionally such a clock may include a carved date of that time. These carved dates were never intended to fool anyone when the clock cases were sold new; these features are plainly anachronistic, so far as both the period of the cases (constructionally) and the clocks which they contain are concerned, but the cases are still in no way 'fakes'.

There was a local fashion, though perhaps not a national one, for carved oak cases towards the latter end of the eighteenth century.

46

Exactly why this carved decoration bears a resemblance to seventeenth-century carving we do not know, unless perhaps it was designed to blend in with other furniture of that period. We have only to count up the products of a local maker whose customers seem to have favoured this type of case to realise that they were a genuine local fashion, especially in the Pennine districts of the Rochdale/Halifax area. A count of cases on clocks by the Listers of Halifax, who we know used cases of Lancashire origin or style, would show that something like one-third were carved black oak ones. I find it impossible to believe that Victorian carvers selected clocks by some makers and not by others.

There are cases where examination makes it obvious that the carving was later than the construction—an afterthought. For instance a case with its door crossbanded in mahogany can hardly have been intended for carving, the beauty of the banding being obliterated by being stained black. I have seen such cross-banded cases where the carving was obviously done later. I have also seen numerous carved cases which I feel sure were made that way, and I think that we should at least examine carved cases very thoroughly before writing them off as 'Victorian' fakes.

By the nineteenth century, case styles had begun to change, in Lancashire as elsewhere. The availability of veneers of figured mahogany, rosewood and satinwoods, and of all manner of fancy stringing work and inlays, meant that the clock could be given a spectacular appearance whilst keeping the cost to a minimum by using a softwood frame. Inlays of shell motifs, fans, vases, were bought in bulk, and applying them was not a great deal more difficult than wallpapering. The results were very effective, yet the cost was not high. Almost every hardware shop of the 1820s sold shell inlays—coloured marquetry panels with a paper backing all ready to be glued into place, rather like a ready-assembled jigsaw puzzle.

I do not mean to belittle case decoration of this sort. It was very popular and can be most attractive. However it *was* cheaper to make. It had indeed become vital to get the cost down lower and lower in order to reach a wider market and to compete against imported clocks. Increasing mechanisation meant that veneers, inlays and

47

brass case fittings (escutcheons, capitals, etc) all became cheaper. A mid-nineteenth-century case might show a far more abundant use of superficial decoration than its mid-eighteenth-century counterpart, yet be cheaper to make and to sell. Cheapness and availability of materials led to an over-exuberant use of them. Cases became even broader, giving wider surface areas to display the new wealth of ostentatious decoration. Balance, restraint, harmony (and some would say sanity) were lost. The county which had been capable of producing some of the finest provincial casework ever made was now able to produce some of the most gaudy and ill-designed. The heavy Lancashire scrolled pediment, when filled in with a wide expanse of plain wood as on mid-nineteenth-century cases, can look most un-gainly. Whilst a fine Lancashire case can be superb, a poor one can be truly repulsive—to our present-day tastes, that is! We must not forget that the ostentatiousness of the broad cases of the 1850s and 1860s was in accord with the tastes of the day.

This last wild fling of exuberant decoration in casework failed to win the battle for the longcase clock against the incoming shiploads of cuckoo clocks, wooden-wheeled German wall clocks, American wall and shelf clocks and 'Vienna' regulators. By 1870 local case-making had virtually died, as local clockmakers were forced to become merely retailers and repairers, and turned to piano-tuning, musical boxes and barometer selling.

# 4

# PRICES AND VALUES

The original prices of clocks are very interesting. They are also difficult to study because few original receipts are preserved. A further problem is that we often have difficulty in knowing exactly what type of clock was involved. Descriptions in old inventories were often vague, and we cannot be sure how accurate the valuation of an item was; some valuations were deliberately inaccurate, some were inaccurate because of the valuer's ignorance. An inventory, moreover, gives a second-hand value, presumably less than the current new value.

It has long been known that the clockmaker did not make the case, which was the product of a carpenter or cabinetmaker. The assumption has normally been that the clockmaker bought in the case in order to supply it with the clock as a complete item. No doubt this happened on occasions—indeed, we know it did. However I am interested to find in examples of original prices that I come across that the price was quite plainly the price of the clock alone *without* the case. Let us initially consider that a provincial lantern clock (30-hour of course and with no wooden case) cost about £2 10s in 1650. It would not be unreasonable to assume that a 30-hour brass-dial longcase clock (without case) cost the same, about £2 10s. We know that this level of prices is correct from examples in other counties. We further know that prices of clocks remained relatively stable from 1650 to about 1800, there being none of the rapid inflation in those days that we are accustomed to today.

From contemporary records elsewhere we know that the following

49

price scale would apply throughout most of the eighteenth century for clocks without cases.

| | |
|---|---|
| Square brass-dial 30-hour, single-handed | £2  5s |
| Square brass-dial 30-hour, two handed | £2  10s |
| Square brass-dial 8-day | £4  5s |

These were for simple country versions. A town clock with extra features might exceed £4 5s. We can thus see in perspective that the £4 put on Joseph Pryor's clock and case in 1720 is a second-hand value and therefore not helpful as a 'price' guide (we can safely assume that a clockmaker's own clock would be an 8-day one). The same applies to James Barton's 1715 pair of clocks at £3 10s and George Taylor's 1722 clock and case at £5. Hence inventory prices tend only to confuse the picture of 'at new' costs. It is worth noting however that the £14 valuation of Pryor's 'two spring clocks'—their second-hand value—indicates that such a spring-driven table clock (often called a 'bracket' clock) was about twice the price of a good 8-day clock without its case. This is one good reason why the bracket clock was never a very popular form in the county. Apart from its cost, it had the disadvantage that its spring-driven performance could seldom equal the consistency of that of the weight-driven longcase clock with longer pendulum.

The records of Gillows of Lancaster give occasional glimpses of prices, as in those instances where they purchased a clock to sell in a case of their making. In 1771 they paid £4 4s for a clock (which must have been an 8-day arched brass dial one) to go into a 'handsome' mahogany case they were supplying. In 1797 they paid £4 10s for one, probably of the same type, though this may well have been a painted-dial 8-day. In 1799 they bought a 13-inch-square painted-dial 30-hour clock from Newbys, the Kendal clockmakers at £2 11s. We may wonder why they sent to Kendal when there were many clockmakers closer to hand—there was nothing special about Newby's clocks, so perhaps they had some sort of reciprocal trading agreement with them.

The above are all cost prices for the clocks alone. The cases were additional, and we shall look at their prices shortly. In 1804 John

50

*Page 51* (*left*) Fine quality eight-day clock by 'Jo. Burges de Wigan' c 1730, with a most unusual layout of calendar work in the arch and lunar dial above the VI; (*right*) thirty-hour clock signed 'Joshua Browne Leverpool fecit' c 1740. The dummy winding holes and squares simulate an eight-day clock, and the seconds dial is unusual on thirty-hour but normal on eight-day clocks

*Page 52*   (*left*) Eight-day clock by Standring of Bolton c 1750–60 in top quality mahogany case, standing 7ft 8in. Many of its features are in the best Lancashire tradition, including the brickwork base; (*right*) eight-day clock by Fearnley of Wigan c 1780 in finest mahogany, standing 8ft. It is typical of better-quality Lancashire style and proportions, and the reeding of the hood door, giving the appearance of double pillars, is a Lancashire feature

Wignall of Ormskirk charged £7 14s for an 8-day clock (no doubt a painted-dial one) complete with case, offsetting £1 1s against this for an old clock which the customer traded in.

In 1822 Isaac Simpson of Chorley charged £2 16s for a 30-hour painted-dial clock, probably an arched dial as the square dial was now very much out of favour. Again this was *without* the case. The order was obtained through his cousin, William Fell, of Slaidburn, Yorkshire, who advised Isaac to make it a good one with as handsome a face as possible for the customers were relying entirely on William. So some customers bought clocks completely unseen, entrusting the choice of dial and style wholly to the clockmaker. In 1823 William also got Isaac an order for a watch at about 4 or 5 guineas for a local farmer who was not particular to a shilling or two. This proved rather an unfortunate deal, as six months later, the watch was still not working properly, and William finally returned it to Isaac packed up in feathers in a consignment of butter!

From the Gillows records, an average clock case took between one and a half and two weeks for one man to make. In deal, it cost Gillows altogether about £1 5s to £1 10s; in oak £1 10s to £2. A mahogany case might range between £2 15s and £5, making a mahogany one 2½ to 5 times the cost of a deal one. (It is interesting to note that the deal case was sold painted.) To these cost prices the firm would add their profit of about 12 per cent.

To a cabinetmaker then earning roughly £1 a week, a good mahogany case and 8-day brass-dial clock (costing perhaps £10 in all) represented ten weeks' wages. Translating this into today's values would put the 'new' cost at £300 to £400, assuming a similar tradesman's wages today might range from £30 to £40 a week. A deal-cased 30-hour painted-dial clock might have cost £4 or four weeks' wages—£120 to £160 in today's terms. This comparison enables us to see how clocks at this time were still quite costly items, beyond the aspirations of many; and further, why the expensive 8-day brass-dial clock in a mahogany case was the least common type.

With increasing mechanisation the prices of clock parts actually decreased and by the 1850s (when most clocks were being made almost entirely in the 'factories' and merely sold by the man whose name they bore) one could buy an 8-day clock complete with case for 5 or 6 guineas. This was not a great deal more than the clock alone had cost fifty years earlier, and these later cases often involved much more cabinet work than the plainer earlier ones.

Such price structures as we can formulate in Lancashire seem to work out much like those throughout the rest of the country, a pattern which had applied since the introduction of the pendulum in 1658. That the 8-day clock was about one and a half times to twice the price of the 30-hour one, and the 8-day spring-driven table (bracket) clock was more than twice the price of the weight-driven 8-day one. It follows that in all provincial areas the number of people who could afford the 30-hour clock was comparatively large and the wealthier bracket clock customers were very few. Consequently the 30-hour clock was always the commonest type, the 8-day one rarer, the bracket clock much rarer still and in some country areas was virtually unknown. In the nineteenth century bracket clocks became more common.

# GLOSSARY

*Arbor*   Clock axle.

*Birdcage movement*   See Post-framed movement.

*Capitals and bases*   Tops and bottoms of hood pillars.

*Chapter ring*   The separate brass ring bearing hour numbers fixed to the main dial sheet on brass-dial clocks.

*Chiming/striking*   All longcase clocks normally strike the hour. A few are chiming, ie play a chime at each quarter-hour in addition to normal hourly striking.

*Count wheel*   See Locking plate.

*Dial centre*   The area inside the chapter ring.

*Eight-day clock*   A clock driven by two weights on catgut lines and wound by a key. Can run from seven to ten days at one winding, according to height of case.

*Escutcheon*   Decorative lock-plate, usually of brass.

*Falseplate*   Rectangular iron bracket fixed to rear of some 8-day painted dials to assist clockmaker fit his movement. Often bears name of dialmaker, NOT movement maker.

*Finials*   Brass (or sometimes gilded wooden) terminals set on top of a clock case for decoration. Often a ball topped by a spire or eagle.

*Fret*   Pierced fretwork decoration. A 'blind' fret has a pierced surface but is applied to a solid background.

*Lenticle*   Glazed aperture in trunk door through which pendulum can be seen swaying.

*Locking plate* (also called count wheel)   The striking system used on virtually all 30-hour clocks and some earlier 8-day ones. It consists of a wheel with notches at increasing intervals allowing the clock to strike 1, 2, 3, blows, and so on.

*Movement*   Correct terminology for the 'works' of both clocks and watches.

*Ogee moulding*   S-shaped in cross-section.

*Patera* (plural paterae)   Decorative brass discs often fixed to ends of scrolled or swan-necked pediments. Sometimes made of carved or turned wood instead, when termed 'rosettes'.

*Plate-framed movement*   A movement housed between two upright plates held by horizontal corner pillars.

*Post-framed movement*   The opposite, constructionally, to a plate-framed one. It has horizontal plates top and bottom held by upright pillars.

*Regulator*   A precision timepiece, non-striking, plain and functional.

*Spandrels* (on clock dials)   Cast-brass decoration appearing in each of the four corners of a brass dial and sometimes in the arch.

*Spandrels* (on clock cases)   The area of casework appearing immediately at each side of the archway on a clock hood, sometimes carved, gilded, or made of painted glass.

*Thirty-hour clock*   A clock driven by one weight (with small ring-shaped counter-weight). Wound by pulling rope or chain. Can run between 24 and 48 hours according to layout, case height and length of rope.

*Timepiece*   A non-striking clock.

*Trains*   A set of clock wheels; the going train is the timekeeping set which makes the clock go; the striking train is that operating the bell.

# LIST OF MAKERS

*Abbot and Garnet.* Farnworth. Watch-makers 1834–51.

*Abbott, Francis.* Manchester. No 1 Smithy Door, 1834.

*Abbott, James.* Farnworth. Watch-maker, married Ellen Pierpoint there 1806.

*Abbott, John.* Liverpool. 21 Cop-peras Hill in 1822.

*Abbott, John.* Bold. Watchmaker. Baptised children at Burton-wood, by wife Mary: 1793 George, 1797 William, 1800 Peter. One of the same name apprenticed in 1757 to John Williamson, watchmaker, for £21.

*Abbott, John.* Prescot. Watchmaker. Had issue there by wife, Mary: 1818 Thomas; 1823 Mary.

*Abbot, Nathan.* Farnworth. Watch-maker. Married Mary Alcock there in 1757. One such, son of Thomas Abbot, apprenticed in 1747 to John Miller of Liverpool, watchmaker, for £10.

*Abbot, Nathan.* Farnworth. Watch-maker, married Catherine Heys there in 1833.

*Abbott, Thomas.* Farnworth. Watch-

maker married Dorothy Marsden there in 1788.

*Abbot, William.* Burtonwood. Watchmaker there in 1776 when son, Thomas, baptised by wife, Mary.

*Abbott, William.* Prescot. Watch-maker. Son, Thomas, baptised 1795 by wife, Ann.

*Abbot, William.* Prescot. Watch-maker. Issue by wife, Jane, baptised: 1818 William, 1823 Joseph. In 1822 working in Atherton St.

*Abram, George.* Poulton, nr Preston. Clock and watchmaker in Market Place 1834–58.

*Abraham, John.* Warrington. Watch-maker. Will proved 1776.

*Abram, Thomas.* Prescot. Watch-maker at Rainhill in 1823 when son, Samuel, baptised by wife, Margaret.

*Abraham/Abram, Thomas.* Liverpool. Watchmaker at Dig Lane 1754 and 1761. Will proved 1767.

*Abrahamson, William.* Liverpool. 11 Kent Square in 1851.

*Ackers, Edward.* St Helens. Watch-maker at Sutton. Issue: 1767

*Ackers, Edward.* cont.
John, 1769 Margaret, 1772 William, 1775 Thomas, 1779 Mary, 1783 James and Edward.

*Ackers, John.* Prescot. Watchmaker, son of Edward above? Married at Farnworth in 1788 to Alice Sephton. Living at Rainhill when issue born: 1794 Edward, 1796 Abraham.

*Adams, Nathaniel.* Liverpool. 15 Great Newton St in 1851.

*Adamson, Henry.* Liverpool. 125 Park Lane in 1834.

*Addison, Thomas.* Ulverstone. Working 1744 as clockmaker. Died 1766, will proved 1767—mentions wife, Jane, and son, John. A T. Addison of Liverpool, recorded in mid-18th century, may be the same man.

*Agar, Thomas/Mary & Sons.* Bury. Clock and watchmaker at Silver St in 1822, 5 Union St in 1824, Bolton St in 1834. Presumably died before 1848 as Mary listed there in that year, then Mary & Sons till 1858.

*Agar, W. & Co.* Bolton. Clockmaker at Deansgate in 1858.

*Agnew, Thomas & Son.* Manchester. Mantel clock reported dated 1874.

*Ainsworth, James.* Prescot. Clock and watchmaker at Atherton St in 1834.

*Ainsworth, John.* St Helens. Watchmaker at Sutton. Issue baptised: 1774 William, 1776 Mary, 1779 Thomas, 1781 James, 1784 Mary.

*Ainsworth, Robert.* Liverpool. Watchmaker. Will proved in 1747.

*Airey, Thomas.* Liverpool. Clock and watchmaker at 29 Moorfields in 1848, then at 67 Dale St in 1851.

*Alcock, John.* Prescot. Watchmovement maker. Married at Farnworth in 1781 to Mary Monkhouse.

*Alcock, John.* St Helens. Watchmaker. Daughter, Agnes, born 1782 by wife, Elenor (Worral). Lived at Windle.

*Alcock, Joseph.* Prescot. Watchmovement maker. Married Catherine Claughton at Farnworth, 1757.

*Alcock, Thomas.* Farnworth. Watchmaker. Married Catherine Kilshaw in 1785.

*Aldridge, Thomas.* Oldham? Son of Thomas senior. Apprenticed clockmaker in 1752 to Stephen Wilmshurst of Oldham. Not known if worked there later.

*Alker, James.* Wigan. Clockmaker at Scholes in 1832.

*Alker, James.* Chorley. Watchmaker in Market St 1851–8.

*Alker, John.* Wigan. Working by 1797. Son, James, born 1798 by wife, Margaret, who died in 1808. Many clocks recorded, including Ribchester church clock. Shop in Market Place. Believed died 1832.

*Alker, John* (II). Wigan. Watchmaker in Market Place 1851–8, probably as successor to Nicholas, qv.

*Alker, John and Nicholas.* Leyland. Watchmakers there 1851 — branch of Wigan firm?

*Alker, Nicholas.* Wigan/Chorley. At Wigan 1830–50. Moved to Market St, Chorley, c 1851 and still there 1858.

*Alker, Thomas.* Wigan. Clock and watchmaker. Lived at Millgate 1822 when daughter Margaret born by wife, Catherine; in Hallgate 1824 when daughter, Alice, born. At Market Place in 1848.

*Alkerton, Henry.* Ditton/Halewood. Watch-spring maker, apprenticed in 1713 to William Barrow of Halewood. Listed as early example of specialisation.

*Allen/Allin, Thomas.* Manchester/ Salford. Clockmaker, married Jane Hall 1787. In 1824 listed at 2 Spear St, Salford.

*Allison, William.* Liverpool. Watchmaker at Gildarts Gardens 1795.

*Anderson, Alexander.* Liverpool. Clock and watchmaker. Liverpool Museum have 3 watches, c 1787. Lost watches advertised 1775–8. Clocks recorded 1760–75.

*Anderson, George.* Liverpool. Watch recorded c 1800.

*Anderson, Richard.* Preston. Watchmaker and silversmith. Preston museum have watch made in 1792. Died before 1817 in which year son, Robert, became a Lancaster freeman.

*Anderson and Robinson; Anderson, William.* Lancaster. William Anderson apprenticed 1750 to Thomas Ogden of Halifax for £30—a high premium. In business by 1758. Partnership with Robinson dissolved 1789. His shop was in Market St. Will proved 1801. Several clocks and watches recorded, including watch at Lancaster museum and clock at Blackburn museum.

*Anderson, William.* Liverpool. At 29 High Park St, Toxteth Park, in 1848.

*Anderton, J.* Liverpool. Watch by him c 1800 in Liverpool museum.

*Andrews, Nathan.* Yatebank? Son of Nathan senior. Apprenticed to William Yates, clockmaker, of Yatebank 1724 for £30.

*Angus, William.* Liverpool. Regulator by him in Birkenhead museum, c 1870.

*Ansdell, James.* St Helens. Watchmaker at Sutton. Issue: 1755 Anne, 1758 James.

*Ansdle, John.* St Helens. Watchmaker at Bold in 1761 when took Matthew Bushell as apprentice for £30. Married in 1762 to Eleanor Bramhill. Issue born 1763, at Sutton, James; 1764, at Bold, Clostacker; 1768, at Rainford, James; 1774, at Rainford, John.

*Antrobus, John.* Manchester. Clockmaker. Married there in 1772 to Frances Hobun.

*Antrobus, Philip* (senior). Manchester. See Philip junior below. Thirty-hour clocks noted c 1740–50.

*Antrobus, Philip* (junior). Manchester. Clockmaker and farmer.

59

*Antrobus, Philip* cont.
Born c 1741. Married Alice
Booth 1783. Died 5 October
1820, aged 79, then of Butler
Lane. Will proved 1821. Described as 'junior' at marriage,
which implies existence of a
Philip senior, and clocks re-
corded with this name made
c 1740–50 also suggest his existence.
*Appleby, Thomas.* Manchester.
Watchmaker 1791–5.
*Appleton, John.* Prescot. Watch-
maker. Married Mary Pye at
Farnworth 1783. Child Ann
born 1796.
*Appleton, Richard.* Cronton? Watchmovement maker. Apprenticed
1756 to William Garnett of
Cronton for £23.
*Appleton, Thomas.* Prescot. Watchmaker. Wife Ellen had issue:
1795 Rachel, 1798 Henry.
*Archer, George.* Rochdale. Clock and
watchmaker and jeweller at
Packer St, 1824.
*Archer, John.* Liverpool. Watch-
maker at 44 Dale St, 1767–84.
*Archer, Percy.* Liverpool? Son of
Richard Archer. Apprenticed as
watchmaker to Stephen Tilling-
hast of Liverpool for £15 in 1742.
*Arden, John.* Liverpool. Watch-
maker at 32 Shaw's Alley 1775–
80. Died 1780.
*Armitage, J. H.* Warrington. Clock
and watchmaker at 25 Market
St, 1858.
*Armstrong, Alfred.* Manchester.
Watchmaker. Son of Joseph
Armstrong, silversmith. Born

1851. Lived at Withington with
wife Catherine, 1884–7.
*Armstrong, Asnath.* Manchester. Sold
imported clocks at 9 Long Millgate in 1851.
*Armstrong, Edward.* Manchester.
Sold imported clocks at 24 Long
Millgate in 1851.
*Armstrong, George Booth.* Manchester.
Clock and watchmaker, also
jeweller and optician. Born 1836,
son of Joseph Armstrong, silver-
smith (qv). Had six children
1877–87 by wife, Rita.
*Armstrong, Joseph.* Manchester.
Clock and watchmaker, silver-
smith and jeweller at 88 Deans-
gate. Had 13 children by wife,
Sarah, including 1829 Thomas,
1831 Joseph Boyd, 1836 George
Booth, 1851 Alfred, all of whom
followed same trade. Still at
Deansgate 1851.
*Armstrong, Joseph Boyd.* Manchester.
Son of Joseph A. above. Born
1831. Watchmaker at Douglas
in 1859 when children Edgar and
Emma born, by wife Caroline.
*Armstrong, Robert.* Manchester.
Clockmaker. Married Susan
Needham 1811. In 1834 listed at
19 Fennel St.
*Armstrong, Thomas.* Manchester.
Born c 1755. Married as widower
in 1814 to Sarah Wardle. Clock-
maker. Shop at 2 Half St, 1824–
8. Died at Ardwick 1835, aged 80.
*Armstrong, Thomas.* Manchester.
Jeweller and silversmith, eldest
son of Joseph Armstrong. Born
1829. Premises in Deansgate.
Issue by wife, Eliza: 1862 Frank,

*Armstrong, Thomas.* cont. 1867 Clara Emily, 1870 Kate, 1873 Mary Alice.

*Armstrong, Thomas.* Milnthorpe. Letter of 1836 addressed to 'Mr. Thomas Armstrong, clockmaker, Millthorp, nr Lancaster' quoted by Hobbs—may be same man as at Warton?

*Armstrong, Thomas.* Lancaster. Clock and watchmaker at Adelaide in 1851.

*Armstrong, T.* Warton. Clockmaker there in 1858. St Helens library has longcase clock by him, 30-hour, painted-dial.

*Arnet/Arnold, Henry.* Farnworth. Watchmaker, married Mary Appleton there in 1803. Alternative spellings leave name uncertain.

*Arrowsmith, John.* Farnworth. Watchmaker. Married there 1791 to Mary, daughter of James Ansdale—she was born 1752.

*Arrowsmith, John.* St Helens. Watchmaker at Sutton in 1825 when daughter, Margaret, born by wife, Margaret.

*Ashall, Charles.* Bolton. Watchmaker at Mealhouse Lane in 1848, Church Bank in 1851, then Bradshawgate in 1858.

*Ashall, John.* Bolton. Clock and watchmaker at Manor St in 1834.

*Ashall, William.* Bolton. In 1848 listed at Church Gate and at 4 Manor St—successor to John? In 1851 at Market St.

*Ashburton, ——.* Liverpool. Liverpool museum have watch c 1785

*Ascroft, James.* Wigan. Made sundial in 1718, according to Hawkes.

*Ashcroft, John.* Liverpool. Apprenticed watchmaker in 1752 to Robert Miller of Prescot for £14. Liverpool museum have late 18th-century watch by him, with place as Kirby.

*Ashley, Thomas.* Liverpool. At 6 Heath St in 1851.

*Ashton, James.* Manchester. Watchmaker. Took John Berry apprentice in 1717 for £18. His sons, James and Thomas, admitted to school in 1735-6; son William admitted 1738.

*Ashton, John.* Prescot. Watchmaker. Had child, Ellen, by wife Alice 1825.

*Ashton, Nicholas.* Prescot. Watchmaker. Child, Ann, baptised 1796 by wife, Martha.

*Ashton, Samuel.* Manchester. Clockmaker. Married Sarah Booth in 1793.

*Ashurst, James.* Chorley. Watchmaker. Died 1793.

*Ashworth, John.* Bacup. Clock and watchmaker and engraver at Newgate 1848-51.

*Ashworth, J.* Rochdale. Watchmaker at 74 Whitworth Rd in 1858. May be from Bacup?

*Aspinall, Henry.* Liverpool. Watchmaker at 26 Bixteth St in 1790; 61 Tythebarn St in 1795.

*Aspin(w)all, James.* Wigan. Clockmaker. Believed came from Heaton near Bolton. Free 1712. Believed moved away after 1717 (Hawkes).

*Aspinwall, James.* Liverpool. Lost watch advertised in 1800 (No 704).

*Aspin(w)all, John.* Liverpool. Watchmaker at 90 Old Dock Gates 1781–1800.

*Aspinall, Peter.* Ashton-in-Makerfield, nr Wigan. Makers of spurs, also guns and maybe clocks too. Free 1664. Repaired church clock 1666 and 1672. Died 1677. Will mentions wife and three sons, William, Peter and Edward.

*Aspinwall, Robert.* Liverpool. At 3 Richmond St, 1814.

*Aspin(w)all, Thomas.* Manchester. Watchmaker. Married Sarah Burton from Wakefield in 1787.

*Aspinall, William.* Bolton. Watchmaker at Old Hall St in 1848, Great Moor St 1851, then Newport St in 1858.

*Astley, Edward.* Liverpool. Clock and watchmaker in 1834 at 5 Duckworth St.

*Asworth, Richard.* Manchester. In 1848 at 12 Chester St, Hulme.

*Atherton, John.* Prescot. Watchmaker. Married Sarah Leech in 1767 at Farnworth.

*Atherton, John.* Prescot. Watchmaker. Had daughter, Elizabeth, by wife, Alice, in 1823.

*Atherton, S.* Liverpool. Liverpool museum have watch c 1785.

*Atherton, Thomas.* Liverpool. Liverpool museum have watch c 1770–80.

*Atherton, Thomas.* Prescot. Watchmaker. Married in 1820 at

Farnworth to Ann Booth. Child, Mary, born 1826.

*Atkin, Francis.* Liverpool. Watchmaker at 28 Church St in 1800. In 1824 at 55 Lord St as wholesaler. At 38 Chapel Walk in 1828.

*Atkin, Robert.* Liverpool. At 13 Limekiln Lane in 1822.

*Atkinson, Elizabeth.* Barrow-in-Furness. Watchmaker at 19 Strand in 1869.

*Atkinson, Jonathan.* Manchester. Clockmaker. Married Alice Dickinson, 1833.

*Atkinson, Richard.* Liverpool. Watchmaker. Son of John Atkinson of Lancaster, mason. Free at Lancaster in 1785, though working at Liverpool. In 1790 at 13 Tempest's Hay.

*Atkinson, Robert.* Lancaster. Lancaster museum have watch.

*Atkinson, Robert.* Liverpool. Watchmaker at 6 Knight St in 1800.

*Atkinson, Thomas.* Ulverston/Dalton. Market St, Ulverston in 1862. Market St, Dalton in 1866.

*Atkinson, Thomas.* Lancaster/Ormskirk. Clockmaker, free at Lancaster 1767. Son of Nicholas Atkinson. By 1786 listed at Ormskirk as watch, clock, and jack maker. Various clocks noted, both brass and painted dials.

*Backhouse, James* (I). Lancaster. Watchmaker. Married Ann Jackson in 1744. Died 1747. Son John was a merchant; son Wil-

*Backhouse, James (I)*. cont. liam went to New York. Silver watch reported c 1730.
*Backhouse, James* (II). Lancaster? Son of Alice Backhouse of Newbarns. Apprenticed watchmaker in 1749 to Thomas Smoult of Lancaster for £15. May be son of James (I).
*Bagot, John*. Lancaster. Watchmaker and jeweller. Born 1808 Scotforth, Lancs. Established at Lancaster by 1834 in Market St. Then at 29 Cheapside in 1848, and 11 Wood St, 1851–69. Children by wife, Isabella: 1835 Isabella, 1842 Mark, 1845 John.
*Bailey, Joseph*. Liverpool. Apprenticed watchmaker in 1756 to William Blore of Liverpool for £35.
*Bailey, Thomas*. Liverpool. At 4 Kensington Terrace, Kirkdale in 1848.
*Baker, William*. Liverpool. In 1851 at 60 Mill St.
*Ball, Isaac*. Prescot. Watchmaker. Daughter, Mary, baptised there 1819 by wife, Mary.
*Ball, John*. Liverpool. Clockmaker. Married 1699. Issue included sons 1706 James, 1712 Benjamin, 1715 Joseph. He, and his wife, Catherine, both died in 1716. Lived at Hackins Hey.
*Ball, Thomas*. Wigan/Warrington. Apprenticed watchmaker to Matthew Holt of Wigan in 1752 at £4 4s. Married in 1767 at Warrington to Ellen Dootson, widow.
*Ball, William*. Prescot. Apprenticed

watchmaker to Thomas Glover in 1760 at £15.
*Ball, William*. Farnworth. Watchmaker. Married Catherine Ellison there in 1807. Same man as above?
*Ball, William*. Liverpool. At 9 North Side, Old Dock in 1822.
*Balmer, Thomas*. Liverpool. Clock and watchmaker at 18 Downe St, 1814. At 28 London Rd in 1834.
*Balmer, William*. Prescot. Variously styled as watchmaker and watchhand maker. Married Ellen Brown at Farnworth in 1795. Daughter, Ann, born 1797.
*Bamber, Abraham*. Preston. Watchmaker at 10 Avenham Lane, 1851–8.
*Bamber, John*. Aughton. Son of John Bamber, gentleman. Apprenticed 1701 to William Wolfall (Walpole?) watchmaker of St Martin-in-the-Fields, London. Probably worked in London.
*Bamber, Samuel*. Bolton. At Bradshawgate in 1848.
*Bamber, S*. Blackpool. Watchmaker at 34 Market St in 1858. May be above man from Bolton?
*Banks, Ellen*. Preston. At 128 Fishergate in 1848.
*Banks, James*. Ormskirk. Clock and watchmaker at Moor St, 1848–54.
*Bankes, John*. Oldham. Square dial longcase reported—late 18th century?
*Banner, Richard*. Liverpool. Clockmaker there in 1734

63

*Banister, Thomas.* Liverpool. Clockmaker there 1734. Connected with William?

*Ban(n)ister, William.* Liverpool. Son of John Banister of Liverpool, yeoman. Apprenticed watchmaker in 1719 to Richard Whalley of Liverpool for £10. Still listed there in 1754.

*Barber, E.* Bury. Watchmaker at Bridge St, Heywood in 1858.

*Barker, Thomas.* Wigan. Clockmaker. Free there 1737.

*Barker, William.* Wigan. Well-known clockmaker and gunsmith. Working there by 1748, but not officially 'free' there till 1754. Issue by wife, Ellen, Daye 1747 and Thomas 1755. Clocks signed mostly without Christian name, as probably worked together with son, Daye. Numerous clocks recorded including 8-bell musical clock and astronomical world-time clock. Believed died 1786–7. Also famous for making steel crossbows and the 'best fowling pieces in the kingdom'— one in Wigan museum. Son, Thomas, known as a gunmaker.

*Barker, Daye.* Wigan. Clockmaker. Born 1747, son of William Barker above. Not known to have worked after father's death (1787). Liverpool museum have painted-dial bracket clock c 1800 signed 'Barker of Warrington and Wigan'—may be by him?

*Barlow, Benjamin.* Oldham. Clockmaker. Longcase clock noted c 1775.

*Barlow, Edward.* Warrington. See *Booth, Edward.*

*Barlow, Edward.* Oldham. Several brass-dial clocks noted of mid-18th century, c 1750–70.

*Barlow, James.* Eccles/Oldham. Clockmaker. Daughter, Mary, 1788 at Eccles by wife, Elizabeth. May also have worked at Oldham.

*Barlow, Richard.* Manchester. At 15 Great Ducie St in 1851.

*Barlow, Robert.* Liverpool. At 13 Hood St in 1848.

*Barned, Israel & Co.* Liverpool. At 3 Lord St in 1822–5. Probably connected with next entry.

*Barned & Co.* Liverpool. No 2 Lord St, 1814–15.

*Barnes, George.* Manchester. At 18 Brook St, Chorlton-on-Medlock, 1848–51.

*Barnes, Robert.* Liverpool. Watchmaker at Dale St, 1751–61.

*Barnish, John.* Rochdale. Born c 1760. Brass-dial and painted-dial clocks noted by him. At Great Drake St, 1822–5; at The Crescent, 1828. Died 25 May 1829 aged 69. May be son of William (qv).

*Barnish, William.* Rochdale. Clockmaker. Several clocks reported. Born c 1734. Died there 1776 aged 42.

*Barow, John,* Rochdale. Watchmaker. Died 1769.

*Barr, ——.* Bolton. Painted-dial clock noted c 1815–20.

*Barr, Henry.* Prescot. Apprenticed watchmaker to James Diverton in 1751 for £18.

*Barret, James.* Manchester. Watchmaker. Son, Micah, born 1678.

*Barrington, Isaac.* Liverpool. At 118 London Rd in 1834.

*Barron, James.* Prescot. Watchmaker. Issue by wife, Ellen: 1823 Henry; 1825 Joseph.

*Barron, Thomas.* Liverpool. Son of Henry Barron of Knowlsley, husbandman. Apprenticed in 1710 to William Laithwaite of Liverpool, watch-case maker, for £15. Worked at Templars Hey pre 1722, then at Strand post 1722. Various children born between 1718 and 1724. Believed to have made watches as well as cases.

*Barrow, David Ratcliffe.* Prescot. Watchmaker and watch-hand maker. Various issue born to wife, Jane, between 1819 and 1826.

*Barrow, Edward.* Warrington. Apprenticed in 1728 to William Denton, watch-tool maker, at £4.

*Barrow, John.* Prescot. Watchmaker. Issue by wife, Elizabeth: 1823 John; 1825 Thomas; 1826 John.

*Barrow, Robert.* Farnworth. Watchmaker, 1848–51.

*Barrow, Thomas.* Farnworth. Watchmaker at Widnes in 1818 when daughter, Hannah, born to wife, Elizabeth.

*Barrow, William.* Halewood. Watchspring maker. Took Henry Alkerton apprentice in 1713 for £18.

*Barry, John.* Bolton-le-Moors. Clock and watchmaker at Ashburner St in 1824. White-dial clock noted.

*Barry, Thomas.* Bolton. Clock and watchmaker at 125 Bradshawgate, 1822–9.

*Barry, Thomas.* Ormskirk. Clock and watchmaker there in 1786.

*Barton & Esplin.* Wigan. Established 1831. Wallgate in 1838.

*Barton, James.* Ormskirk. Clockmaker. Repaired house clock for Nicholas Blundell in 1704. Died 1718. Left all tools to his apprenticed grandson, James Barton, son of his son, Henry Barton of Eccleston. Left widow, Ellen, and two daughters.

*Barton, James.* Ormskirk/Eccleston? Clockmaker. An apprentice working for his grandfather, James Barton (qv) of Ormskirk in 1718 when the latter died.

*Barton, John Wand.* Manchester. Watchmaker. Son, John, admitted to school in 1744. Advertised 1746. Died 1770 leaving will.

*Barton, Joseph.* Liverpool. Clock and watchmaker at Derby St, Edgehill in 1834.

*Barton, Richard.* Walton? Son of William Barton, deceased. Apprenticed in 1722 to Lawrence Dewhurst of Walton, clockmaker, for £20.

*Barton, Thomas.* Manchester. Watchmaker. Married 1752 to Mabel Seddon. Died 1791. Sold business 4 June 1782 to Mr Runcorn.

*Barton, William.* Wigan. At Wallgate in 1834. See Barton and Esplin.

*Basnet, James.* Liverpool. Clock,

65

*Basnet, James.* cont.
watch, and chronometer maker
at Roberts St North, 1834–51.

*Basnett, Thomas.* Prescot. Watchmaker. Married Ann Pickern in
1816. Issue: 1818 John; 1823
Thomas; 1826 William. At
Eccleston St in 1834.

*Battinson, John.* Colne/Burnley.
Clock, watch, and gold balance
maker. At Colne 1807–12 when
issue born to wife, Betty. Lived
near Colne church gates. Had
John Spencer (III) as trainee for
a while. At 5 Hall St, Burnley,
1822–5.

*Batty, William.* Manchester. Lower
King St in 1851.

*Bayliff, John.* Manchester. Clockmaker. Married as widower to
Mary Warmishaw, widow, in
1816. May be from Halifax
where a man of this name worked
in 1770.

*Baynes, R.* Bolton. Watchmaker at
108 Higher Bridge St in 1858.

*Beaver, Louis.* Manchester. At 70
Cross St (King St), 1848–51.

*Beaver, William.* Wigan. Clock and
watchmaker at Wallgate in 1822.

*Beesley, George & Richard.* Liverpool.
Clock, watch and chronometer
makers at 56 Great Crosshall St
in 1834. See also under Richard
& George.

*Beesley, James.* Manchester. Watchmaker in *Manchester Mercury* in
1766.

*Beesley, James.* Lancaster. Clock and
watchmaker in 1869 at 18 Cheapside.

*Beesley, James.* Farnworth. Watch-

maker. Married Mary Hoom,
spinster, 1799.

*Beesley, James.* Farnworth. Watchmaker. Married Rachel Bromilow, spinster, in 1812.

*Beesley, James.* Prescot. Watchmaker. Married Ann Lyon,
spinster, in 1819, by whom
daughters born in 1823 and 1825.

*Beesley, John.* Prescot. Watch
movement-maker. Married Margaret Forshaw, spinster, in 1778.

*Beesley, John.* Farnworth. Watchmaker. Married Elizabeth
Roscow, spinster, in 1809.

*Beesley, John.* Prescot. Watchmaker.
Had son, Thomas, by wife,
Sarah, in 1823.

*Beesley, Joseph.* Farnworth. Watchmaker. Married Sarah Thoma-
son, spinster, in 1782.

*Beesley, Joseph.* Farnworth. Watchmaker. Married Jane Abram,
spinster, in 1806.

*Beesley, Joseph.* Farnworth. Watchmaker. Married Mary Lyon,
spinster, in 1810.

*Beesley, Richard & George.* Liverpool.
Watchmakers—see also under
George and Richard. Liverpool
museum have two watches by
them. At 59 Great Cross Hall
St in 1828. At 4–6 Boundary St
in 1848.

*Beesley, Thomas.* Farnworth. Watchmaker. Married Margaret Hitch-
mough, spinster, in 1796.

*Beesley, Thomas.* Liverpool. Watch
and chronometer maker. May be
same man as above. At 16 Lambert St in 1824.

*Beesley, William.* Farnworth. Watch-

*Beesley, William.* cont. maker. Married Mary Leather, spinster, in 1810.

*Beesley, William.* Prescot. Watchmaker. Married Alice Brown in 1817, by whom he had various issue including 1818 William and 1826 John.

*Bell, A.* Whalley. Clockmaker at Oswaldtwistle in 1858.

*Bell, Henry.* Lancaster. Clock and watchmaker. Watch No 288 hallmarked Chester 1800. Bought bracket clock case from Gillows of Lancaster in 1800. Died 1801. Succeeded by Thomas Worswick and Thomas Dickinson.

*Bell, J.* Burnley. Watchmaker at 13 St James St, 1851–8.

*Bell, J.* Garstang. Longcase clock recorded with four seasons spandrels, c 1750.

*Bell, John.* Stretford. Clock and watchmaker there 1848.

*Bell, John.* Lancaster. Clockmaker. Son of John Bell of Poulton, shipwright. Free 1825. May be same man as working at Kirby Lonsdale, Westmorland, in 1828.

*Bell, Peter.* Garstang. Market Place, 1824–5.

*Bell, Thomas.* Liverpool. Liverpool museum have watch, early 19th century.

*Bell, William.* Lancaster. Watchmaker. Lancaster museum have watch by him. Born Coniston in 1836. In 1851 was apprentice to his uncle, William Batty Hodgson, whom he succeeded in business in New Market, where Bell worked 1858–69.

*Bellion, Edward.* Liverpool. Sold imported clocks at 5 Cookson St in 1848 and then at 58 Greenland St in 1851.

*Bellion, William.* Liverpool. Liverpool museum have watch hallmarked Chester 1877–8.

*Bellman, Daniel.* Broughton-in-Furness. Watch and clockmaker. Born 1799, son of William Bellman. Had premises in New St. Son, Thomas, died 1851 aged 11. He died 10 December 1865 aged 66. Widow, Biddy, died at Ulverston in 1877 aged 76. Numerous white-dial clocks recorded.

*Bellman, Thomas.* Ulverston. Watchmaker in Soutergate 1848–51, then still a bachelor. Born 1806 at Broughton, son of William Bellman (qv).

*Bellman, William.* Broughton-in-Furness (and Kendal?). Clockmaker. Issue by wife, Christian: 1790 William; 1792 Susan; 1795 Robert; 1799 Daniel; 1805 John (died 1806); 1806 Thomas. Probably died after 1812. May have gone to Kendal after 1818. Had Henry Hird as apprentice in 1801. Sons, Daniel and Thomas (qv), followed same trade.

*Bennett, William.* Liverpool. At 81 Christian St, 1824–5.

*Bennit, George.* Manchester. Watchmaker. Married Mary Clarkson of Stockport in 1766.

*Benson, Thomas.* Kirkham. Clock and watchmaker at Poulton St in 1848.

*Benton, William.* Liverpool. At 162 London Rd in 1848.

*Berrick, Bernard.* Liverpool. At 19 Great Howard St, 1848–51.

*Berrington, James.* St Helens. At Church St, 1822–34.

*Berrington, James.* Bolton. Clock and watchmaker at Bradshawgate in 1834. May be from St Helens.

*Berrington, John Johnson.* Bolton. Clock and watchmaker and silversmith at 151 Deansgate, 1822–51.

*Berry, Arthur.* Liverpool. Chronometer maker at Great Nelson St, 1824–9.

*Berry, James.* Prescot. Watchmaker. Married Ann Brownbill in 1769.

*Berry, John.* Manchester. Son of Sarah Berry. Apprenticed watchmaker in 1717 to James Ashton for £18.

*Berry, Joseph.* Manchester. At 41 Chapel St, Ardwick in 1848.

*Beswick, William.* Farnworth. Watchmaker. Married Ellen Wilson, spinster, in 1828.

*Bethell, John.* Warrington. Clock and watchmaker at Bridge St, 1822–34.

*Bibby, George.* Prescot. Watchmaker. Son, Ralph, born 1795 to wife, Isabel.

*Bibby, H.* Bolton. Clockmaker in 1858 at Bradshawgate.

*Bibby, Ralph.* Prescot. Watchmaker. Daughter, Mary, born 1819 to wife, Ellen. May be son of George above.

*Bibby, Thomas.* Liverpool. At 7 Renshaw St in 1828.

*Bickerstaff, Peter.* Liverpool. Clock and watchmaker and jeweller at Byrom St in 1814; Hunter St in 1822; then Byrom St again in 1828.

*Bickerstaff, Robert.* At 29 Circus St, 1822–5.

*Bickerstaff(e), William.* Liverpool. Watchmaker and jeweller at 95 Highfield St in 1795; 55 High St in 1800; 11 Strickland St in 1828.

*Billinge, James.* Liverpool. Watchmaker at 10 Highfield St, 1795–1814.

*Billinge, John.* Wigan. Watchmaker, free there 1671.

*Billinge, Topping.* Liverpool. Watchmaker at 16 Cropper St in 1790.

*Binch, James.* Liverpool. Clockmaker at Plumb St in 1767; then at Lombard St in 1777.

*Birch, James.* Liverpool. Clock and watchmaker at 12 Standish St in 1834.

*Birch, John.* Farnworth. Watchmaker. Married Mary Atherton in 1795. Son Joseph born same year.

*Birch, Joseph.* Farnworth. Watchmaker. Married Elizabeth Lythgoe, spinster, 1793.

*Birch, Richard.* Heywood. Watchmaker there in 1828.

*Birchall, G.* Warrington. Liverpool museum have early 19-century watch movement.

*Birchall, George.* Prescot. Watchmaker. Married in 1766 Mary Birchall (*sic*).

*Birchall, James.* Prescot. Watchmaker. Issue by wife, Sarah: 1823 Mary; 1825 Sarah.

68

*Birchall, John.* Liverpool. Watch-maker. Died 1686.

*Birchall, John.* Prescot. Watch-maker. Son, Joseph, entered Manchester school in 1820 aged 15.

*Birchall, Joshua & Mary.* Liverpool. Watchmaker/watch finisher at 4 Edmund St, 1781–9, when died. Widow, Mary, succeeded him there in 1790.

*Birchall, William.* Liverpool. Watch-maker at 7 Ray St in 1796.

*Birchall, William.* Prescot. Watch-maker. Son, James, born to wife, Mary, in 1797. May be same man as above.

*Birchall, William.* Prescot. Watch-maker. Son, Edward, born 1818 to wife, Ann.

*Birckley, Frederick.* Manchester/ Rochdale. Dealer in imported clocks at 6 Gorton St, Salford in 1834; then at West Hill, Roch-dale in 1848.

*Bird, Charles.* Liverpool. Watch-maker. Son, William, born to wife, Margaret in 1822. At 14 Limekiln Lane, 1824–9.

*Birtles, Edward.* Liverpool. Clock-maker at 1 Button St, 1777–97, when died.

*Blackburn, James.* Prescot. Son of William Blackburn. Appren-ticed in 1742 to William Faza-kerly, watchmaker, for £20. A man of this name died there in 1774, described as 'watch wheel finisher'.

*Blackburn, John.* Liverpool. Watch-maker. Son, William, born to wife, Ellen, in 1822.

*Blackburn, Robert.* Liverpool. Watch-maker. Son of John Blackburn, cordwainer. Free at Lancaster in 1817, though worked at Liver-pool.

*Blackhurst, George.* Warrington. Clock and watchmaker at Bridge St, 1851–8.

*Blackmore, Thomas.* Liverpool. At 25 Torbock St in 1824.

*Blakeborough, Charles.* Todmorden. At Patmos in 1848.

*Blakeborough, Henry.* Burnley. Clock and watchmaker, jeweller and silversmith at Market St in 1822; 85 St James St, 1824–34; Blucher St in 1848; 33 St James St in 1851. Wall clocks recorded.

*Blakeborough, John.* Bacup. Clock and watchmaker and jeweller at Union St in 1848; Market St in 1851.

*Blackborough, John Mangle (Man-gie?).* Burnley. Watchmaker at 33 St James St, 1858. May be from Bacup.

*Blakeborough, William R.* Heywood. Market St in 1851.

*Blakeburn, W.* Burnley. Watch-maker at Padiham in 1858.

*Blakely, John.* Liverpool. Clock-maker there in 1784.

*Blore, William.* Liverpool. Watch-maker. Took Henry Brown apprentice in 1752 for £19 5s and Joseph Bailey apprentice in 1756 for £35.

*Blundell, Thomas.* Liverpool. Liver-pool museum have watches hall-marked Chester 1837 and 1883. At 4 Slater's Court, Castle St in 1822; 26 Rupert St in 1824; 54

*Blundell, Thomas.* cont. Upper Pitt St, 1828–34; 50 Great George St, 1848–51, in which latter years also listed as chronometer maker.

*Boardman, Samuel.* Manchester. Son of James Boardman. Apprenticed clockmaker in 1742 to William Kay for £2 10s. Deceased by 1760, when son, James, admitted to school.

*Bold, John.* Prescot. Watchmaker. Son, William, born to wife, Hannah, in 1794.

*Bold, John.* Liverpool. At 37 St Ann St in 1851.

*Bold, Matthew.* Bold near Farnworth. Longcase clock noted, 3 train, chiming on 8 bells—c 1780.

*Bold, William.* Liverpool. Clock and watchmaker and jeweller at 20 Gerard St, 1828–34. Longcase clock reported c 1820.

*Bolton, Henry.* Liverpool. At 32 Oldhall St, 1848–51.

*Bolton, Robert.* Wigan. Clockmaker. There by 1797. Also a gunsmith, and later listed as such. Wife, Alice, died in 1811 aged 44. Son, William, born 1783, died 1791.

*Bolton, T.* Liverpool. Liverpool museum have watch hallmarked Chester 1857.

*Bolton, Thomas.* Manchester. Watchmaker in *Manchester Chronicle* in 1791.

*Bond, ——.* Manchester. Watch by him reported stolen from William Anderson's shop in Lancaster in 1798.

*Bond, John Turner.* Preston/Blackpool. Clock and watchmaker at 58 Friargate, Preston in 1848; then at Church St, Blackpool in 1851.

*Bond, Samuel.* Liverpool. At Albert St, Toxteth Park in 1848.

*Bond, William.* Liverpool. Sold imported clocks in Limekiln Lane, 1848–51.

*Boore, John.* Liverpool. Watchmaker. Advertised 1782. Retired 1784.

*Booth, Charles.* Manchester. Watchmaker. Married Hannah Dobsworth in 1792.

*Booth, Edward.* Warrington. Born 1636. Changed name to Edward Barlow later in life. Credited with invention of rack striking c 1676. Did not work in Lancashire however, though born there.

*Booth, George.* Manchester. Watchmaker from Pontefract. Married Mary Bowker in 1760. Son, James (qv) admitted to school in 1773. Advertised in *Manchester Mercury* in 1762. Died 1788.

*Booth, George.* Manchester. Listed at Turner St, 1822–5.

*Booth, James Bawker (Bowker?).* Manchester. Presumably son of George Booth above. Listed at Friday St, Spear St, 1822–4.

*Booth, John.* Manchester. Watchmaker mentioned in *Manchester Mercury* in 1782.

*Booth, John.* Stalybridge. At Rossbottom in 1824.

*Booth, John Richard.* Ashton-under-Lyne. Clock and watchmaker at 55 Oldham Rd in 1834.

*Bootle(s)*, *Thomas*. Wigan. Watchmaker at 52 Wallgate, 1851–8.

*Bosket*, *R*. Liverpool. Liverpool museum have early 19th-century watch.

*Bott*, *Thomas & Co*. Liverpool. Watchmakers and jewellers at 79 St James St, 1848–51. Liverpool museum have watch hallmarked Chester 1853.

*Bowden*, *George*. Rainhill/Liverpool. Son of Thomas Bowden. Apprenticed watchmaker in 1747 to John Yates of Rainhill for £35. In 1781 listed at 6 Sharehill St.

*Bowker*, *Mrs*. Manchester. Watchmaker there in 1762 (*Manchester Mercury*).

*Bowler*, *Joseph*. Manchester. Seller of foreign clocks at 48 Carruthers St in 1851.

*Bowler*, *Richard*. Manchester. Clockmaker. Married Ann Bardsley in 1802.

*Bowman*, *Richard*. Manchester. At 8 Barton St, Hulme in 1851.

*Bowness*, *George*. Lancaster. Watchmaker. Born 1836. In 1851 still an apprentice living in Upper King St with widowed mother, who was a charwoman. In 1869 in business in North Rd.

*Bradberry*, *Matthew*. Bolton. Clock and watchmaker in Great Moor St in 1824.

*Braddock*, *John*. Manchester. Son of John Braddock of Hatfield, Derbyshire. Apprenticed clockmaker in 1744 to John Oliver of Manchester for £20.

*Bradford*, *J*. Liverpool. Reported as working in 1815.

*Bradley*, *James Gibbon*. Liverpool. Clock, watch and chronometer maker, also jeweller in Richmond Row, 1828–34.

*Bradley*, *John*. Blackburn. Clock and watchmaker at Salford Bridge in 1824.

*Bradley*, *John*. Todmorden. Supposedly working there 1822.

*Bradley*, *William*. Lancaster. Clockmaker. Born in 1785 at Liverpool. At Lancaster by 1831 where children Thomas and Jacob born. Resided in Germany St in 1851.

*Bradshaw*, *James*. Blackburn. Clock and watchmaker at Darwen St in 1834; 18 King William St in 1848; Church Street, 1851–8.

*Bradshaw*, *James*. Prescot. Watchmaker. Issue by wife, Elizabeth: 1818 Caroline; 1823 George Woodward; 1825 Elizabeth.

*Bradshaw*, *John*. Manchester. Clock and watchmaker. Married there in 1766 Elizabeth Barnett, widow. Mentioned there in 1788 as a Quaker. Said to have come from York, though I cannot confirm this. Might be same man as below. See also Cooper & Bradshaw.

*Bradshaw*, *John*. Manchester. Watchmaker. In Deansgate, 1822–34. Salford museum have watch hallmarked 1823.

*Bradshaw*, *John*. Liverpool. Watchmaker. Son, James, born to wife, Alice, in 1834. At 31 Clayton St in 1834. At Wavertree, 1840–51.

*Bradshaw, Peter.* St Helens. Watchmaker at Sutton, 1769–80. Sons, John, born 1769, Richard 1772.

*Bradshaw, T. and W.* Bolton. Watchmakers at 21 Hotel St in 1858.

*Bradshaw, Thomas.* Manchester. Watchmaker there in 1764 (*Manchester Mercury*).

*Bradshaw, Thomas.* Prescot. Watchmaker. Married Elizabeth Bold in 1793. Issue born 1795–7.

*Bradshaw, William.* Liverpool. At 39 Leeds St in 1814; 4 Leigh St in 1824; 72 Gerard St in 1834.

*Bradshaw, William.* Blackburn. Watchmaker, jeweller and silversmith at King William St in 1851.

*Bradshaw, W.* Bolton. Watchmaker at 22 King William St in 1858.

*Braithwaite, William.* Hawkshead. Listed there 1824–6. Died 1829 aged 47 (according to Hobbs).

*Bramble, William.* Liverpool. Watchmaker in 1790 at Mill Lane, Islington.

*Breckell, Richard.* Holmes. Clockmaker. Died 1756. Administration proved Richmond.

*Brewer, John.* Rochdale. Died 1720. Recorded as a clockmaker, but inventory describes him as hardwareman. No clocks in stock when he died.

*Brewer, Richard.* Prescot/Lancaster?/London? Apprenticed in 1760 to John Lancaster of Prescot, watchmaker. Free at Lancaster in 1783, when listed as from Oxford St, London.

*Brewer, Thomas.* Preston. Son of John Brewer of Lancaster. Was watchmaker working at Preston when made freeman of Lancaster in 1817. At 36 Lord St in 1824, then in Market Place, 1828–58.

*Brewer, Thomas.* Clitheroe. Clock and watchmaker at Market St in 1822.

*Brewer, William,* Blackburn. At 1 Lord St in 1824–8.

*Bridge, Henry.* Farnworth. Watchmaker. Married Margaret Fenney in 1794.

*Bridge, Thomas.* St Helens. Watchmaker. Married Rebecca Edwardson 1771, by whom he had several children. Believed married again in 1807 to Mary Knight, though possibly a different watchmaker of the same name.

*Bridge, Thomas.* Manchester. Clockmaker. Married Ann Smethurst there 1739. This might be the Wigan clockmaker of the same name below.

*Bridge, Thomas.* Bolton. Clockmaker. Died there 1717. Widow, Elizabeth, survived him. Inventory of his goods survives.

*Bridge, Thomas.* Wigan. Clockmaker. Free 1712. May be son of above? Married in 1716 Ellen Winstanley. Repaired church clock several times. There till at least 1745. Date of death unknown. Wife died 1727. Sometimes signed clocks 'Bridge de Wigan' *cf* Burgess de Wigan, Hindley de Wigan.

*Brierley, Joseph.* Ashton-under-Lyne. Jeweller at 110 Stamford St in 1848.

*Brimilow, Peter.* Prescot. Watchmaker. Born 1766, son of Thomas Brimilow. Various issue baptised at Burtonwood in 1790s. Died at Eccleston 1808 aged 43. Widow died 1829. *cf* Bromilow.
*Brindle, Ralph.* Liverpool. Clock and watchmaker at Derby St, Edgehill in 1834.
*Broadbent, John.* Ashton-under-Lyne. At 216 Stamford St, 1834-48.
*Broadbent, T.* Ashton-under-Lyne. Watchmaker at 310 Stamford St in 1858.
*Broadhurst, James.* Liverpool. At 4 Trowbridge Place in 1824.
*Brodrick, Thomas.* Preston. 179 Friargate in 1834.
*Bromilow, George.* Prescot. Watchmaker. Son, Thomas, born 1794 to wife, Mary.
*Bromilow, Thomas.* St Helens. Watchmaker at Hardshaigh and Eccleston when issue born by wife, Ellen between 1820 and 1837.
*Brooks, Abel.* Stalybridge. High St in 1848.
*Broom, Charles.* Prescot. Watchmaker. Married Ellen Thomas, 1823.
*Brown, ——.* Liverpool. Liverpool museum have longcase clock signed thus c 1735—see Joshua.
*Brown, Edward.* Manchester. 29 Market Place, 1848-51.
*Brown, George.* Farnworth. Watchmaker. Married Ann Ledward, 1831.
*Brown, Henry.* Liverpool. Watchmaker. Apprenticed 1752 to

William Blore at £19 5s. At Ranelagh St in 1761. Died 1773.
*Brown, Henry.* St Helens. Watchmaker at Windle in 1786 when daughter born.
*Brown, Henry.* St Helens. Watchmaker at Windle when married Alice Lea, by whom several children born 1809-13. Same man as above?
*Brown, J.* Prescot. Chronometer maker at Chorley House in 1858.
*Brown, James.* Liverpool. Clock and watchmaker. Watch No 1413 hallmarked 1814; then at 46 London Rd. At 62 Whitechapel, 1822-34.
*Brown, James.* Liverpool. Liverpool museum have watch Chester hallmark 1888.
*Browne, Jeremy.* Liverpool. Watchmaker. Son, William, admitted to Manchester school in 1744.
*Brown, John.* Manchester. Watchmaker from Warrington. *Manchester Journal* 1772. Son, James, died 1779 aged 5 (by wife Sarah).
*Browne, Joseph.* Manchester. 111 Market St in 1834.
*Brown, Joshua.* Liverpool. Clockmaker. Married Elizabeth Shortcar 1711, by whom children Thomas (1716) and William (1723). Listed at Cable St in 1734 and 1773. May be two men in succession covered this long period?
*Brown, Nathaniel.* Manchester. Clockmaker. *Manchester Mercury* 1762. Blackburn museum have clock. Several brass-dial clocks noted of c 1760-70, including

73

*Brown, Nathaniel.* cont.
one in marquetry case and one in carved oak case.

*Brown, Richard.* Farnworth. Watchmaker. Married Alice Scott 1828.

*Brown, Richard.* Prescot. Watchmaker. Issue by wife, Betty, 1819–24.

*Brown, Robert.* Barrowford, nr Colne. Clockmaker there 1851–8.

*Brown, Thomas.* Liverpool. 33 Renshaw St in 1848. 136 Vauxhall Rd in 1851.

*Brown, Thomas.* Manchester. Watchmaker at 289 Deansgate in 1824; then at Bridge St, 1828–51. Son, Thomas, entered school in 1831 aged 8.

*Brown, William.* Preston. Watch and clockmaker at 133 Church St in 1851; then at 28 Fishergate in 1858.

*Brown, William.* Prescot. Watchmaker. Son, John, born 1794 by wife, Mary.

*Brown, William.* Farnworth. Watchmaker. Married Elizabeth Sparkes, 1815.

*Brown, William.* Manchester. Clockmaker. Married Elizabeth Armitage 1791. Married Hannah Sutton 1796. Not clear whether one maker or two with same name.

*Brown, William.* Prescot. Watchmaker. Married Betty Houghton 1818, by whom son, James, born 1824.

*Brown, William.* St Helens. Watchmaker of Windle. Children born between 1766 and 1786.

*Brown, William.* St Helens. Watchmaker at Sutton in 1836 when son, William, born to wife, Alice.

*Browne, William.* Liverpool. Clockmaker at 32 Castle St. Insolvent 1774.

*Brownbill, Edmund.* Prescot. Watchmaker at Rainhill in 1796 when son, Edmund, born to wife, Martha.

*Brownbill, James.* Liverpool. Several men of this name here including: cannot distinguish. 1795 at 34 Highfield St; 1800 at 10 Bixteth St; 1814 at 47 Prussia St; 1828–34 at 25 Earle St; 1848–51 at 19 Richmond Row; 1848–51 at 6 Prussia St.

*Brownbill, James.* Poulton nr Preston. Watchmaker at Poulton, 1851–8.

*Brownbill, John.* Liverpool. Several of this name, including: 1769 at 16 Prussia St; 1796 at James St; 1814 at Pownall Square; 1822–34 at 48 Prussia St. Child John born to wife, Ann, 1834.

*Brownbill, John.* Prescot. Watchmaker at Rainhill. Issue by wife, Mary, 1818–23.

*Brownbill, Robert.* Liverpool. At 5 Dansie St in 1851.

*Brownbill, R. S.* Fleetwood nr Preston. Watchmaker at Church St in 1858.

*Brownbill, Thomas.* Eccleston. Watchmaker. Married Margaret Pownall 1816. Son, John, born 1819.

*Brownbill, Thomas.* Liverpool. Watchmaker at 15 Prussia St in 1774; 26 Union St in 1781.

*Buchanan, John.* Ashton-under-Lyne. Clock and watchmaker, Scotland St, 1822–8.

*Buckford, William.* Liverpool. Lost watch advertised in 1795 (No 4507).

*Bullman, John.* Liverpool. Clockmaker. Married Ellen Rowson in 1707. Daughter, Mary, born 1708. Lived at Dale St.

*Bullman, Thomas.* Liverpool. Clockmaker. Children born, 1701 Robert; 1702 Sarah; 1704 Rebecca. Lived at Dale St.

*Bunyan & Gardner.* Salford. At 25 Market Place, 1848–51. In latter year also at 51 Chapel St. Salford museum have longcase clock.

*Burb(r)idge, Joseph & Elizabeth.* Manchester. At 60 King St in 1848. In 1851 succeeded by Elizabeth there—his widow?

*Burgess, ——.* Liverpool. Liverpool museum have two late 18th-century longcase clocks. May be Bezaliel (qv)?

*Burgess, Bezaliel.* Liverpool. Watchmaker. Lost watch reported 1751. At Pool Lane, 1769. Listed as Burgess & Langton, 1767.

*Burges(s), John.* Wigan. Clockmaker. Married Margaret Winkley there 1711. Free 1712. Married again in 1737 to Margaret Beisley. Died 1754 aged about 65. Longcase clock in Wigan library. Some signed 'de Wigan' *cf* Hindley.

*Burgess, John.* Liverpool. Watchmaker of Toxteth Park, died 1716.

*Burgess, John.* Manchester. Sold imported clocks at 34 London Rd in 1851.

*Burgess & Langton.* Liverpool. See Burgess, Bezaliel.

*Burgess, Richard.* Manchester. Clock and watchmaker mentioned in *Manchester Herald* in 1793.

*Burgess, Samuel.* Manchester. Clockmaker. Died 1753 leaving will. Apparently no sons to succeed him.

*Burghart, Augustin.* Bolton/Salford. In 1834 at Derby St, Bolton. Sold imported clocks at 44 Greengate, Salford, 1848–51.

*Burns, Richard.* Manchester. Watchmaker. *Manchester Journal* 1778. Died 1806, leaving will.

*Burquart, Augustin.* Manchester. At 44 Green Gate, Ardwick in 1848 selling imported clocks. Probably directory error for A. Burghart (qv).

*Burrows, John.* Farnworth. Watchmaker. Married Margaret Jones, 1782.

*Burrows, Richard.* Liverpool. Bootle Lane, Kirkdale in 1848.

*Burrows, Thomas.* Liverpool. 1848 at 3 Shaws Brow; 1851 at 160 Dale St.

*Burton, Isaac* (senior). Ulverston. Clockmaker. Born 1797 at Backbarrow, son of Jonathan. Married Susannah Parkin from Leicestershire in Ulverston 1821. Children born: 1826 Jonathan (succeeded father qv); 1828 Isaac (became a clockmaker); 1832 Thomas (became a draper); 1837 Margaret. Worked at Soutergate, then after 1822 at King St.

*Burton, Isaac* (senior). cont. Succeeded in 1865 by son, Jonathan. Many white-dial clocks recorded.

*Burton, Isaac* (junior). Ulverston. Clockmaker. Son of Isaac Burton senior, born 1828. Journeyman clockmaker in 1851 at Stanley St with wife, Margaret, and children, George born 1851 and Isaac born 1849. Later worked with brother, Jonathan junior, at Queen St.

*Burton, Jonathan* (senior). Ulverston. Clockmaker. Came from Backbarrow about 1819 after death of first wife. Married again 1819 to Mary Fell. In Duke St, 1822–5. White-dial clocks recorded. Succeeded by son, Isaac (qv), born 1797.

*Burton, Jonathan* (junior). Ulverston. Born 1826, son of Isaac senior. Clockmaker. Succeeded to business in Queen St in 1865. Still there 1869.

*Burton, Thomas.* Ulverston? Place of work uncertain. Repaired local clocks 1808, 1809, 1811.

*Burton, W.* Rawtenstall. Clock and watch cleaner in 1858 at Crawshaw Booth.

*Burtonwood, William.* Farnworth. Watchmaker. Married Hannah Moor, 1801.

*Bushell, Mathew.* Bold. Apprenticed 1761 to John Ansdale of Bold, watch movement-maker, for £30.

*Bushell, Robert.* Liverpool. Watchmaker. Married Jane Kinsey, 1709. Several children born between 1711 and 1724, including

Thomas born 1719. Worked initially at Thomas St, by 1722 at Ormond St, later at Water St, then in 1724 at Chorley St. Still working 1734.

*Bushel/Bushall, Thomas.* Liverpool. Watchmaker at Dale St in 1761. Lost watch No 22 reported 1773.

*Butler, Mrs.* Bolton. Clock and watchmaker at Church Gate in 1822.

*Butler, W.* St Helens. Watchmaker and jeweller at 47 Church St, 1851–8.

*Butterfield, John.* Todmorden. Clockmaker at Dobroyd in 1824.

*Butterworth, H.* Bacup. Watchmaker at Queen Street in 1858.

*Butterworth, H.* Rawtenstall. Watchmaker at Bank St in 1858.

*Byrne, ———.* Liverpool. Liverpool museum have late 19th-century regulator.

*Byron, John.* Prescot. Watchmaker. Married Mary Heaps 1822 by whom daughter, Ann, born 1826.

*Byron, Thomas.* Prescot. Watchmaker. Married Ellen Berry 1820, by whom daughter, Elizabeth, born 1825.

*Caddick, Richard.* Liverpool. Clock and watchmaker at 10 Birkett St in 1834.

*Cairnz(?), John.* Liverpool. 62 Paradise St in 1848.

*Calbrook, James.* Manchester. Clock dealer at 412 Oldham Rd in 1848.

*Calderbanck, Richard.* Farnworth. Watchmaker. Married Elizabeth Hurst, 1783.

*Callwood, John & Susannah.* Liverpool. Clockmaker at 20 Whitechapel in 1790. Died 1800. Succeeded by Susannah.

*Camb, T.* Manchester. Clockmaker at Newchurch in 1858.

*Cameron, A.* Liverpool. Watchmaker working pre-1800. Liverpool museum have 3 watches.

*Cameron, Alexander.* Liverpool. Chronometer-maker at 54 South Castle St in 1848.

*Cameron, John R.* Liverpool. Chronometer-maker at 54 South Castle St in 1851.

*Cammack, Robert.* Ormskirk. Clock and watchmaker at Moor St, 1848–58.

*Campbell, Thomas.* Broughton. Clock and watchmaker 1858–66. Longcase clock reported.

*Cannin, Joseph & Co.* Liverpool. 44 Limekiln Lane in 1848.

*Carnes, John.* Liverpool. 62 Paradise St in 1851.

*Carr, James.* Chipping/Garstang. At Chipping, 1828. High Street, Garstang, 1848–58. Presumably same man.

*Carruthers, John.* Lancaster. Born 1813 in Carlisle. In 1851 lodging with widowed grocer at 18 Chapel St. Bachelor and watchfinisher.

*Carter, James.* Warrington. Clock and watchmaker, silversmith and swordsmith at Bridge St, 1822–48.

*Carter, James* (junior). Warrington. Clock and watchmaker at Horse Market St in 1834.

*Carter, Joseph.* Warrington. Bridge St, 1848–51.

*Carter, Robert.* Warrington. Bridge St in 1822.

*Cartmell, John.* Kirkham. Watchmaker at Freckleton St, 1851–8.

*Case, Henry.* Prescot. Watchmaker. Child, Jane, born to wife, Mary, in 1826.

*Case, James.* Prescot. Watchmaker. Married Mary Helsby 1810. Various children born as late as 1826.

*Catterall, James.* Prescot. Watchmaker. Son, John, born 1797 to wife, Betty.

*Catterall, John.* Liverpool. Watchmaker at 10 Cropper St, 1790–1800.

*Catteral, Joseph.* Bolton. 1828 at Blackhorse St.

*Catterall, Peter.* Liverpool. Watchmaker at Key St in 1763; Cases St in 1773.

*Cawley, John.* Manchester. Watchmaker. Son, Thomas, born 1744.

*Cawson, Edward.* Lancaster. Clockmaker. Born 1759, son of John Cawson. Free 1779. Issue born to wife, Jane: 1780 Ann; 1783 Mary; 1785 Elizabeth. Dates of birth of sons not known. Son, Thomas, cotton spinner; son, John, whitesmith. Died sometime after 1811 and before 1817. Longcase clocks recorded. Known to have bought some cases from Gillows of Lancaster.

*Cawson, James.* Greta Bridge/Liverpool. Clockmaker. Born 1757, son of John Cawson of Lancaster and elder brother of Edward Cawson above. Free 1779, then working at Greta

77

*Cawson, James.* cont. Bridge. By 1790 had moved to Park Lane, Liverpool. Son, Thomas, pilot; son, William (qv), watchmaker. Still working as clock and watchmaker and engraver in 1822. Succeeded by widow, Mary by 1828.

*Cawson, William.* Liverpool. Watchmaker. Son of James Cawson of Liverpool above. Free 1817. In 1834 Ellen Cawson at 110 Park Lane would seem to be his successor.

*Chadwick, Benjamin.* Liverpool. Liverpool museum have watch with Chester hallmark for 1841. Known to have also made chronometers. At 69 Lord St, 1848–51.

*Chadwick, James.* St Helens. Clock and watchmaker and optician at Westfield St, 1848–51.

*Chadwick, John.* Liverpool. Clockmaker at 5 Smithfield St, 1790–6. May be same man as below.

*Chadwick, John.* Manchester. Clockmaker. Married Ruth Worral there 1797. Perhaps worked at Liverpool—see above.

*Chadwick, Joseph.* St Helens. Watchmaker there when son, William, born to wife, Alice, in 1834.

*Chambers, James.* Liverpool. 5 Blake St in 1828–34.

*Chambers, R.* Bolton. Church Bank in 1858.

*Champion, Richard.* Liverpool. Liverpool museum have watch c 1790–1800. Cf Richard Tompion.

*Chapman, Ann.* Liverpool. 45 Castle St in 1834.

*Chapman, Joseph.* Liverpool. 84 Old Hall St in 1822.

*Chapman, Moses.* Liverpool. Chronometer maker at 28 Castle St in 1848.

*Charleston, John.* St Helens. Watchmaker there in 1836 when son, Thomas, born to wife, Ann.

*Cheetham, J.* Leigh. Watchmaker at Market St in 1858.

*Cheetham, Samuel.* Middleton. Clockmaker. Buried there 5 September 1769. Left will.

*Chesworth, Thomas.* Prescot. Watchmaker. Children born there 1819–24.

*Chesworth, William.* Prescot. Watchmaker. Daughter, Mary, born 1825 to wife, Ellen.

*Chethword, John.* St Helens. Watchmaker at Sutton in 1774 when daughter born.

*Chew, John.* Prescot. Watchmaker. Children born 1794–6 by wife, Betty, included son, Thomas who may be Thomas below.

*Chew, Thomas.* Prescot. Watchmaker. May be son of John above, born 1794. Children born there 1819–26.

*Chorley, Matthew.* Prescot. Married Ann Anderson 1817. Working till 1825 at least. Listed as watch tool maker as well as watchmaker.

*Chorley, William.* Prescot. Watchmaker. Married Elizabeth Tickle 1823. Son, Matthew, born 1825.

*Christian, J.* Manchester. Stand Lane, Whitefield, Pilkington in 1858. May be from Liverpool—see below.

*Christian, John.* Liverpool. 20 Plumbe St in 1834. Later at Manchester?

*Clare, Peter* (I). Manchester. Clock and watchmaker of repute. Working by 1764 (*Manchester Mercury*). Married Mary Whittall 1772. Working in Deansgate then. Said to have resided in Cheshire, but clock of c 1765 noted signed at Eccles. Later succeeded by son, Peter, though not known exactly when.

*Clare, Peter* (II). Manchester. Clockmaker, son of above. At 48–50 Quay St, off Deansgate, 1822–9. By 1834 at 16 Quay St where remained till 1851. Dealt in imported clocks too. Regulator dated 1849 in Mosley St Art Gallery, Manchester.

*Clark & Morris.* Liverpool. 33 Church St in 1851.

*Clarke, R.* Liverpool. Liverpool museum have watch hallmarked Birmingham 1824.

*Clark, Thomas.* Ashton-under-Lyne. Clockmaker. Died 1712. Administration and inventory list interesting materials in his workshop.

*Clark, Thomas.* Windle. Clocksmith. Died 1726 leaving will.

*Clark, Thomas.* Cartmel Fell/Ulverston. Clock and watchmaker, son of Cornelius Clark, watchmaker. Free 1767. Believed moved to Ulverston by 1770 till c 1800.

*Clark, Theodore Cuthbert.* Ulverston. Probably worked at Kirkby Lonsdale, Westmorland c 1820.

Watchmaker and auctioneer at Queen St, Ulverston by 1825. Watch No 348 reported made in 1825. At King St in 1828. Various white-dial clocks recorded.

*Clark, William.* Liverpool. Clockmaker at 66 Tithebarn St, 1824–8.

*Claughton, Joseph.* Prescot. Watchmaker. Married Jane Claughton (*sic*), 1759.

*Clay, James.* Manchester. Foreign clocks at Broad St, Pendleton in 1851.

*Clay, Thomas.* Liverpool. 1851 at Limekiln Lane.

*Clayton, John.* Prescot. Clockmaker. Died 1754 leaving will. Widow Joan.

*Clayton, Martin.* Manchester. Watchmaker. Married Mary Watson 1789. Working there by 1800. At 99 Market St in 1822; 58 Picadilly in 1824. Had sons, Martin, George Edward and Japhet.

*Clayton, Peter.* Liverpool. Watchmaker there in 1754.

*Clegg, James.* Manchester. 17 Bradford St in 1848.

*Clegg, William.* Manchester. Three addresses given 1848–51, probably three shops: 19 Travis St, London Rd; 113 Canal St, Gt Ancoats; 63 Oxford St.

*Clegg, William Frederick.* Manchester. 118 River St, Hulme in 1851. Could be fourth shop of above William.

*Clements, Thomas.* Liverpool. Bracket clock c 1790 noted.

79

*Cleminson, George.* Ulverston. Clock-maker. Hobbs records his death as 15 March 1776 aged 76.

*Clewer, William Henry.* Todmorden. Cheapside in 1851; Strand, 1858–66.

*Cliff, John.* St Helens. Watchmaker at Sutton. Daughter born 1769.

*Clifton, John.* Liverpool. Clock-maker. At 16 Fazackerley St in 1777. Died 1794. Various long-case clocks recorded including two in Liverpool museum.

*Clitheroe, John.* Farnworth. Watch-maker. Married Ellen Ackers, 1831.

*Clitherow, John.* Rainhill. Watch-maker. Daughter born 1819.

*Clitherow, Thomas.* Eccleston. Watchmaker. Son, Thomas, born there 1819 to wife, Ann.

*Clitherow, Thomas.* Liverpool. 10 Warren St, 1828–34. May be same man as above, qv.

*Clitherow, Thomas.* St Helens. Watchmaker. Married Elizabeth Leaf 1770.

*Clitherow, William.* Prescot. Watch-maker at Sutton in 1796 when son, Henry, born to wife, Jane.

*Clitherow, William.* Prescot. Watch-maker. Daughters born to wife, Ann, 1823 and 1825.

*Clough, John.* Manchester. Clock-maker. Unusual clock with astrological features known of mid-18th century date. Son, James, born 1744. Married 1756 (?second) Sarah Pimblot—Mr E. L. Edwardes records.

*Clowes, B.* Liverpool. Watch hall-marked 1775, another 1806.

*Clowes, D.* Liverpool. Liverpool museum have watch hallmarked 1806.

*Clowes, John Joseph.* Liverpool. 68 Christian St, 1828–34; 5 Clare-mont Place, Kirkdale, 1848–51, where sold imported clocks.

*Cluley, William.* Manchester. Clock-maker. Married Elizabeth Scott, 1802.

*Coates, Archibald* (I). Wigan. Clock and watchmaker of repute. Working by 1759. Two watches and clock in Wigan museum. Made both brass- and painted-dial clocks. Often signed simply 'Coates-Wigan' probably indi-cating joint family product. Sons Archibald, James and Robert succeeded him. Died 1797 leav-ing will.

*Coates, Archibald* (II). Wigan. Son of above, of age by 1795. Worked till c 1810 then became licensee of 'The Cock' in Millgate (Hawkes).

*Coates, James & Robert.* Wigan. Sons of Archibald (I). Made both watches and clocks, though James seems to have been the watchmaker and Robert the clockmaker. Watches in Liver-pool and Preston museums; watch by James in Wigan museum. Working by 1794. Robert died in 1800 leaving will. James continued till at least 1811.

*Cobb, James.* Liverpool. Imported clocks at 4 Rumford Place in 1851.

*Cobham, Joshua.* Liverpool. Variously described as watch-

*Cobham, Joshua.* cont. maker and watch case-maker. Children born 1674–81.

*Cockshot, Ann.* Liverpool. 81 Gerrard St in 1814.

*Cockshutt, Edmund.* Liverpool. Watchmaker at 12 Highfield St in 1800.

*Cockshott, John.* Liverpool. 18 Rigby St in 1796 as watchmaker.

*Cockshott, William.* Liverpool. 3 Highfield St, 1790–6; 35 Bridport St in 1824.

*Cockshoot, William.* St Helens. 22 Church St in 1848.

*Cohan, Asher & Son.* Liverpool. 53 South Castle St, 1848–51.

*Cohan, John.* Liverpool. Clock, watch and chronometer-maker at 15 Cannon Place in 1834.

*Cohen, Max.* Manchester. Liverpool museum have watch movement c 1850.

*Cohen, Simeon.* Liverpool. 38 Sir Thomas's Buildings in 1834.

*Coigley, James.* Liverpool. Clock, watch and chronometer-maker at 22 Paradise St in 1822; 57 Paradise St in 1824; 77 Hanover St in 1834.

*Coleman, Benjamin & Co.* Liverpool. 69 Church St in 1834.

*Coleman & Chapman.* Liverpool. 60 Castle St, 1824–8. Liverpool museum have bracket clock c 1825.

*Collier, David.* Etchells?, nr Manchester (Eccles?). Various longcase clocks noted by this man signed without place, mostly late 18th-century brass dial. Died 1792—administration.

*Collier, James.* Rochdale. St Mary's Gate in 1834, clock dealer.

*Collier, Peter.* Warrington/Manchester. Watchmaker. In *Manchester Mercury* 1787. Came from Warrington.

*Collier, Robert.* Blackburn. King St, 1828–9. Later to Salford?

*Collier, Robert.* Manchester. 122 Chapel St, Salford in 1848. From Blackburn?

*Collier, Samuel.* Eccles, Manchester. Clockmaker. Buried Eccles 14 June 1806 aged 56.

*Collier, Thomas.* Manchester. 8 Acton St in 1834.

*Collinge, W.* Burnley. 15 Cheapside in 1858.

*Collingwood, Henry.* Rochdale. Blackwater St in 1824; Yorkshire St in 1848; 2 Cheetham St in 1858.

*Collingwood & Rainton.* Rochdale. Albion Place in 1828.

*Collingwood, Robert.* Rochdale. Packer St in 1824.

*Comberbach, Edward Stephen.* Blackburn. 48 Victoria Buildings, New Market Place in 1858.

*Condliff, James.* Liverpool. Clocks, watches and turret clocks. Circus St in 1822; Fraser St, 1824–51. Liverpool museum have 12-bell painted-dial musical clock playing tune every third hour, also two turret clocks (one carillon). Also watch.

*Cooke, John.* Trafford. Liverpool museum have watch movement c 1750–60.

*Cooke, William.* Liverpool. 68 Byrom St in 1834.

*Cookson, Thomas.* Ulverston. Canal St in 1822.

*Cooper, J.* Eccles, Manchester. Church St, Eccles, 1848–58.

*Cooper, T.* Earlestown. Liverpool museum have watch of mid-19th century.

*Coppell, ——.* Liverpool. Lost watch advertisement 1767.

*Coppell, Zallel.* Liverpool. 10 Cases St in 1848.

*Coppock, Thomas.* Prescot. Watchmaker. Married Elizabeth Swift 1769.

*Corlett, James.* Liverpool. Great Howard St in 1848.

*Cornah, James.* Lancaster/Manchester. Watchmaker. Free at Lancaster 1777. Bankrupt 1785. Died 1795 at Manchester. Watch by him stolen from William Anderson's shop in Lancaster in 1798.

*Cornwall, James.* Liverpool. 6 Church Lane in 1824.

*Costala, Thomas.* Liverpool. Watchmaker at 2 Pemberton Alley in 1781.

*Costen, Adam.* Kirkham. Several brass-dial clocks noted of c 1760–80.

*Costen, John.* Kirkham. Watchmaker. Died 1803 leaving will. Wife Ellen. Brother was William Costen (qv) with whom he worked.

*Costen, William.* Kirkham. Watchmaker in association with brother, John (qv) till 1803, after which presumably continued alone.

*Cotterell, Joshua.* St Helens. Clock-

maker at Eccleston in 1785 when son, Joshua, born.

*Coughin, James.* Manchester. At 306 Deansgate, 1828–9; 2 Deansgate in 1834.

*Coulton, John.* Ulverston. Clock and watchmaker. Born 1793 at Kendal. Worked at Duke St, 1822–51. Wife, Margaret, came from Cumberland. Painted-dial clocks recorded.

*Coulton, Thomas.* Ulverston. Recorded by some authorities but I cannot trace him and feel this is an error for John above.

*Coward, J.* Warrington. Clockmaker at 36 Dolman's Lane in 1858.

*Coward, William.* Lancaster. 25 Penny St in 1822.

*Cowburn, Henry.* Kirkham. Poulton St, 1848–58.

*Cowburn, J.* Preston. Clock and watch-cleaner at 18 Fylde St in 1858.

*Cowel, David.* Manchester. 64 Shudehill in 1851. Cf David Cowen.

*Cowell, Henry.* Liverpool. Watchmaker at 8 Little Woolton St, Lowhill in 1848.

*Cowen, David.* Manchester. Dealer at 6 Bradshaw St in 1848. Cf David Cowel.

*Cragg, James.* Milnthorpe/Manchester. Clockmaker. Free 1779. Son of Robert Cragg of Heversham. Was at Milnthorpe in 1779. Probably at Manchester by 1801 and still there 1817. Brass-dial clocks recorded.

*Cragg, John.* Liverpool. Watch-

*Cragg, John.* cont. maker there in 1822 when daughter born to wife, Margaret.

*Cranage, John.* Liverpool. Clock, watch, and chronometer-maker in Hunter St, 1824–34.

*Cranage, Joseph.* Liverpool. 10 Horatio St in 1824.

*Cranage, Thomas Stokes.* Liverpool. At Islington, 1824–34. See Cronage, Thomas.

*Crichlow (also Cricklow and Crunchlow), Thomas.* Liverpool. Clockmaker. Married Catherine Tyrer 1704. At Castle St, 1705–12, when children born.

*Crighton, James.* Manchester. Clockmaker. Married Elizabeth Hercules 1799.

*Critchley, Henry.* St Helens. Watchmaker in 1836 when daughter born to wife, Elizabeth.

*Critchley, Joseph.* Manchester. 230A Deansgate in 1851.

*Critchley/Crouchley, Lawrence.* Prescot. Watchmaker at Eccleston. Son, Thomas, born 1796 (Crouchley); daughter, Mary, born 1824 (Critchley). May be same man or two different men.

*Critchley, Robert.* Liverpool. At Benns Gardens, 1822–5.

*Critchley, William.* Liverpool. At 47 Standish St in 1814; 35 Ben Jonson St in 1828.

*Croasdale, Thomas Roscoe.* Bury. 12 Rock St, 1848–58.

*Cronage, Thomas.* Liverpool. 9 Spitalfields in 1814. *Cf* Cranage, Thomas.

*Crooksll, Richard.* Farnworth. Watch-

maker. Married Margaret Bromilow 1822.

*Cross, James.* Prescot. Watchmaker. Married Elizabeth Wainwright 1788 by whom he had, amongst others, son, William, born 1795.

*Cross, John.* Liverpool. Watchmaker at Crosshall St in 1795.

*Cross, Richard.* Farnworth. Watchmaker. Married Ellen Millineux 1801. Son, John, born Prescot, 1818.

*Cross, Robert.* Farnworth. Watchmaker at Eccleston. Married Margaret Holme 1790. Son, Richard, born 1796.

*Cross, William.* Prescot. Watchmaker. Married Ellen Holyhead 1819, by whom daughter born 1824.

*Crossley, Henry (Humphrey?).* Manchester. At Hunts Bank, 1822–8. One directory calls him Humphrey.

*Crouchley, Thomas.* Prescot. Watchmaker. Died 1773. Another of same name died 1782.

*Crowe, John.* Liverpool. 86 Greenland St in 1848; 6 East Side, Queens Dock in 1851.

*Crowley, John.* Manchester/Liverpool. Watchmaker. Married Mary Harris at Manchester 1821. At 5 Rice St, Liverpool, 1834.

*Crump, Thomas.* Liverpool. Watchmakers—probably error for Thom & Crump (qv). 1 Webster St in 1790; 35 Highfield St in 1795.

*Crumpsty, Thomas.* Liverpool. 60 Harrington St, 1822–5.

*Culverwell, Richard Major.* Liverpool. At 21½ Tithebarn St in 1834.
*Curran, Thomas.* Liverpool. 6 Hawke St in 1824.

*Dagnall, Henry.* Liverpool. Watchmaker. Married Caroline Irwin, 1834.
*Daniels, Henry.* Liverpool. At 39 Castle St, 1814–22. By 1824 was Henry & John below.
*Daniels, Henry & John.* Liverpool. Patent lever watches and chronometers and silversmiths at 39 Castle St in 1824; St George's Crescent, 1828–51. From 1834 also had second shop in Lord St till 1851.
*Daniels, James.* St Helens. Watchmaker at Dutton where children born 1823–6 by wife, Elizabeth.
*Daniel, Thomas.* Kirkham. Son of Mary Daniel. Apprenticed to Henry Hindley in 1761 as clockmaker. Not known whether actually worked in Kirkham.
*Darbyshire, Roger.* Wigan. Watchmaker. Free 1662. Died 1690, according to Hawkes.
*Davenport, ——.* Liverpool. Lost watch reported 1752.
*Davies, Edward.* Dalton/Barrow. At Market St, Dalton in 1866. Also had shop at The Strand, Barrow, 1866–9.
*Davies, George.* Todmorden. There 1837.
*Davies, Henry.* Prescot. Watchmaker. Married Rachel Ackers, 1769.
*Davies, William.* Farnworth/Liverpool. Watchmaker. Married Mary Platt at Farnworth 1818. At 64 Church St, Liverpool in 1814.
*Davison, R.* Liverpool. Watch reported c 1790.
*Dawes, John.* Ulverston. Married Margaret Walker, 1792 (Hobbs).
*Dawson, Stewart & Co.* Liverpool. Liverpool museum have watch hallmarked 1887.
*Dean, J.* Leigh. Watchmaker at Bradshawgate in 1858.
*Dean, Joseph.* Clitheroe. At Lowergate in 1824.
*Dean, Richard.* Leigh. Market St in 1828–51.
*Dean, Thomas.* Leigh. Market St in 1824.
*Dean(s), Thomas.* Eccles, Manchester. Church St, 1828–58.
*Decachent, Stephen.* Manchester. Watchmaker in *Manchester Mercury* 1794.
*Dellesser, Ellis.* Liverpool. 48 Castle St in 1824.
*Dennett, James.* St Helens. 5 Market St, 1822–48. Bracket clock reported.
*Dennett, John.* Wigan. Cross Keys Yard in 1851; 7 Market Place in 1858.
*Dennett, Thomas.* St Helens. Tontine St in 1851.
*Denton, George.* Prescot. Watchmaker. Child born to wife, Mary, in 1795.
*Denton, William.* Warrington. Watch tool-maker. Took Edward Barrow apprentice in 1728 for £4.
*Deveny, Thomas.* Lancaster. Watchmaker. Born 1817 in Liverpool.

*Deveny, Thomas.* cont. Bachelor lodging in Market St, Lancaster in 1851.
*Dewhurst, Laurence.* Walton. Clockmaker. Took Richard Barton apprentice in 1722 for £20.
*Dewhurst, William.* Ribchester. Shopkeeper. Dressed church clock for 2s 4d in 1670.
*Dewhurst, William Bolton.* Clitheroe. Watchmaker at Church St, 1824–8. At Castle St, 1834–58.
*Dewsbury, Samuel.* Salford. 51 King St in 1851—see Duesbury, Samuel.
*Dickinson, John.* Warrington. Died 1722.
*Dickinson, John.* Lancaster/Cartmel. Clocksmith. Free at Lancaster 1750. Married same year Catherine Noble. After 1755 moved to Cartmel. By 1778 had moved to Egremont, Cumberland. Believed died 1780 aged 56.
*Dickinson, John.* Manchester. Watchmaker. Son of William Dickinson, architect. Working at Manchester in 1817 when made a freeman of Lancaster.
*Dickinson, Richard.* Liverpool. Watchmaker at Oldhall St by 1714, when daughter born. Died 1743.
*Dickinson, Thomas.* Lancaster. Watchmaker. Free 1796. Lancaster museum have two watches, one signed 'Dickinson (successor to H. Bell) Lancaster'.
*Dickon, Mary Ann.* Manchester. 109 Market St in 1848.
*Dillon, Jonathan.* Manchester.

Watchmaker. Married Ann Prockter 1804.
*Dismore, Thomas.* Liverpool. Bold St, 1848–51. Maker to the Queen.
*Diverton, James.* Prescot. Watchmaker. Took Henry Barr apprentice in 1751 for £18.
*Dixon, James.* St Helens. Watchmaker at Eccleston in 1819 when daughter born to wife, Ann.
*Dixon, William.* St Helens. New Market in 1851.
*Dodsworth, James.* Liverpool. Liverpool museum have watch Chester hallmark for 1879.
*Doke, Richard & Sarah.* Liverpool. 33 Lord St in 1834. Sarah Doke at 11 Lord St in 1848, probably his successor.
*Doke, William.* Farnworth. Watchmaker. Married Mary Woodward there 1820.
*Doncaster, Thomas.* Wigan. Watchmaker and silversmith. Working there by 1756 when married Hannah Rizley. Married secondly Ann Scott 1792, who died 1800 aged 51. Later he was also a banker and mayor in 1795 and 1798 (Hawkes). Preston museum have watch of 1773.
*Done, William.* Manchester. Watchmaker in *Manchester Journal* 1778.
*Donkin, Gerard.* Liverpool. Imported clocks at 83 Dale St, 1848–51.
*Donking, James.* Liverpool. Importer and manufacturer of brass and wood clocks and toys at 42 Dale St, 1828–34. At 74 Richmond Row, 1848–51.

F

85

*Donney, W. J.* Liverpool. Liverpool museum have watch c 1860.

*Douglas & Co, Robert.* Liverpool. Watchmaker at 4 Plumb St in 1781. At 53 Ranelagh St, 1822–8.

*Douglas, Samuel & Robert* (junior). Liverpool. 53 Renshaw St in 1814.

*Doward, H.* Widnes. Crow Wood, 1851–8.

*Doward, Henry.* Farnworth. Watchmaker. Married, 1786, Mary, daughter of William Garnett (qv), watchmaker of Cronton.

*Doward, William.* Farnworth. Watchmaker at Appleton in 1834; Widnes in 1848.

*Dowell, Daniel.* Liverpool. 11 Croston St, 1790–6.

*Dowling, William.* Liverpool. 29 Circus St in 1834.

*Downing, John.* Liverpool. Watchmaker. Duke St in 1790; Cheapside in 1800. Wigan museum have watch made in 1815.

*Downing, Samuel.* Liverpool. Dale St in 1761; Castle St in 1769. Working still 1784.

*Drescher, Simon (Samuel?).* Manchester. 1 Coop St, 1824–8 (marked as Samuel in 1828). At 44 Shudehill in 1834, listed as maker of German and Dutch clocks. White-dial longcase clock noted c 1820.

*Drielsma, Isaac Jones.* Liverpool. Clock, watch and chronometer maker at Hanover St, 1834–51.

*Drielsma, Morris.* Liverpool. 40 Elliot St in 1848; 18 Parker St in 1851.

*Drinkwater, John.* Liverpool. Watchmaker at 30 Pool Lane in 1777.

*Drummond, Thomas.* Liverpool. 15 Ben Jonson St in 1814.

*Duesbury, Samuel.* Manchester. 1 Lever St in 1822. See Dewsbury.

*Duff, William & Co.* Liverpool. 25 Tithebarn St, 1834–51.

*Duggan, Thomas.* Liverpool. Watchmaker at Dry Dock in 1781.

*Dumbell, John.* Liverpool. 100 Scotland Rd, 1828–34.

*Dumbell, Joseph.* Liverpool. Watchmaker at 9 Newhall St in 1800.

*Dumbell, Joseph.* Rochdale. Yorkshire St in 1828; The Walk in 1834.

*Dumbell, Thomas.* Rochdale. Watchmaker and jeweller at Blackwater St in 1822; 4 New Market in 1824.

*Dumbell, William.* Prescot. Fazackerly St, 1828–58.

*Dumville, John.* Hulme. Clockmaker, son of Nathaniel Dumville (qv), clockmaker. Married there in 1857 to Ann Slater.

*Dumville, Nathaniel.* Hulme? Clockmaker. Alive in 1857 when son, John, married. Must have been working by 1836 when son born.

*Duncan, R.* Liverpool. Liverpool museum have watch hallmarked 1805.

*Dunks, David.* Accrington. Abbey St in 1848. See Tunks.

*Dutton, John.* Liverpool. Watchmaker at 20 Highfield St in 1800; 3 Temple Court in 1822.

*Dutton, Samuel.* Liverpool. Watchmaker in 1790.

*Dyke, William.* Liverpool. Watch and watch spring-maker at 67 Plumb St, 1777–90.

*Dyson, George.* Manchester. Watch-maker. Married Sarah Ralphs 1847. At 15 Scott St, Hulme in 1848; Moss Lane in 1853; then Tamworth St in 1855 and Lower Moss Lane in 1858, when son, George, born.
*Dyson, Humphrey.* Manchester. Watchmaker at 168 Deansgate in 1824; 6 Churchgates in 1828.
*Dyson, Jacob.* Farnworth. Watch-maker. Married Ellen Berry 1787. Still there 1795.

*Eaton, Joseph.* Prescot. Watchmaker. Daughter born 1824 by wife, Mary.
*Eckersley, Richard.* Chowbent. Cinderhills in 1848.
*Eden, Ralph.* Liverpool. Working 1773–96. See also Vernon & Eden.
*Edmonds, B.* Liverpool. Lost watch reported 1778. Could be same man as below.
*Edmonds, D.* Liverpool. Liverpool museum have nine watches dated between 1775 and 1810.
*Edmondson, John.* Liverpool. Watch-maker at Ray St, 1790–6.
*Edwards, D.* Liverpool. Lost watch reported 1783. *Cf* D. Edmonds above.
*Edwards, Francis.* Liverpool. Clock and watch dial-enameller at 24 Park St, Toxteth in 1848.
*Edwards, James.* Manchester. Clock-maker. Married Susanna Moston, 1792.
*Edwards, Richard.* Liverpool. 170 Dale St in 1851.

*Edwardson, John.* Liverpool. Watch-maker. Advert 1751. Dale St, 1754–61. May be son of William below?
*Edwardson, William.* Liverpool. Watchmaker. Probably born 1695. Issue between 1715 and 1722 including John born 1718.
*Eggleston, J.* Salford. Salford museum have papier mâché wall clock of late-19th century.
*Eld, Richard.* Manchester. Watch-maker. Son, Richard, born 1702.
*Eldershaw, Thomas.* Manchester. Clockmaker. Married Ann Hardman, 1803.
*Ellam, William.* Sutton. Clock-maker. Will proved 1777.
*Ellis, George.* Manchester. Clock-maker. Married Mary Smith there 1792.
*Ellis, James E.* Liverpool. Whole-saler. York Chambers, 22 North John St in 1848.
*Ellison, Henry.* Childwall (nr Liver-pool). Clockmaker. Died 1750 leaving will mentioning sons, William, Arthur and Robert. To grandson 'my watch which I generally carry about with me'.
*Ellison, Robert.* Eccleston. Watch-maker. Died 1798 leaving will. May be same man as below.
*Ellison, Robert.* St Helens. Watch-maker of Windle. Married Mar-garet Pickavance 1771. Children born 1772–83.
*Ellison, Samuel.* Liverpool. Watch-maker at 64 Preston St, 1767–77.
*English, David & Mary.* Manchester. Watchmaker. Married Mary Chadwick 1803. Mary English

87

*English, David & Mary.* cont. listed at 7 Blackfriars in 1824, presumably his widow and successor.

*Ensworth, Robert.* Liverpool. Clockmaker there in 1734.

*Entwistle, William.* Prescot. Watchmaker. Children born by wife, Jane, 1824–6.

*Erlam, Job.* Sutton. Watchmaker. Probably born 1738. Married Alice Garnet 1759. Children born: 1760 Job and 1763 Parcival (qv).

*Erlam, Parcival.* Sutton. Watchmaker, son of Job Erlam above, born 1763. Had twins by wife, Mary, 1795.

*Erling, Jonathan.* Wigan. Clockmaker. Fined in 1699 for working without being free, and not heard of again (Hawkes).

*Esplin, George.* Wigan. Clockmaker. Established in 1831. Succeeded in 1858 by Royle and Rawson. Premises in Wallgate. Watch and clock recorded.

*Etchells, Matthew.* Manchester. Clockmaker. Married Mary Radford, 1766.

*Etches, John.* Liverpool. 29 Lime St in 1828.

*Evans, Edward.* Liverpool. 67 Brunswick Rd in 1848. Liverpool museum have painted-dial longcase clock signed 'E. Evans-Liverpool' supposedly c 1800.

*Evans, George.* Liverpool. 8 Exchange St East, 1848–51.

*Evans, W. T.* Haslingden. Painted-dial longcase clock noted, dated 1824.

*Eyett, John.* Liverpool. Watch No 1879 hallmarked 1864—then at 64 Netherfield Rd North.

*Fairclough, Edward.* Liverpool. Watchmaker at Castle St, 1774–1800.

*Fairclough, Henry.* Liverpool. Watchmaker at Castle St in 1773.

*Fairclough, Jeffrey.* St Helens. Clock tool forger in 1822. In 1834 listed as movement maker and clock materials supplier.

*Fairclough, John.* St Helens. Watchmaker at Windle in 1833 when child born by wife, Ann.

*Fairclough, Richard.* Liverpool. Watchmaker. Richmond St in 1781; Bevington Bush in 1796.

*Fairhurst, John.* Liverpool. 143 N Scotland Rd in 1824.

*Falk, David & Co.* Manchester. 53 Market St in 1851.

*Fallar, Theodor Kuss.* Manchester. Imported clocks at 2 Broughton Rd South, 1851.

*Fallows, John Baptist.* Manchester. Maker of German and Dutch clocks (ie importer) at 5 Old Bridge St in 1834.

*Fallows, Thomas.* Preston. 21 Adelphi St in 1851.

*Farnworth, John.* Liverpool. 11 Mill St in 1851.

*Farnworth, Thomas.* Blackburn. 55 King William St in 1858.

*Farran/Farrow S.* Ashton-under-Lyne. Clockmaker at 40 Cavendish St in 1858.

*Farrer, John.* St Helens. Watchmaker. Married Mary Evans 1815. Daughter born 1819.

*Fawcet(te)*, ——. Liverpool. Brass-dial longcase clock c 1715 noted signed 'Fawcette in Leverpoole fecit'. Liverpool museum have one, c 1725.

*Fayrer, James.* Lancaster. Clocksmith. Free there 1783. Son of Thomas (qv).

*Fayrer, Thomas.* Lancaster. Clocksmith. Free 1744. Probably still alive in 1783 when son, James, was free there. Clocks, longcase and bracket and watches recorded.

*Fazakerley, Henry.* St Helens. Watchmaker. Married Thomasin Bolton 1787.

*Fazakerly, James.* Rainford. Watchmaker. Married Margaret Standish there as bachelor 1824.

*Fazakerley, James.* St Helens. Watchmaker at Sutton. Married Martha Beech, 1819. Children born 1820–30.

*Fazackerly, John.* Liverpool. Watchmaker. Lost watch reported 1744. Pool Lane in 1766. Died 1770 leaving will.

*Fazackerly, John.* St Helens. Watchmaker at Sutton. Married Ann Peeling, 1785.

*Fazakerley, Richard.* Manchester. Watchmaker. Born c 1785. Died at Angel St, 1836, aged 51.

*Fazakerley, Thomas.* Prescot. Watchmaker. Died 1771.

*Fazakerley, William.* Prescot. Watchmaker. Took James Blackburn apprentice in 1742 for £20.

*Fearnley, Peter.* Wigan. Clockmaker at Wallgate. Married Ann Lawson 1776. Nine children born before 1795. Worked at Standishgate, 1801–26. Wife died 1821 aged 67. He died 1826 aged 77. Many longcase clocks recorded. Made clock for Wigan church in 1788 (Hawkes).

*Fell, Abraham.* Ulverston. Clock noted c 1740. Attended clocks at Holker Hall in 1733 and 1744. Man of same name later attended Cartmel church clock till 1800 (Hobbs).

*Fell, James.* Lancaster. Free there as watchmaker 1767. Probably still alive in 1806 when son, Robert, was also free there.

*Fell, John.* Blackburn/Chorley. Blekeley Moor in 1834. May be the same John Fell who was apprenticed c 1825 to Isaac Simpson of Chorley.

*Fell, Joseph.* Ulverston. Clockmaker. Married Eleanor Lowry there 1779. Children born between 1780 and 1787, when also listed as watchmaker (Hobbs).

*Fenny, James.* St Helens. Watchmaker of Bold. Married Elizabeth Woodward 1780, by whom several children.

*Ferns, Richard.* Prescot. Movement maker (for watches?). Married Mary Eaton, 1768.

*Fewller, John.* Liverpool. Clockmaker at Georges St, 1761–80.

*Fielding, Robert.* Liverpool. Lost watch No 23 reported in 1784.

*Fietzen, Andrew.* Liverpool. 10 Jamaica St in 1834; 4 Park Place in 1848.

*Fillingham, Robert.* Prescot. Watch-

89

*Fillingham, Robert.* cont.
maker. Daughter born 1794 to
wife, Hannah.
*Finch, Jonathan.* Prescot. Watchmaker. Married Alice Baker
as bachelor 1819 there.
*Finlow, Ralph.* Prescot. Watchmaker. Son, Ralph, born 1796
to wife, Esther.
*Finney, James.* Prescot. Watchmaker. Son, Thomas, born 1823
to wife, Ann.
*Finney, John.* Liverpool. Clockmaker free 1761. At New Market
in 1761, later Thomas St. Died
1795.
*Finney, Joseph* (I). Liverpool. Born
c 1708, son of John Finney MD
of Wilmslow, Cheshire. Free at
Liverpool 1732-3. At 1 Finney
Lane, Thomas St, 1761-6.
Clockmaker and architect.
Known to have designed the
Octagon Chapel, Temple Court,
Liverpool, later St Catherine's
Church, demolished 1820. Made
turret clocks and musical and
astronomical clocks as well as
ordinary longcase clocks. Two
regulators recorded with year
movements and annual calen-
dars, also various watches and
barometers and scientific instruments. Married Jemina
Whitehurst, who survived him
when he died in 1772, his
business then passing to Thomas
Harrison.
*Finney, Joseph* (II). Liverpool. At 8
Richmond St in 1796, at which
address Jemina, widow of Joseph
(I), was listed in 1790. Uncertain

whether this is a second Joseph
or simply a directory error.
*Finney, Richard.* Liverpool. Bootle
Rd in 1828; Claremont Place,
Kirkdale in 1834.
*Finney, Thomas.* Liverpool. Falkner
St in 1848.
*Fisher, Henry.* Preston. Preston
museum have watch—no date
known.
*Fisher, John.* Preston. Square brass-
dial longcase clock noted c 1740-
50. Early 18th-century clock re-
ported with 'Henry Watson'
engraved in place of VII to V
numerals, right round dial.
*Fisher, Richard.* Liverpool. 11 James
St, 1814-28; at 13 Tarleton St in
1834.
*Fitzer, William.* Liverpool. Maguire
St in 1814; 20 Baptist St in 1822;
11 Gerard St in 1828.
*Fleetwood, Henry.* Prescot. Watchmaker. Married Sarah Hunt,
1769.
*Fleetwood, James.* Liverpool. 74
Highfield St in 1814.
*Fleetwood, Joseph.* Liverpool. Liverpool museum have watch No 29,
c 1750-60.
*Fleetwood, Robert,* Liverpool. Watch-
maker at Dale St in 1790.
*Fleetwood, Thomas.* Prescot. Watch-
maker. Son, Henry, born 1769
to wife, Mary.
*Fleetwood, Thomas.* Liverpool.
Watchmaker in 1754.
*Fleming, James.* Liverpool. Watch-
maker. Married Mary Fresh at
Dalton, 1803 (Hobbs). Listed at
12 Princess St, 1790-5.

*Fleming, Richard.* Liverpool. 13 Blake St in 1814.

*Fletcher, J.* Newton-in-Makerfield. At Earlestown in 1858.

*Fletcher, James.* Ashton-under-Lyne. 205 Stamford St, 1851–8.

*Fletcher, James.* Liverpool. 15 Gay St in 1834.

*Fletcher, John.* Manchester. 89 Brook St; David St in 1851.

*Fletcher, John.* Ulverston. Watchmaker. Born Broughton, 1820. Trading 1848–54 at Fountain St. Wife Caroline from Lincolnshire, by whom had son, John.

*Fletcher, Robert.* Roby-with-Huyton. Clockmaker. Died 1743. Mentions wife, Mary, stepson, John Winstanley and Thomas Fletcher of London, watch casemaker.

*Fletcher, William Frederick.* Ashton-under-Lyne. Old St in 1848; Market Avenue in 1858.

*Flower, Edward.* Liverpool. 77 Renshaw St in 1851.

*Fogg, James.* Manchester. Clockmaker. Married Elinor Bateman there 1801.

*Fogg, John.* Liverpool. 22 North Side Old Dock, 1814–28.

*Fogg, William.* Prescot. Watchmaker. Married Ann Copple, 1756.

*Fogg, William.* Farnworth. Watchmaker. Child born 1818 by wife, Sarah.

*Forber/Forbes, Edward.* Liverpool. 42 Kitchen St in 1814 as Forbes; 75 Gerard St in 1834 as Forber.

*Forber, Joseph.* Liverpool. 105 Park Lane in 1820.

*Forbes, Joshua.* Liverpool. Park Lane, 1834–51.

*Ford, Thomas.* Liverpool. 68 Circus St in 1834.

*Ford, William.* Prescot. Watchmaker. Issue by wife, Sarah, 1824–6.

*Foster, Henry.* Prescot. Watchmaker. Son Henry born to wife, Martha, 1826.

*Foster, Henry.* Liverpool. 7 Williamson Square, 1848–51.

*Forster, James.* St Helens. Watchmaker at Hardshaw and Sutton when children born 1760–7.

*Fo(r)ster, John.* Liverpool. Watchmaker at 2 Lombard St, 1774–7.

*Foster, John.* Manchester. 57 Turner St in 1848.

*Foster, John & Thomas.* Manchester. Imported clocks at 57 Turner St in 1851.

*Foster, John.* Liverpool. Watchmaker. Sons Henry and John born 1823 to wife, Hannah. At 15 Lawrence St in 1824; 18 Gerard St in 1828; 5 Williamson Square in 1834.

*Fo(r)ster, John.* St Helens. Watchmaker at Sutton, 1752–64; then Eccleston, 1764–72. Died 1806, leaving will.

*Foster, John.* Prescot. Watchmaker. Children born to wife, Mary, 1795 and 1797.

*Foster, Ralph.* St Helens. Watchmaker at Parr, 1778–82. He died in 1786, same year as wife, Mary.

*Forster, Ralph.* Farnworth. Watchmaker. Married Beatrix Mather 1824.

91

*Forster, William.* St Helens. Watchmaker at Sutton in 1755 when daughter born.

*Foster, William.* Manchester. Eight-day quarter chiming clock reported c 1750.

*Fothergill, William.* Manchester. Clockmaker. Married Ann Mills, 1791.

*Fox, William.* Liverpool. 22 Lime St in 1848.

*Frame, John.* Manchester. 81 Gt Ancoats St in 1848.

*France, Richard.* Warrington. Clockmaker. Died 1740 leaving will. Apparently died childless. 'To the clockmakers that come to my burial each a pair of gloves . . .' Eight-day square brass-dial clock c 1720 noted signed 'France-Warrington'. Oak case with sunburst inlay on door.

*Franklin, Abraham.* Manchester. 1 St Ann's Place, 1824–34; also at 64 Bridge St in 1824. Watchmaker, jeweller, silversmith and toy warehouse.

*Frederick, Leonard.* Preston. 133 Church St in 1848.

*Freeman, Charles.* Liverpool. 74 Cable St in 1848.

*Friendly, Ralph.* Prescot. Fazackerley St in 1822.

*Frodsham, David.* Liverpool. Clockmaker at 1 Mason St in 1774.

*Frodsham, Henry.* Liverpool. 17 South Castle St, 1848–51. Watches and chronometers.

*Frodsham, Samuel.* Manchester. Clockmaker. Married Jane Lydiate as bachelor 1815.

*Furnival, Benjamin.* Liverpool. Grange St, Birkenhead in 1834.

*Gallimore, Joseph.* Manchester. Clockmaker in 1795 directory.

*Gant, John.* Farnworth. Watchmaker. Married Mary Molyneux, 1787.

*Ganter, Matthew.* Manchester. Imported clocks at 22 New Islington in 1851.

*Gardner, Edward.* Lancaster. Watchmaker. Born 1826 at Halton. Wife, Betsey, from Lancaster. Established by 1851 at Church St and also at 27 New St; at North Rd in 1858 and 6 New Rd in 1869.

*Garner, James.* Liverpool. 1 Rose St in 1834.

*Garner, William.* Manchester. Clockmaker. Married Mary Kelsall, 1799.

*Garnett, Edmund.* Lancaster. Born there 1833, son of Edmund Garnett (senior) a joiner. Apprentice watchmaker in 1851 living with parents.

*Garnett, John.* Bold. Son of William (II). Born 1765. Watchmaker and farmer. Married Rebecca Broadbent 1796. Issue born 1801–11.

*Garnett, Richard.* Bold. Watchmaker and farmer. Born 1757, son of William (II). Married Sara Morris, 1785.

*Garnett, Robert* (I). Bold. Watchmaker and farmer, son of William (II). Born 1770. Married Amelia Gandy 1805, who died

*Garnett, Robert (I).* cont.
1808. After 1808 lived at Penketh. Died 1843 aged 72.

*Garnett, Robert* (II). Farnworth. Son of Robert (I). Born Farnworth 1805. Apprenticed a carpenter in 1819 but later became a watchmaker. Wife named Mary. He died 1877.

*Garnett, Thomas.* Rainhill. Watchmaker. Died 1786.

*Garnett, Thomas.* Sutton/Warrington. Watch and watch-tool maker. Married Elizabeth Bachus 1755 at Warrington. Died 1760.

*Garnett, Thomas.* Bold. Watchmaker and farmer. Son of William (II). Married Jane Moss in 1799. Died 1812.

*Garnett, William* (I). Bold. Watchmaker and farmer. Built Hayfield House in 1744. Son, William, born 1731. Died 1789. Widow, Sarah, died 1795.

*Garnett, William* (II). Cronton. Watchmaker and farmer. Son of William (I). Born 1731. Married Elizabeth daughter of Richard Hankinson, watch-tool maker 1753. Issue included: 1757 Richard (qv); 1765 John (qv); 1768 Thomas (qv); 1770 Robert (qv). Died in 1796. Widow died 1798. In 1756 took Richard Appleton as apprentice for £23.

*Garnett, William* (III). Bold. Watchmaker and farmer, son of William (II). Born 1760 at Farnworth. Married Elizabeth Moss 1799. Issue born 1800–7.

*Garratt, Henry.* Ormskirk. Burscough St in 1824; Moor St in 1828. May be same man as Hugh Garratt below.

*Garrett, Hugh.* Ormskirk. Watchmaker 1786. May be same man as Henry above.

*Gaskes, Samuel Lockett.* Manchester. Broad St in 1851.

*Gatton, Edward.* Liverpool. Watchmaker at Church St in 1769; Pool Lane in 1773.

*Gawne, Charles E.* Barrow. Watchmaker at Church St in 1869.

*Gee, James.* Manchester. Clockmaker. Married Mary Radford, 1774.

*Gee, John.* Farnworth. Watchmaker. Married Sarah Williams, 1812.

*Gee, William.* Warrington. Watchmaker. Died 1750.

*Gerrard, Edward.* St Helens. Watchmaker. Married Martha Boardman, 1776.

*Gervin, Thomas.* Manchester. Clockmaker. Married Elizabeth Smith, 1798.

*Gibbons, John.* Manchester. Clockmaker. Married Hannah Allwood, 1806.

*Gidman, Hugh.* Prescot. Watchmaker. Children born to wife, Margaret, 1795–7.

*Gidonan/Gedman, Joshua.* Prescot. Watchmaker. Children born 1823–5 to wife, Elizabeth.

*Gilhooly, Ephraim.* Manchester. 97 Chester Rd, 1848–51.

*Gill, Isaac.* Manchester. Imported clocks at 141 Higher Chatham St, Chorlton-on-Medlock in 1851.

93

*Gill, John.* Manchester. 141 Upper Chatham St in 1848. See also Isaac Gill.

*Gillet, Charles Edward.* Manchester. Clock and watchmaker. Came from Leek, Staffordshire. Married Alice Barber at Farnworth 1768. At Manchester, 1772–1800. Also hardwareman, hosier and clockmaker, living at Market Lane. Believed also to have been in partnership with John Healey.

*Gillis, Frederick Ludwig.* Liverpool. 57 Ashton St in 1848; 17 Basnett St in 1851.

*Gillows.* Lancaster and London. Firm of cabinet makers, founded at the end of the 17th century by Robert Gillow. The firm flourished and ultimately opened a branch in London c 1770. Records preserved number about 180 volumes. Made clock cases, including some early mahogany ones—eg three for exporting to West Indies in 1744 at £2 5s each. Known to have sold clocks with some of their cases, which they bought from local clockmakers, eg Newbys of Kendal. Some clocks exist with Gillows name on dial, eg one with movement made by Thomas Fayrer, but Gillows on dial. See *Gillows' Clock Cases* by Nicholas Goodison.

*Glatz & Wunderley.* Manchester. Brass, wood and musical clocks at 4 Old Bridge St in 1824. See also below.

*Glatz, Joseph.* Manchester. Successor to above at 4 Old Bridge St, 1828–34, selling German clocks. At Blackfriars St, 1848–51.

*Gleave(s), John.* Liverpool. 36 Highfield St in 1814; 1 Hill St, 1822–51.

*Gleave, Matthew.* West Derby. Watchmaker. Died 1705 leaving will.

*Gleave, Thomas.* Farnworth. Watchmaker. Married Sarah Whitfield, 1805.

*Gledhill, Richard.* Manchester. 240 Oldham Rd in 1834.

*Glover, Alexander.* Prescot/Rainhill. Watchmaker from Rainhill. Married Alice Houghton 1726 at Prescot.

*Glover, Henry.* St Helens. Watchmaker at Sutton when children born including son, Henry, in 1759. Painted-dial longcase clock noted c 1790 signed 'H. Glover —St. Helens'. Another in St Helens library.

*Glover, James.* Prescot. Watchmaker. Died 1765 leaving will.

*Glover, James.* Farnworth. Watchmaker at Widnes in 1834; at Cronton, 1848–51.

*Glover, James.* Sutton. Watchmaker. Child born 1806 by wife, Margaret.

*Glover, John.* Prescot. Watchmaker. Child born to wife, Margaret, in 1795. Died 1801 leaving will.

*Glover, John.* St Helens. Watchmaker at Sutton. Children born 1766–85.

*Glover, John.* St Helens. Watchmaker at Windle in 1819 when son born to wife, Rachel.

*Glover, John.* Widnes. Watchmaker in 1851.

*Glover, Joseph.* Manchester. 63 Shudehill in 1824.

*Glover, Thomas.* Farnworth. At Cronton, 1848–51.

*Glover, Thomas.* Rainhill/Prescot. Watchmaker. Took William Ball apprentice in 1760 for £15. Died 1798.

*Goad, Thomas Turner.* Lancaster. Born Ulverston, 1837. Watchmaker (aged 14) at Marton St in 1851.

*Godwin, William.* Manchester. 54 Great Ancoats St in 1834. See also William Goodwin.

*Goldstein, Jacob.* Liverpool. 110 Whitechapel in 1848.

*Goldstone, Michael.* Manchester. 14 Fountain St, 1848–51.

*Goodwin, Martin.* Manchester. 9 London Rd, 1848–51.

*Goodwin, William.* Manchester. 19 Chester St, Chorlton-on-Medlock, 1848–51.

*Goore, Giles.* Prescot. Watchmaker. Child born to wife, Esther, 1825.

*Goore, John.* Prescot. Movement maker. Married Ellen Summer, 1768.

*Gore, James.* Farnworth. Watchmaker. Married Hannah Garnet, 1798.

*Gore, John.* Prescot. Watchmaker. Married Margaret Lyon 1819. Children born there, 1824–6.

*Gore, John.* Liverpool. Gerard St in 1834.

*Gorsuch, Fleetwood.* Liverpool. 11 Clayton St in 1814.

*Gorsuch, Henry.* Prescot. Watch-

maker. Married Lydia Yates 1773. Died 1784, leaving will.

*Gostage, Samuel.* Liverpool. At Birkenhead in 1834.

*Gowland, George.* Liverpool. 76 South Castle St in 1851. Also chronometers.

*Grace, William.* Liverpool. 66 Crosshall St in 1814.

*Graham, John.* Liverpool. Roscoe St in 1851.

*Graham, Joseph.* Prescot. Watchmaker. Daughter born 1825 to wife, Esther.

*Graham, Joseph.* Farnworth. Watchmaker. Married Ann Pendleton, 1834.

*Graham, Thomas.* St Helens. Watchmaker. Son, Joseph, born 1777.

*Gray, James.* Manchester. Clockmaker. Married Grace Chantler, 1797.

*Grayson, James.* Liverpool. 72 Highfield St in 1814.

*Greaves, Thomas.* Manchester. Watchmaker in 1800.

*Green, E.* (late Thomas). Liverpool. 59 Fleet St in 1822. See Thomas Green below.

*Green, James.* Liverpool. Watchmaker at 10 Peter St in 1800.

*Green, Peter.* Liverpool. Watchmaker listed in 1734.

*Green, Robert.* Liverpool. Watchmaker. Castle St in 1767. Lost watch No 340 reported in 1780.

*Green, Thomas.* Wigan/Kendal. Watchmaker. Born Wigan 1843. By 1870 working at Kendal.

*Green, Thomas.* Liverpool. Watchmaker at Temple St, 1781–96. Listed in 1822 as *late* Thomas

*Green, Thomas.* cont.
Green at 59 Fleet St—see Green,
E. Liverpool museum have
bracket clock and watch.
*Green, Thomas.* Liverpool. Sir
Thomas's Buildings in 1796.
Second shop of above man or a
second man of same name?
*Green, William.* Wigan. Clock and
watchmaker and jeweller in
Wallgate, 1834–51.
*Green, William.* Liverpool. Watch-
maker. Son, William, born to
wife, Margaret, in 1825 at Rose
Hill.
*Green, William.* Prescot. Clock-
maker. Market Place in 1822;
Eccleston St, 1824–34. Children
born to wife, Margaret, there
1819–26.
*Greenall, ——.* Parr (Prescot). Brass-
dial clocks noted signed 'Greenall-
Parr' c 1770–80.
*Greener, C. & F.* Liverpool. Brass
and wood clocks at 4 Richmond
St in 1822.
*Greener, Francis* (& Co). Liverpool.
Dutch and German clocks at 34
Whitechapel, 1824–34. Succes-
sors to above?
*Greenhalgh, Henry.* Manchester. 3
John Dalton St in 1851.
*Greenhalgh, J.* Bury. Liverpool
museum have watch movement
c 1840.
*Greenhalgh, John.* Accrington.
Watchmaker at 86 Abbey St,
1848–58.
*Greenhalgh, John* (& Sons). Man-
chester. German and Dutch
clocks at London Rd, 1828–34;
17 St Mary's Gate, 1848–51.

Also at 33 Market St in 1848
('& sons').
*Greenwood, Charles.* Liverpool. 112
Brownlow Hill in 1848.
*Gregory, James.* Ormskirk/South-
port. Moor St, Ormskirk in 1824.
At Southport, 1828–34.
*Gregory, John.* Ashton-under-Lyne.
117 Stamford St in 1848.
*Gregory, Thomas.* Liverpool. Brass-
dial 30-hour clock, late 18th
century noted.
*Gregson, John.* Lancaster/Ulverston.
Watchmaker of Lancaster. Free
there 1811. Son of Matthew
Gregson, cooper. By 1822 work-
ing at Ulverston Market Place as
clockmaker / silversmith. Still
alive in 1830.
*Gregson, John.* Liverpool. Liverpool
museum have watch c 1825–30.
Same man as above?
*Grener & Co.* Manchester. 4 Old
Bridge St in 1822. See also
Greener.
*Grice, Job.* Ormskirk/Lancaster.
Longcase 8-day clock reported,
second quarter 18th century,
signed Ormskirk. Several re-
corded signed at Lancaster. Seem
to have no actual dates for him.
*Griffiths, David.* Liverpool. 62 Stan-
hope St in 1851.
*Grimshaw, John.* Liverpool. 39 Sir
Thomas's Buildings in 1828.
Also tool dealer.
*Grimshaw, Thomas.* Liverpool.
Chronometer-maker. Married
Ann Robinson, 1834.
*Grocot, Thomas.* Liverpool. Liver-
pool museum have watch move-
ment of late-18th century.

*Grounds, Gabriel.* Dutton. Watch-maker. Died 1724—administra-tion and inventory.

*Grounds, Johnson.* Wigan. Watch-maker at 13 Standish Gate in 1858. Wigan museum have two watches.

*Grundy, John.* Whalley. Brass-dial 30-hour clock noted c 1775–80. Another reported and a third in Blackburn museum.

*Guest, Ralph.* Prestwich. Clock-maker. Died 1728 leaving will. Widow Alice named.

*Gutteridge, Charles.* Hulme. Watch-maker. Son of Edward Gut-teridge, weaver. Married in 1851, aged 30, to Jane Phillips. Lived at 4 Hurlbutt St.

*Guy, John.* Liverpool. Watchmaker. Old Dock in 1790. Died 1799.

*Guy, Peter.* Liverpool. Working by 1689. Died 1741. Clockmaker.

*Hadfield, John.* Manchester. Clock-maker. Son, George, born 1738.

*Hadwen, Isaac.* Liverpool. Clock and watchmaker. Born 1723, son of Isaac Hadwen, senior, clock-maker of Sedbergh and Kendal. Moved to Liverpool shortly after 1737 with widowed mother. Died there 1767.

*Hadwen, Hannah.* Liverpool. Clock-maker at Pool Lane, 1767–9. Widow of Isaac?

*Hadwen, Isaac.* Liverpool. Watch-maker at Pool Lane, 1777–84.

*Hadwen, Joseph.* Liverpool. Clock-maker at Church St, 1761–9.

*Hall, Eaton.* Liverpool. Watch-maker at 31 Pitt St in 1795.

*Hall, James.* Prescot. Watchmaker. Married Betty Hunt 1773.

*Hall, John.* Manchester. 56 King St, 1848–51.

*Hall, Samuel.* Bickerstaffe, nr Orms-kirk. Watchmaker. Died 1737.

*Hall, Thomas.* Prescot. Movement-maker (watch?). Married Esther Erlam, 1778.

*Hall, Thomas.* Farnworth. Watch-maker. Married Ellen Taylor, 1805.

*Hall, Thomas.* Liverpool. Clock, watch and chronometer-maker at 18 Park Rd in 1834.

*Hall, William.* Farnworth/Liver-pool. Watchmaker. Married Elizabeth Lawrenson 1827. Son, Thomas Cummins, born 1834.

*Halliwell, David.* Warrington. Clockmaker at Bridge St in 1834. See also below.

*Halliwell, John.* Warrington. Clock-maker at Bridge St in 1822. See also above.

*Hallows, John.* Liverpool. 1 Holly St in 1851.

*Hallows, Jonathan.* Liverpool. 36 Lionel St in 1824.

*Halpern, Bros.* Manchester. Liver-pool museum have watch c 1870.

*Halsall, Edward.* Liverpool. Watch-maker. Died 1783 leaving will.

*Halsall, Henry.* Halewood. Watch-maker. Died 1767.

*Halsall, Robert.* Ormskirk. Church St in 1828.

*Halshey, Henry.* Lancaster. Watch-maker. Died 1683.

*Halton, G. C.* Lancaster. Lancaster museum have watch.

*Halton, John.* Manchester. Clock-maker. Married Margaret Jones, 1803.

*Hamlet, William.* Liverpool. 128 Richmond Row in 1851.

*Hammond, George & Thomas.* Manchester. 42 Cross St, King St, 1848–51.

*Hampson, Robert* (& Thelwell). Warrington / Wigan / Manchester. Clockmaker. Child born 1758 at Warrington by wife, Betty. Clocks of c 1760 noted made there. Said to have been at Wigan in 1791, when son, Joseph, aged 23, died there (Hawkes). By 1824 was at Manchester as Hampson and Thelwell, jewellers, silversmiths and watchmakers at 2 St Anne's Square. By 1828 was alone again at 2 Ducie Place.

*Hampson, Thomas.* Liverpool. Arched brass moon dial longcase clock noted c 1780.

*Hancock, Daniel.* Manchester. Watchmaker. Married Harriet Roberts 1846. At Hassal St, Hulme in 1850; 94 Clopton St in 1855.

*Hardie & Christie.* Manchester. Clock dial makers in 1824 at 17 Oak St.

*Hardman, Gerrard.* Liverpool (Whiston). Watchmaker. Worked twenty years with father, John Hardman (qv) whom he left in 1768 to work alone. Died 1771 at Whiston.

*Hardman, Gerrard.* Farnworth. Move-ment-maker (watch?). Married Alice Ashton, 1784.

*Hardman, Henry.* Liverpool. Watchmaker. Advertised 1767. At St Paul's Square in 1773.

*Hardman, John.* Wavertree. Watch and clockmaker. Working by 1748. Advertised 1768, when son, Gerrard, left him, having then worked together for 20 years. Some clocks signed simply 'Hardman–Wavertree' probably from this partnership. Liverpool museum have longcase clock and watch. Died 1773.

*Hardman, Samuel.* Prescot. Watchmaker. Son, William, born to wife, Mary, in 1819.

*Hardman, Thomas.* St Helens. Watchmaker. Married Sarah Abbot, 1787.

*Hardman, William.* Manchester. Clockmaker. Married Mary Lee, 1809.

*Hardy, John.* Preston. 19 Fishergate in 1822.

*Hargreaves, Thomas.* Burnley. Painted-dial longcase clock noted c 1780–90.

*Harker, James.* Liverpool. Watchmaker. Probably born 1689. In 1719 at Queen St; 1721 (when son, Thomas, born) near Dock; 1723 (when son, Garnet, born) at Strand St; still there 1725, when son, William, born.

*Harper, William.* Prescot. Watchmaker. Son, James, born 1797 to wife, Esther.

*Harris, Charles.* Liverpool. Clock and watchmaker, 26 Paradise St in 1834.

98

*Harris, Frederick.* Manchester. 3 Corporation St in 1851.

*Harris, Henry James.* Manchester. 6 New Richmond Place, 1828–48. At 6 Broad St in 1851.

*Harris, J. & A.* Liverpool. Salford museum have watch hallmarked 1863.

*Harris, L(azarus).* Liverpool. Salford museum have watch hallmarked 1827, initial L. Lazarus H. at 34 Duncan St in 1851.

*Harris, L.* Manchester. Watch reported made 1881. Watches in Salford museum and Blackburn museum.

*Harrison, James.* Farnworth. Watchmaker. Married Tabitha Leyland, 1834.

*Harrison, John.* Liverpool. Lost watch advertised in 1753.

*Harrison, John.* Liverpool. Watch and chronometer maker at 60 Great Crosshall St, 1824–8; Castle St, 1834–51. In 1848 also had shop at 24 Park St, Toxteth Park. Watch No 10234 hallmarked 1818.

*Harrison, Richard.* Ormskirk. Liverpool museum have watch movement c 1790–1800.

*Harrison, Thomas.* Liverpool. Clock and watchmaker at Finneys Lane, 1774–1800. In 1778 advertised for journeyman. Watch in Liverpool museum. Successor to Joseph Finney in 1772. Died 1814.

*Harrison, William.* Farnworth. Watchmaker. Married Margaret Parr, 1833.

*Harrocks, Joshua.* Lancaster. Clock-maker. Free 1748. Probably worked for the Parkinsons, as some of their clocks have movements bearing his name. One such dated 1746. Made parish church clock in 1759. Still at Lancaster in 1764 when daughter, Sarah, born there. Later moved to Eamont Bridge and clocks signed with this place exist made c 1770. Believed still alive in 1783.

*Hart, Moses.* Liverpool. 134 Park Lane in 1848.

*Hart, Napthali.* Liverpool. Lord St, 1848–51.

*Harvie, William.* Wigan. Repaired church clock 1651. Probably a blacksmith (Hawkes).

*Hatfield & Hall.* Manchester. 56 King St in 1834.

*Hatter, Thomas.* Wigan. Watchmaker at Queens St in 1821 when son, James, born to wife, Catherine.

*Hatton, George Cooper.* Lancaster. Watchmaker, jeweller and silversmith. Claimed to have been born there in 1811, but probably earlier, as he was free there in 1826. Son of Joseph Hatton. At Church St by 1834 but in 1851 moved to Market St. In 1869 was at 17 Cable St. Issue by wife, Ann (Cook), included George Cooper junior, born 1848. His 1851 household included two undergraduates from Durham University.

*Hatton, James.* St Helens. Watchmaker of Sutton in 1768 when son, William, born.

99

*Hatton, Thomas.* Preston. Preston museum have watch c 1790.
*Hatton, William.* St Helens/Liverpool. Watchmaker of Liverpool when issue by wife, Margaret, baptised at St Helens (1827–36).
*Haworth, Richard.* Liverpool. 38 Pitt St in 1834; 77 Pitt St in 1851.
*Hawson, James.* Liverpool. 41 Sir Thomas's Buildings in 1834 as clock and watch dial enamellers.
*Hayes, Christopher.* Oldham. Manchester St, 1848–51.
*Hayes, Edward.* Leigh. Market St, 1848–58.
*Hayes, James Henry.* Oldham. 45 Yorkshire St, 1848–51.
*Hayes, W.* Oldham. 6 Manchester St in 1858.
*Hayes, William.* Liverpool. 20 Paradise St in 1851.
*Hayhurst, John.* Preston. 8 Oxford St in 1851; 133A Church St in 1858.
*Haywood, David.* Manchester. Watchmaker. Married Ann Higgins 1843. In 1848 at 149 Medlock St, Hulme; late 1848 at Foster St, Hulme; 1851 at 13 Regent St, Salford.
*Hayworth, Richard.* Liverpool. 77 Pitt St in 1848.
*Heald, T.* Chorley. Market St in 1858.
*Healey, John.* Manchester. Watch noted made 1793.
*Healey, Thomas.* Manchester. 1822–4 at Old Bridge St, Salford. In 1824 also at 306 Deansgate.
*Heap, John.* Burnley. 29 Cheapside, 1848–51; 18 Market St in 1858.
*Heckle, Alanson / Atkinson / Alison.*

Liverpool. Christian name uncertain due to directory errors. At 73 Park Lane, 1822–4; 2 St James St in 1828. Some authorities list him as Anthony, which is wrong.
*Heckle, Henry Harrison.* Liverpool. 118 Bold St, 1848–51.
*Heinekey, Robert.* Liverpool. 19 Gerard St in 1834.
*Helm. ———.* Ormskirk. Brass-dial 8-day longcase clock noted c 1780.
*Helsby, Edward.* Sutton/Wigan. Watchmaker with wife, Ann and children at Sutton in 1822, Wigan in 1824.
*Helsby, James.* St Helens. Watchmaker at Parr in 1786 when son, James born.
*Helsby, James.* Farnworth. Watchmaker. Married Elizabeth Forshaw 1821.
*Helsby, James Gooden.* Liverpool. 7 Elliot St in 1834.
*Helsby, John.* St Helens. Watchmaker at Sutton in 1820, when son, John, born to wife, Lydia.
*Helsby, John.* Liverpool. Bevington Hill in 1834.
*Helsby, Richard.* St Helens. Watchmaker. With wife, Esther, at Sutton, 1810–32, when children born.
*Helsby, Thomas.* Prescot. Watchmaker. Married Mary Dyson 1817. Child born 1824.
*Helsby, William.* St Helens. Watchmaker at Hardshaw, 1769–87. Children included: 1771 William; 1774 John; 1777 Samuel; 1787 Richard.

*Page 101* (*right*) Eight-day clock
by J. Standring of Bolton
c 1750–60. This is a quarter-
chiming (ting-tang) clock

(*left*) Hood and dial of eight-day
clock by Peter Fearnley of Wigan
c 1780, showing more detail of
this superb workmanship. The
dial has a very unusual pierced
centre, centre seconds and
centre date hands

*Page 102* (*left*) Thirty-hour cottage clock by Grundy of Whalley c 1775, in oak with mahogany trim and standing 6ft 11in. The restriction in height makes for less elegant proportions; (*right*) eight-day clock by Nathaniel Brown of Manchester c 1760–70 in carved case of blackened oak, height about 6ft 10in. The carving is thought to be contemporary with construction

*Helsby, W.* St Helens. Watch-maker at Windle in 1858.

*Hemingway, John.* Manchester. 86 Market St in 1822; Piccadilly, 1828–34.

*Henderson, Alexander.* Bury. 39 Rock St in 1851.

*Henderson, E.* St Helens. Longcase clock of 28-day duration by him in St Helens library. Probably an only clock as thought not to have been a regular clockmaker.

*Hendrick, John.* Liverpool. Tarleton St in 1790; Dawson St in 1800; 6 Williamson Square in 1814.

*Hendrick, John & Peter.* Liverpool. Clock, watch and chronometer-makers. At Church St in 1822. Liverpool museum have watch hallmarked 1840 and a longcase clock c 1830. Semi-regulator noted c 1820.

*Henret, John.* Prescot. Watchmaker. Wife, Mary, had child 1818.

*Heppet, James.* Didsbury. Watch-maker. Died 1781 leaving will.

*Herman, James (Jacob).* Manchester. Son, William, entered school 1831 aged 10. Imported clocks at Chapel St, Salford, 1848–51.

*Hermann, Joseph.* Manchester. German clocks at 47 Shudehill in 1824; 71 Long Millgate in 1828.

*Heron, William.* Liverpool. Listed as clock and watchmaker in 1800.

*Herr, J.* Bolton. 43 Newport St in 1858.

*Hesketh, Thomas & John.* Farnworth. At Cronton, 1848–51.

*Heskey, Henry.* Manchester. Watch-maker in 1781 directory.

*Hesmondhalgh, Edward.* Ribchester. Paid in 1813 for clock face of church—may be a local joiner?

*Hess(s), Ralph & Co.* Liverpool. Wholesaler at 17 South John St, 1848–51.

*Hess, Rosetta.* Liverpool. 36 Pool Lane in 1834.

*Hewit, George.* Prescot. Watch-maker there 1823–5 when children born.

*Hewitt, John.* Prescot. Watchmaker there 1819–24, when children born.

*Hewit, Joseph.* Prescot. Watch-maker. Son, John, born 1796.

*Hewit, Joshua.* Prescot. Watch-maker. Married Ann Rimmer 1788 by whom children born in 1790s. Married (secondly?) Margaret Byrom 1801. Died 1802 leaving will.

*Hewit, Joshua.* Prescot. Watch-maker. Son, Joshua, born 1818 by wife, Elizabeth.

*Hewit, Joshua.* Huyton. Watch-maker. Daughter born by wife, Lydia, in 1794.

*Hewitson, Richard.* Liverpool. Watch-maker. Son of Thomas Hewit-son of Liverpool. Free at Lan-caster in 1817.

*Heyes, Christopher.* Oldham. Market Place in 1822; High St, 1824–34.

*Heys, William.* Liverpool. Watch-maker in directory 1780.

*Hiatt, Henry.* Prescot. Chronometer-maker at Toll Bar, 1848–51.

*Hibbert, Thomas.* Manchester. 6 Victoria Bridge St, Salford, 1848–51.

G

*Hicks, Charles.* Liverpool. 43 Ray St, 1822–8.

*Higginson, Charles.* Prescot. Watchmaker. Child born to wife, Alice in 1796.

*Higginson & Fairclough.* Liverpool. Liverpool museum have watch movement c 1775.

*Higginson, Henry.* Liverpool. Working there as watchmaker by 1675. Wife, Martha, died 1676. Second wife, Elizabeth, died 1679. He died 1694.

*Higham, Robert.* Manchester. 18 Deal St, Salford in 1848.

*Higham, Thomas.* West Derby, Liverpool. Watchmaker. Children born to wife, Mary, 1799–1821.

*Highfield, Joseph / Josiah.* Liverpool. Watchmaker. Listed as Joseph in 1761, Josiah in 1773.

*Highfield, Nathan.* Liverpool. Watchmaker there 1780–90.

*Highfield, William.* Liverpool. Watchmaker at Dale St in 1761. Later to Wrexham and then Oswestry where insolvent 1778.

*Hill, C.* Preston. 9 Market Place in 1858.

*Hill, Richard.* Liverpool. 52 Fontenoy St in 1824.

*Hill, Thomas.* Farnworth. Watchmaker there in 1800 when married Elizabeth Shaw.

*Hill, Thomas.* Rochdale. Guide Post in 1828; Drake St in 1834.

*Hill, William.* Farnworth. Watchmaker. Married Sarah Preston there 1798.

*Hilton, Evan.* Wigan. Watchmaker working there by 1667. Free 1670. Died 1699 (Hawkes).

*Hilton, John.* Liverpool. 10 Earle St, 1848–51.

*Hinchcliff, J.* Oldham. Greenacres Moor in 1858.

*Hind, William.* Oldham. 4 Curzon St in 1851.

*Hindley, (Henry).* Wigan. A maker of repute. Earliest mention seems to be when paid in 1726 for repairing church clock (Hawkes). Clocks known signed 'Hindley de Wigan', include one bearing date of 1730 and one wooden movement. He is believed to be the man who went to York in 1731 and worked there till his death in 1771. His year of birth is calculated as 1701. Can hardly have worked more than 10 years at most in Wigan, hence his Wigan clocks are not numerous. His York clocks include some exceptional items.

*Hird, Henry* (I). Broughton/Scotland. Son of William Hird, blacksmith, of Grisebeck. Apprenticed 1801 to William Bellman of Broughton for 6½ years. By 1815 had moved to Thornhill, Dumfries. Died 1854 when on a visit to Whitehaven aged 65.

*Hird, Henry* (II). Ulverston. Nephew of Henry (I). Succeeded to business of Henry Philipson (junior) after 1851. Longcase clocks recorded. Also jeweller. In Market Place in 1869.

*Hird, Edward & William.* Barrow/Ulverston. Edward succeeded his brother, Henry (II), at

*Hird, Edward & William.* cont. Ulverston c 1880. Had previously begun business at Barrow c 1864. Longcase clocks recorded and also made clocks for the Furness Railway Co. William joined him c 1870. Edward had a very small shop at the head of Market St. An apprentice, Henry Myers Todd, bound in 1889 for six years received 2s 6d weekly the first year, 3s 0d the next year, rising to 8s 0d in the final year. I am told that Edward Hird 'looked like King Edward, with a little pointed beard'.

*Hislop, Alexander.* Liverpool. 56 Pool Lane in 1828; 40 Great Homer St in 1851.

*Hodgson, Henry.* Lancaster. Watchmaker. Son of John Hodgson, ropemaker. Free in 1817.

*Hodgson, John.* Lancaster. Watchmaker and jeweller at Cheapside in 1834, then entrance to Shambles in 1851.

*Hodgson, William Batty.* Lancaster. Watchmaker. Son of John Hodgson, cabinet maker. Free 1820. Shop at 18 Penny St in 1848. In 1851 moved to 2 New Market. Had three employees, including his nephew, William Bell (qv) as apprentice in 1851. Wife, Mary, came from Coniston. Longcase clocks recorded too.

*Hodson, Thomas.* Chorley. Clockmaker. Died 1756. Left stock to wife, Dorothy, and son, James. One clock signed 'Hodson–Chorley' with date 1690 on dial.

*Hoffmayer, Alexander.* Liverpool. Imported clocks at 51 Park Lane in 1851. See next entry.

*Hoffmayer & Cley.* Liverpool. 51 Park Lane in 1848. See previous entry.

*Hoffmayer, Martin.* Liverpool. German clocks at 90 Dale St in 1834.

*Holcroft, John.* Prescot. Watchmaker. Child born to wife, Elizabeth, 1794 and 1797.

*Holden, Joseph.* Liverpool. 58 Sir Thomas's Buildings, 1848–51.

*Holgate, William.* Wigan. Wallgate in 1822. Wigan museum have longcase clock.

*Holison, ——.* Liverpool. Liverpool museum have watch hallmarked 1831.

*Holland, James.* Manchester. Watchmaker. Married Elizabeth Kay, 1791.

*Holland, Richard.* Liverpool. Watchmaker. Died 1747 leaving will.

*Hollingsworth, George.* Liverpool. Watchmaker there 1780–4.

*Hollinrake, James.* Todmorden. 64 York St in 1866.

*Hollinson(e), Alexander.* Liverpool. Liverpool museum have watches hallmarked 1802–7. Also one c 1790 and another c 1795 recorded.

*Hollinson, William.* Liverpool. Liverpool museum have watch movement c 1800.

*Holliwell, John.* Warrington. Clockmaker at Bridge St in 1828.

*Holliwell, Thomas.* Farnworth. Clockmaker. Married Grace Jackson, 1812.

*Holliwell, William.* Liverpool. Clock-maker at Strand St in 1773. Liverpool museum have long-case clock by him c 1770.

*Holme, James.* Manchester. Watch-maker of Newton. Married Mary Hayward of Rochdale, 1665.

*Holme, John.* Cockermouth/Lan-caster/Broughton. Watchmaker. Free at Lancaster in 1783, though of Cockermouth. Born c 1760 at Burton-in-Kendal (Penfold). Married at Broughton in 1785 to Mary Barker by whom children born 1787–8. A man of this name was an inn-keeper there in 1808.

*Holme, Joseph.* Prescot. Watch-maker. Son, Nathan, born to wife, Hannah, in 1825.

*Holme, Lawrence.* Liverpool. Liver-pool museum have watch hall-marked 1758. At Old Dock in 1781; Pitt St in 1790.

*Holmes, Peter.* Liverpool. 49 Green-land St in 1834.

*Holme, Thomas.* Liverpool. Watch-maker at Edmund St in 1767; Plumb St in 1769.

*Holme, Thomas.* Prescot. Watch-maker. Married Ann Varley 1807, by whom children born 1819–26.

*Holt, George.* Manchester. 156 Great Ancoats St in 1851.

*Holt, John.* Rochdale. Clockmaker. Wife, Sarah, buried there 1808. Painted-dial longcase clock noted c 1790–1800.

*Holt, Matthew* (I). Wigan. Watch-maker. Took Thomas Ball ap-prentice in 1752 at £4 4s. Wife

named Isabel. Died c 1782 (Hawkes).

*Holt, Matthew* (II). Wigan. Watch-maker. Son of Matthew (I). born 1745. Free 1789, though already advertising 1782. Died 1805 aged 60 (Hawkes). Left will.

*Holt, Robert.* Haslingden. Cranshaw Booth in 1851.

*Holt, T.* Rochdale. Smallbridge, Wardle in 1858.

*Holt, Thomas.* Lancaster. Watch-maker, free 1747. Married Mar-garet Sherson 1743. Died 1775 leaving will mentioning sons James and William, the latter being a watchmaker in London in 1767.

*Holt, Valentine.* Rochdale. Bank Yard, 1824–34.

*Holt, William.* Lancaster. Watch-maker of London. Free at Lan-caster in 1767 but doubtful whether worked there. Men-tioned in will of father (Thomas) in 1775.

*Holt, William.* Wigan. Watchmaker, born about 1735, believed son of Matthew (I). Working there 1768. Died 1780 aged 45 (Hawkes). Watch in Wigan library hallmarked 1767.

*Hooten, Peter.* Liverpool. Watch finisher. Married Sarah Eckers-ley, 1834.

*Hope, Peter.* Liverpool. Liverpool museum have watch hallmarked 1795.

*Hordern, Joseph.* Manchester. 8 Princess St in 1848.

*Hornby, George.* Liverpool. 3 Cross-hall St in 1795.

*Hornby, George.* Liverpool. Waterloo Rd in 1848; 29 Park Lane in 1851.

*Hornby, Gerrard (& Son).* Liverpool. 10 Hales St in 1795; 12 Princess St 1814–24. Liverpool museum have watch signed '& Son' hallmarked 1837.

*Hornby, Henry.* Liverpool. 34 Cunliffe St in 1814; Vernon Court in 1822.

*Hornby, James.* Liverpool. 34 St Paul's Square, 1824–34; 5 Juvenal Place and also at Lawrence St in 1848.

*Hornby, John.* Liverpool. Watch spring-maker. Working there 1707–24. Example of early specialisation.

*Hornby, John.* Liverpool. 32 Lombard St, 1781–1800; 57 Oldhall St, 1814–28. Also at 19 Myrtle St, 1822–34. Presumably had two shops in this period. Seems to have moved from Oldhall St branch to 49 Prussia St in 1834.

*Hornby, Richard.* Liverpool. Clocks, watches and chronometers. New Scotland Rd, 1814–24; 41 Pool Lane 1828–34; 36 South Castle St, 1848–51. Liverpool museum have watch c 1830.

*Hornby, Thomas.* Liverpool. Watchmaker. Listed in 1784. May be same man still there in 1814 when at 43 Bevington St and 1822 at 61 Gildart's Gardens.

*Hornby, Thomas.* Prescot. Liverpool museum have watch c 1790–1800.

*Hornby, William.* Liverpool. Watchmaker listed there in 1734.

*Horridge, Robert.* Liverpool. Watchmaker in 1800 directory.

*Horrocks, Christopher.* Warrington. Watchmaker. Died 1663 leaving will.

*Horrocks, Joshua.* Lancaster. See Harrocks, Joshua.

*Houghton, James.* Burtonwood/Rainhill. Watch movement-maker. Children born to wife, Hannah, include: 1783 John; 1785 Samuel; 1797 William.

*Houghton, James.* Ormskirk. Watch and gold balance maker. Church St, 1822–51. Liverpool museum have watch hallmarked 1855.

*Houghton, James.* Prescot. Watchmaker. Children born by wife, Elizabeth, 1818–26.

*Houghton, James.* St Helens. 15 Ormskirk St in 1848; 34 Church St in 1858.

*Houghton, John.* Prescot. Watchmaker. Married Margaret Carter, 1779.

*Houghton, John.* Prescot. Watchmaker. Children born to wife, Mary, 1824–6.

*Houghton, John.* St Helens. Watchmaker at Hardshaw in 1778 when daughter born.

*Houghton, John.* St Helens. Watchmaker at Hardshaw in 1824 when wife, Sarah, had son, Thomas.

*Houghton, Michael.* Liverpool. Watchmaker. Son, James, born to wife, Mary, 1819.

*Houghton, Richard.* Liverpool. Watchmaker at Moorfields in 1715 when daughter born. Liverpool museum have watch

107

*Houghton, Richard.* cont. c 1705–10. At Tythe Barn St, 1734–61.

*Houghton, Richard.* Wigan. Clockmaker at Standishgate in 1781 when daughter died. A gunsmith in Hallgate in 1806 when son, Isaac, died aged 12 (Hawkes).

*Houghton, S.* Wigan. 56 Millgate in 1858.

*Houghton, Stephen.* St Helens. 57 Church St, 1848–51.

*Houghton, Stephen & Son.* Ormskirk. Moor St in 1824.

*Houghton, T.* Wigan. Wallgate in 1858.

*Houghton, Thomas.* Kirkham. Poulton St in 1851.

*Houghton, Thomas.* Prescot. Watchmaker. Son, Thomas, born 1794 to wife, Hannah.

*Houghton, William.* St Helens. Watchmaker at Hardshaw. Married Sarah Webster 1821. Working 1822–8.

*Houghton, William.* St Helens. Watchmaker. Married Margaret Stock 1782. Children include: 1783 John; 1785 George.

*Houlbrook, Henry.* Liverpool. 27 Cropper St in 1781; 25 Lawton St in 1790; 6 Soho St in 1814.

*Houlgrave, Edward.* Liverpool. Watchmaker. Bankrupt in 1764.

*Houlgreave, Charles.* Childwall. Watchmaker. Son, William, by wife, Nancy, buried 1795.

*Housman, Jacob.* Lancaster. Clockmaker. Came from Bardsea Urswick near Ulverston to marry in Lancaster Ellen Crank in 1733.

Three daughters born 1734–9. Free there in 1732. Wife died there in 1780, when Jacob still alive. Date of his death unknown. Fine longcase clock reported c 1740.

*Howard, Edward.* Prescot. Watchmaker. Married Esther Johnson 1808. Daughter born, 1819.

*Howard, Henry.* Liverpool/Wigan. Listed at Liverpool, 1784–90; at Wigan in 1796.

*Howard, James.* Manchester. 1 Corporation St, 1848–51. In 1851 also at 17A Market St.

*Howard, John.* Liverpool. 99 Christian St in 1851.

*Howard, John.* Prescot. Watchmaker. Married Martha Almand, 1776.

*Howard, Thomas.* Rainhill. Watchmaker. Son, John, born 1818 to wife, Molly.

*Howard, Thomas.* Farnworth. Watchmaker. Married Ann Sixsmith, 1833.

*Howard, Thomas.* Liverpool. Kirkdale Rd, 1848–51.

*Howard, Thomas Wardle.* Liverpool. 28 Berry St in 1851.

*Howarth, Squire.* Ramsbottom. Stubbins Lane in 1848.

*Howarth, William.* Manchester. Clockmaker. Married Hannah Blackwell, 1804.

*Howe, George.* Rochdale. 2 The Walk, 1848–58.

*Howhorth (Howarth), Peter.* Ribchester. Set up church clock in 1719. Probably not a clock*maker.*

*Hoyle, Joseph.* Stalybridge. Stamford St in 1848.

*Hoyle, William.* Bolton. 6 New Market Place in 1824.
*Hoyle, William.* Rochdale. 16 New Market in 1824; The Walk in 1828.
*Hughes, James.* Ashton-under-Lyne. Fleet St in 1851.
*Hughes, Lewis.* Liverpool. 15 Liver St in 1848.
*Hughes, Thomas Roger.* Manchester. 46 Oxford St, Chorlton-on-Medlock, 1848–51.
*Huguenin, Aimé/Sarah.* Liverpool. 33 Lime St in 1824. In 1828 Sarah Huguenin at this address.
*Hulme, James.* Stretford. Watchmaker in 1834.
*Hulme, Thomas.* Manchester. Clockmaker. Married Maria Park 1844. At 105 York St, Hulme in 1848.
*Hulse, Henry.* Manchester. 72 Deansgate in 1822; 57 Piccadilly in 1828.
*Humphreys, Joseph.* Liverpool. Park Rd, 1848–51.
*Hunt, Edward.* Farnworth. Watchmaker. At Widnes in 1818 when wife, Jane, had daughter.
*Hunt, Henry.* Farnworth. Watchmaker. Son, Thomas, born 1818 by wife, Martha.
*Hunt, Henry.* Farnworth. Watchmaker. Married Mary Johnson, 1831.
*Hunt, Isaac.* Farnworth. Watchmaker. Married Hannah Ardern, 1827.
*Hunt, James.* Farnworth. Watchmaker at Appleton, 1834–51.
*Hunt, John.* Farnworth. Watchmaker. Wife, Ann, had child in 1818. Then at Widnes.

*Hunt, Peter.* Prescot. Watchmaker. Married Sarah Appleton, 1819.
*Hunt, Richard.* Manchester. 5 Richmond Row, Pendleton in 1822.
*Hunt & Roskell.* Manchester. 38 Princess St in 1851.
*Hunt, Thomas.* Farnworth. Watchmaker at Appleton, 1848–51.
*Hunt, Thomas.* Prescot. Watchmaker. Married Sarah Gilbert, 1775.
*Hunt, W.* Farnworth. Watchmaker there 1858.
*Hunter, Henry.* Prescot. Watchmaker. Wife, Alice, had child in 1824.
*Hunter, James.* Liverpool. 75 Byrom St in 1824.
*Hunter, John.* Farnworth. Watchmaker. Married Ellen Wilcock, 1824.
*Hunter, Thomas.* Liverpool. 12 Georges St, 1774–1800. No 2 Litherland Alley, 1781–1800. Two men or two shops? Another of this name listed in 1828.
*Hurst, George.* Farnworth. Watchmaker. Married Jane Porter, 1834.
*Hurst, James.* Prescot. Watchmaker. Married Alice Ackers, 1778.
*Hurst, M.* Middleton. Long St in 1858.
*Hurst, Stephen.* Liverpool. Liverpool museum have watch hallmarked 1806.
*Hurstfield, John.* Farnworth. Watchmaker. Married Alice Dagnal, 1823.
*Hutchinson, John.* Clitheroe. Watchmaker. His son, William, was

109

*Hutchinson, John.* cont. buried in 1803. In 1824 at Church Brow.

*Iliffe, Henry T.* Ashton-under-Lyne. Mill Lane, 1851–8.

*Imison, John.* Manchester. Clock and watchmaker. Listed in 1784 directory. Arched brass-dial long-case clock reported in carved case signed 'Imison–Mossley'.

*Ingham, Henry.* Todmorden. York St in 1851.

*Ingham, S.* Bury. Clock and watch cleaner at Edenfield in 1858.

*Ingham, William.* Todmorden. York St, 1848–66.

*Ingleby, ——.* Liverpool. Lost watch reported in 1770.

*Inglish, David/Mary.* Manchester. Blackfriars Bridge in 1822. Succeeded there 1824–8 by Mary (his widow?).

*Inman, James.* Colne. Clock and watchmaker and jeweller at Windy Bank in 1824.

*Inman, John A.* Liverpool. Preston museum have watch dated 1859.

*Inman, Sophia.* Liverpool. 24 Cornwallis St in 1851.

*Inman, William.* Liverpool. 12 Prussia St in 1851.

*Ireland, William.* Prescot. Watchmaker. Married Mary Fairclough, 1781.

*Irving, James.* Blackburn. Blackburn museum have watch movement.

*Isaacs, Ralph.* Liverpool. 35 Castle St in 1822; 19 Pool Lane in 1828; 2 St George's Crescent North in 1834.

*Isaacs, Solomon.* Liverpool. 268 Deansgate in 1828; 44 School Lane in 1834.

*Isherwood, J.* Bolton. 12 Newport St, 1851–8.

*Isherwood, W.* Bolton. Baldwin St in 1858.

*Ivison, Henry.* Liverpool. 5 Benson St in 1834.

*Jackson, Abraham.* Liverpool. Clock, watch and chronometer maker. 55 Lord St, 1814–22; then at Castle St, 1828–34.

*Jackson, Frederick.* Liverpool. Chronometer maker at 37 Castle St, 1848–51.

*Jackson, George.* Lancaster. Market Place, 1851–8.

*Jackson, J.* St Helens. 65 Bridge St in 1858.

*Jackson, James.* Accrington. Blackburn Rd in 1851.

*Jackson, John.* Kirkham. Freckleton St in 1834.

*Jackson, John.* Lancaster. Born 1797 in Shropshire. Watchmaker and jeweller at Lancaster by 1822 at New St; at Market St, 1834–51; then at Church St, 1858–69. Lancaster museum have watch signed 'J. H. Jackson–Lancaster'.

*Jackson, John.* Liverpool. Listed there in 1734.

*Jackson, John.* Liverpool. Liverpool museum have watch hallmarked 1799. At 55 Lord St in 1814. One of this name at 65 Parliament St in 1848 is probably a different man.

*Jackson, Joseph.* Liverpool. 13 Gerard St in 1834.

*Jackson, Joseph.* Warton. Clocksmith. Free at Lancaster in 1730.

*Jackson, S(amuel).* Lancaster. Lancaster museum have watch, perhaps by Samuel Jackson, son of George Jackson, born 1831, living with parents in 1851 as watch cleaner.

*Jackson, Thomas.* Farnworth. Watchmaker. Married Rachel Downall, 1787.

*Jackson, William.* Liverpool. Liverpool museum have semi-regulator c 1850. At 15 Richmond St, 1848–51.

*Jagger, Aaron.* Ashton-under-Lyne. 158 Stamford St in 1834.

*Jagger, Richard.* Oldham/Manchester. Yorkshire St, Oldham in 1834; 30 Medlock St, Hulme, 1848–51.

*James, J.* Bury. 14 Moorside in 1858.

*James, John.* Liverpool. 67 Wapping, 1848; 22 Mulberry St in 1851.

*Jameson, William.* Leigh. Bedford St in 1851.

*Jarvis (Gervis), Henry.* Prescot. Watchmaker. Children born between 1795 and 1826.

*Jefferys, Thomas.* Liverpool. Liverpool museum have watch c 1815.

*Jeffreys, William.* Liverpool/Lancaster. Watchmaker. Born Liverpool in 1809. At Bridge St, Lancaster in 1851, having moved there from Liverpool between 1836 and 1845. At Anchor St in 1858. Wife, Martha, came from

Boston, Lincs. Son, George born 1834; William born 1845.

*Jerome & Co.* Liverpool. Imported clocks at 6 New Quay in 1851. Must be a branch or office of the Newhaven, Connecticut, USA company. This is the first recorded English 'branch' to my knowledge.

*Jessop, George.* Manchester. 107 Chapel St, Salford in 1851.

*Joel, Isaac.* Preston. 122 Church St in 1824.

*Joel, Jacob.* Manchester. Foreign clocks at 6 Swan St, 1848–51.

*Johnson, Charles.* Wigan. Market Place, 1848–51; 22 Wallgate in 1858.

*Johnson & Co.* Bolton. 17 Manor St in 1824.

*Johnson, Henry.* Liverpool. Salford museum have watch early 19th century.

*Johnson, James.* Prescot. Watchmaker. Married Catherine Higginson 1788, by whom child born 1796.

*Johnson, James.* Prescot. Clock and watchmaker. Children born to wife, Elizabeth, 1823–5.

*Johnson, James.* Liverpool. In 1768 assigned property to Rowland Johnson (qv). In 1774 at Johnson St.

*Johnson, James.* Liverpool. Liverpool museum have watch c 1785–1800.

*Johnson, John.* Manchester. Clockmaker. Married Jane Green, 1792.

*Johnson, Joseph.* Liverpool. Clock, watch and chronometer maker

III

*Johnson, Joseph.* cont
at 1 Blake St in 1814; 25 Church
St, 1822–34; 87 Brownlow Hill,
1848–51.
*Johnson, Owen.* Manchester. Clockmaker. Married Catherine Con-
way, 1803.
*Johnson, Richard.* Eccleston. Liver-
pool museum have watch move-
ment c 1770. See below.
*Johnson, Richard.* St Helens. Watch-
maker of Sutton. Married Ann
Ansdell 1751. Issue include: 1762
Richard; 1772 Joseph.
*Johnson, Richard.* Oldham. West St,
1848–58.
*Johnson, Ro(w)land (R. & J.).*
Liverpool. Lost watch recorded
in 1758. After 1773 listed as R.
Johnson & Son. R. & J. Johnson
in 1781. Rowland alone in 1790
at Harrington St.
*Johnson, Samuel.* Liverpool. 20
Roscoe Arcade in 1848.
*Johnson, Thomas and Isaac.* Prescot.
Atherton St in 1834.
*Johnson, Thomas.* St Helens. Watch-
maker at Sutton. Children born:
1763 Robert; 1770 John.
*Johnson (alias Roberts), William.*
Flixton. See Roberts.
*Jonas, Isaac Aaron.* Liverpool. 15
Manchester St in 1848.
*Jones, James.* Liverpool. Lost watch
advertised in 1766.
*Jones, John.* Liverpool. Impossible
to separate several of this name.
One had daughter, Eleanor bap-
tised 1822 by wife, Margaret.
Another had daughter, Emma,
by wife, Bridget, in 1824. One a
Dutch and German clockseller at

16 Renshaw St in 1828. In 1834
one at 37 Gerard St, another at
3 Parliament St, yet another at
6 Mary Ann St. In 1851 the
imported clock man was at 4
Norfolk St.
*Jones, John.* Manchester. Watchmaker. Married Elizabeth Mad-
den 1796. May be same man
listed at 32 Long Millgate in 1834.
*Jones, John.* Prescot. Watchmaker. Married Mary Hurst,
1771.
*Jones, Morres.* St Helens. Watchmaker at Sutton in 1763 when
son, John, born.
*Jones, Peter.* Prescot/Liverpool.
Watchmaker. Children born at
Prescot to wife, Ann, 1818–24. In
1834 at 15 Highfield St, Liverpool, where also made chronometers.
*Jones, Robert (& Son).* Liverpool.
At Castle St in 1796 (alone). '&
Son' in 1814.
*Jones, Robert.* Gloverstone. Watchmaker. Died 1747 leaving will.
*Jones, Robert.* Liverpool. Liverpool
museum have watch hallmarked
1850, also bracket clock c 1830.
*Jones, Thomas.* Liverpool. Queens
Arcade in 1848; 10 Clarence St
in 1851.
*Jones, Thomas.* Prescot. Watch-
maker. Married Elizabeth Platt
1777, by whom several children
as late as 1796. Took James
Tyrer apprentice in 1797.
*Jones, William.* Manchester. 161
Chapel St, Salford, 1824–48.
*Jones & Wally.* Liverpool. Adver-
tised as watchmaker in 1788.

*Jordan, John.* Manchester. 8 Hanging Ditch in 1834; 38 Market St, 1848–51.

*Joseph, Brothers.* Liverpool. 32 South Castle St in 1851.

*Joseph, B. L.* Liverpool. 42 Bold St, 1848–51 (patent lever watches).

*Joseph, Elias.* Liverpool. Watchmaker at Pool Lane, 1790–1800.

*Joy, Julius.* Manchester. 3 London Rd in 1822.

*Joyce, Thomas Price.* Manchester. Watchmaker and jeweller at Stretford Rd. Children born to wife, Emily, 1856–70.

*Jump, Thomas.* Prescot. Watchmaker from Knowsley in 1795 when daughter born to wife, Hannah.

*Kane, Thomas.* Liverpool. 35 Sir Thomas's Buildings, 1848–51.

*Kaye, John.* Manchester. 68 Shudehill, 1848–51.

*Kaye, John.* Liverpool. Advertised for journeyman 1773. Wykes Court, Dale St in 1796. See also Key.

*Kay, Samuel.* Manchester. 268 Deansgate in 1822.

*Kay, Thomas.* Southport. Jeweller at 137 Lord St in 1851.

*Kay, William.* Manchester. Clockmaker. Took Samuel Boardman apprentice in 1742 for £2 10s. Died before 1745, in which year son, Peter, admitted to school there.

*Kaye, William.* Liverpool. Clockmaker at 11 Princess St in 1781.

*Kells, R.* Preston. 101 Friargate in 1858.

*Kelly, John.* Liverpool. Clock watch and chronometer-maker in Richmond Row, 1822–34.

*Kember, Joseph.* Shaw (nr Oldham?). Preston museum have watch inscribed 'James Elgar 1743'. Longcase clock noted of middle 18th century. Some authorities list this man under Shaw as his surname.

*Kemshead, Harvey (& Son).* Manchester. Watchmaker and jeweller at 28 Market St, 1822–34. '& son' in 1824.

*Kemshead, Robert (& Son).* Manchester. Robert '& Son' at 101 Market St in 1828. Alone at 4 St Mary's Gate in 1834.

*Kendrick, John.* Liverpool. Watchmaker at 1 Dawson St in 1800.

*Kennedy (Kenerder), Thomas.* Wigan. Liverpool museum have watch movement c 1770. Born 1727. One watch dated 1759. In directory for 1797. Died 1806 aged 79 (Hawkes).

*Kent, John.* Manchester. Watchmaker 1769–1822, in which latter year at 5 Market Place. Bracket clock reported. Son, William Worsley (qv), born 1804 at Salford.

*Kent, R.* Widnes. Widnes Dock in 1858.

*Kent, William Worsley.* Manchester. Born 1804 son of John Kent (qv). Watchmaker. Married Jennet Hulme 1825. Succeeded father at 5 Market Place in 1828. Moved to 63 Deansgate where worked 1834–51.

*Kenworthy, John.* Oldham. Soho Buildings in 1848.

*Kenyon, ——.* Liverpool. Liverpool museum have painted-dial longcase clock c 1815.

*Kenyon, James.* Liverpool. Clockmaker. At Redcross St in 1715 when son, John, born. At Newmarket in 1725 when son, James, born. Insolvent 1743.

*Kenyon, William.* Liverpool. Clockmaker. Believed born 1667. Various children born between 1708 and 1720.

*Kerfoot, Robert.* Liverpool. Working by 1754. Hanover St in 1761. Died 1774 leaving will.

*Kerfoot, Robert (junior)* Liverpool. At Peter St in 1796. See also next entry.

*Kerfoot, Robert.* Liverpool. Watchmaker. Married Jane Kirn, widow, 1822. May be same man as above.

*Kerkham, Hugh.* St Helens. Watchmaker. At Hardshaw in 1786 when son, Hugh, born.

*Kerr, Joseph.* Bolton. 74 Newport St in 1851.

*Kerry, John.* Farnworth/Liverpool. Watchmaker. Married Christiana Litherland at Farnworth, 1821. At 72 Brownlow Hill, Liverpool in 1851.

*Kershaw, John.* Oldham. Greenacres Moor, 1851–8.

*Ketterer & Co.* Oldham. German clocks at Bow Lane in 1834.

*Key, John.* Warrington. Clockmaker. Married Sarah Crosby there 1761.

*Kilner, Samuel.* Ulverston. Clockmaker in 1760 (Hobbs).

*Kilshaw, Nehemiah.* Prescot. Movement-maker at Farnworth. Married Ellen Stephenson, 1759.

*Kind, John.* Liverpool. 1 Church St, 1834–48.

*King, Alexander.* Liverpool. Watchmaker from Hampshire—insolvent here 1772.

*Kingsley, William.* Wigan. Millgate in 1811 (Hawkes).

*Kirk, William.* Manchester/Stockport. Clockmaker. Married Elizabeth Mills 1778. In 1794 directory. Buried at Stockport 10 April 1830 aged 82. Wife died 1830 aged 79.

*Kirk(h)all, Thomas.* Bolton. Married Ann Bonfourne 1625. Made Brindle church clock in 1637. Liverpool museum have timber-framed clock from Brindle church said to be 1673.

*Kitchen, John.* Liverpool. 22 Cheapside in 1774.

*Knight, Stephen Wintruph.* Manchester. Clockmaker. Married as widower Mary Roberts 1827.

*Knight, Thomas.* Manchester. Oldham St, 1822–48. In 1851 at 128 Oxford St, Chorlton-on-Medlock.

*Knowles, Andrew.* Bolton. Clockmaker. Children born there 1724–38. Thirty-hour one-handed clock noted signed by name only without town c 1740.

*Knowles, John.* Farnworth. Watchmaker. Married Ann Plumley, 1802.

*Knowles, Robert.* Liverpool. Working by 1800. At 19 Renshaw St in 1814; 114 Whitechapel in 1822; Sir Thomas's Buildings in 1828.

*Knowles, Thomas.* Bolton (and Cartmel?). Clockmaker. Died 1787 leaving will. Salford museum have longcase clock by him c 1780. A clockmaker of this name married at Cartmel in 1784 to Grace Barrow—probably same man.

*Labrow, Thomas Scott.* Manchester. Watchmaker. Issue by wife, Alice, born 1845-7. At 158 Gt Ancoats St in 1848; New Church in 1858.

*Lacker, Michael.* Manchester. Dutch and German clocks at Deansgate, 1824-34.

*Laithwaite, John.* Liverpool. Watchmaker listed in 1754. May be son of Robert?

*Laithwait, Robert.* Liverpool. Watchcase maker at Dayle St, 1715-34. Children included John, born 1715.

*Laithwaite, William.* Liverpool. Watch-case maker. Took Thomas Barron apprentice in 1710 for £15. See Lewthwaite.

*Lambie, Hugh.* Liverpool. 9 Redcross St in 1851.

*Lancaster, Francis.* Liverpool. Clock, watches and chronometers at 50 Brownlow Hill in 1824.

*Lancaster, James.* Liverpool. Clocks, watches and chronometers at 82 Copperas Hill.

*Lancaster, John.* Prescot. Watch-

maker. Took Richard Brewer apprentice in 1760 for £20.

*Langley, Thomas.* Liverpool. 63 Cross St, Little Bolton in 1848.

*Langshaw, Hugh.* Prescot. Watchmaker. Children born to wife, Mary, 1795-7.

*Langton, Francis.* Liverpool. Partner of Burgess and Langton 1767; leaves firm 1768.

*Large, John.* Manchester. Clockmaker. Married Catherine Wright 1792. See also below.

*Large, John.* Farnworth. Watchmaker. Married Elizabeth Hornby 1803. See also above.

*Lassell, Thurston.* Liverpool. Clockmaker of Toxteth Park. Died 1758 leaving will. Mentions wife, Ann, and son, William, his sole heir.

*Lassell, William.* Liverpool. Clockmaker at Toxteth Park. Mentioned in will of father (Thurston Lassell) in 1758. At High Park in 1790. Birkenhead museum have longcase clock, as do Liverpool museum, latter signed 'William Lassell–Toxteth Park'.

*Latham, John.* Wigan. Clockmaker, supposedly from Clifton, Westmorland. Free at Wigan in 1749. Still there in 1757. Clocks signed 'Latham–Wigan' (Hawkes).

*Lathom, George.* St Helens. Watchmaker at Eccleston in 1837 when son born to wife, Alice.

*Law, Samuel.* Rochdale. Clockmaker at Rope St in 1824.

*Law, William.* Burnley. Clock repairer 1848.

115

*Lawley, Theodore.* Manchester. German and Dutch clocks at 10 Lower Mosley St in 1828.

*Lawrence, John.* Lancaster. Clockmaker. Working there 1762–72 when children born, including son, William, in 1762, who later became a clockmaker too. Probably still alive in 1801. Lancaster museum have brass-dial clock by him.

*Lawrence, William.* Manchester. Clockmaker from Halifax. Married Ann Nichol, Manchester, 1788, but not known whether he worked there.

*Lawrence, William.* Lancaster/Cark. Probably not same man as in previous entry. Born 1762 at Lancaster, son of John Lawrence (qv). Free there 1785. Married Jane Bispham at Cartmell in 1787. Believed still there in 1818. Various clocks recorded, mostly with painted dials.

*Lawrenson, James.* Prescot. Watchmaker. Son, Thomas, born there in 1819 to wife, Alice.

*Lawson, Henry.* Hindley, nr Wigan. Clockmaker there in 1834. May be son of Ramsay Lawson (qv), born 1792?

*Lawson, John.* Wigan. At Ince in 1851.

*Lawson, Ramsay.* Wigan. Clockmaker at the Wiend. Married Betty Meadows 1791. Son, Henry, born 1792 (Hawkes).

*Lawson, Robert.* Manchester. Clockmaker. Married Elizabeth Unsworth, 1776.

*Lawson, William.* Newton-le-Willows. Born 1735. Clockmaker. Brass-dial clock c 1770 noted. Died at Winwick, 15 November 1805, aged 67.

*Lawson, William.* Todmorden. At Stansfield, 1824–8; at Millwood, 1848–66.

*Layfield, Robert.* Grindlestone Thorn. Watchmaker. Free at Lancaster in 1785.

*Lea, Henry.* St Helens. Watchmaker at Windle. Wife, Elizabeth, had children 1821–5.

*Lea, James.* Liverpool. 9 Hart St, 1824–8.

*Leach, Henry.* Chorley. Market St, 1828–34.

*Leach, Henry.* Preston. 31 Friargate in 1851.

*Leach, J.* Preston. 31 Friargate in 1858.

*Leadbetter, Charles.* Wigan. Wallgate in 1824; Hindley in 1828.

*Leadbeater, Thomas.* Manchester. Watchmaker. Married as bachelor Frances Dunning, 1830.

*Leadbetter, Thomas.* Prescot. Watchmaker. Married Jane Heyes 1802. Son, William, born 1819.

*Leadbetter, William (& Timothy).* Wigan. At Market Place alone in 1828; with Timothy 1834–48; alone again 1851.

*Leaf, Leigh.* Prescot. Watchmaker. Died 1785 leaving will.

*Leah, Henry.* Stalybridge. High St in 1848.

*Leather, Richard.* Prescot. Watchmaker. Children born 1823–5 by wife, Esther.

*Leatherbarrow, Charles.* Liverpool.

*Leatherbarrow, Charles.* cont. Watchmaker. Listed there in 1784.

*Leder(s), John.* Liverpool. Lambert St in 1834; London Rd, 1848–51.

*Lee, Henry.* Bolton. 134 Spring Gardens, 1851–8. Longcase clock reported.

*Lee, Isaac.* Liverpool. 68 Seel St in 1834.

*Lee, James.* Farnworth. Watchmaker. Married Margaret Ashton, 1785.

*Lee, J.* Bolton. 49 Great Moor St in 1858.

*Lee, John.* Liverpool. 19 Whitechapel in 1824.

*Lee, Peter.* Prescot. Watchmaker. Son born 1819 to wife, Ann.

*Lee, Thomas.* Bury. 40 Fleet St in 1851.

*Lee, Thomas.* Farnworth. Watchmaker. Married Elizabeth Ansdale 1760.

*Leech, John.* Kirkham. Watchmaker and silversmith at Poulton St, 1822–8.

*Leech, Thomas.* Prescot. Movementmaker (watch?). Married Elizabeth Walklet, 1768.

*Lees, J. & Co.* Ashton-under-Lyne. 144 Stamford St in 1858.

*Lees, J. H.* Bury. 40 Fleet St in 1858.

*Lees, James.* Middleton. King St in 1848.

*Lees, James.* Ashton-under-Lyne. Clockmaker. Two of his children died there 1697 and 1706.

*Lees, James.* Middleton. Clockmaker. Buried there 10 August 1797, a bachelor.

*Lees, John.* Manchester. Clockmaker. Married Hannah Ogden, 1802.

*Lees, John.* Middleton. Clockmaker. Died 22 September 1804. Watch in Oldham museum.

*Lees, John.* Middleton. Rochdale Rd in 1824; Long St, 1828–34.

*Lees, Jonathan.* Bury/Middleton. Longcase clock noted c 1730 signed at Bury. Died Middleton, 9 May 1785. One clock reported dated 1770.

*Lees, Samuel.* Ashton-under-Lyne 54 Stamford St, 1824–48. Also jeweller.

*Lees, Thomas.* Middleton. Long St, 1848–58.

*Lees, Thomas.* Bury. Believed son of Jonathan, carrying on after his death. Fleet St, 1822–48. Salford museum have early 19th-century wall clock. Longcase clock recorded c 1790.

*Lees, William.* Accrington. Abbey St in 1848; Warner St, 1851–8.

*Lees, William (W.T.?).* Haslingden. George St, 1828–34; W. T. Lees at Dearden Gate, 1848–58.

*Leicester, Laurence.* Wigan. Repaired church clock 1704–10. Worked in Wallgate. Was denied freedom in 1703. Thereafter fined regularly for trading, till hi death in 1711, the same year tha his wife, Mary, had died (Hawkes).

*Leigh, James.* Bold. Born 1762, son of Thomas Leigh, watchmaker. Married Margaret Ashton 1785. Children born 1785–1808.

*Leigh, Joshua.* Liverpool. 48 Gerard St in 1834.

*Leigh, Peter.* Wigan. Clockmaker at Wallgate in 1793 when son born to wife, Elizabeth (Hawkes).

*Leigh, Thomas.* Farnworth. Apprenticed in 1752 to John Willcock of Sutton, watchmaker, for £15. Married Elizabeth Ansdale 1760. Son, James (qv), born 1762. Died 1795 at Bold.

*Leigh, William.* Liverpool. Clockmaker in 1780.

*Leigh, William.* Liverpool. 170 Mill St, Toxteth Park in 1851.

*Leigh, William.* Newton-in-the-Willows. Maker of clocks and watches in 1822 and also tower clocks.

*Leighton, James.* Warrington. Clockmaker. Buried at Wigan in 1776.

*Leighton, John.* Lancaster. In 1838 cleaned clock by John Lawrence of Lancaster.

*Levi, Barnet.* Liverpool. 1828–34 at Lime St; 1848 at 27 Seel St; 1851 at 13 Benson St.

*Lever, Peter.* St Helens. Watchmaker. Children born to wife, Elizabeth, 1831–7.

*Levy & Denziger.* Liverpool. Quadrant St, Lime St, 1848–51.

*Levy, Henry & Co.* Manchester. Watch in Wigan museum, early 19th century.

*Lewis, George.* Manchester. 327 Oldham Rd in 1824.

*Lewis, Morris.* Liverpool. Watchmaker. Married Mary Ann Garner, 1834.

*Lewis, Peter.* Liverpool. Watchmaker. Children born 1695–9. He died 1699.

*Lewis, Robert.* Liverpool. Watchmaker. Married Selina Mitchell, 1834.

*Lewthwaite, William.* Liverpool. Watchmaker and case maker at Edmond St. Children born 1696–1710. Still working 1725.

*Leyland, Thomas.* Prescot. Clock and watchmaker. Children born to wife, Elizabeth, 1818–23. At Atherton St, 1824–58.

*Liddell, Adam.* Liverpool. Bold St, 1848–51.

*Lightfoot, Roger.* St Helens. Watchmaker at Sutton. Children born to wife, Mary, 1770–9.

*Lightfoot, Roger.* Farnworth. Watchmaker. Married Catherine Taylor, 1779.

*Linaker, Henry.* Liverpool. 21 Torbock St in 1834.

*Linton, John.* Liverpool. 4 L. Harrington St in 1824.

*Litherland, Ann.* Liverpool. Brownlow Hill in 1828.

*Litherland & Co.* Liverpool. Watch No 1729 hallmarked 1800. Liverpool museum have watch hallmarked 1806.

*Litherland, Davies & Co.* Liverpool. Makers of chronometers and 'inventors, patentees and manufacturers of the lever watch'. Church St, 1814–34; 37 Bold St, 1848–51, where also sold imported clocks.

*Litherland, John.* Liverpool. Watchmaker. Children born 1677–84. Died 1687.

*Litherland, John.* Liverpool. Watchmaker in 1800. At 5 Russel Place in 1814.

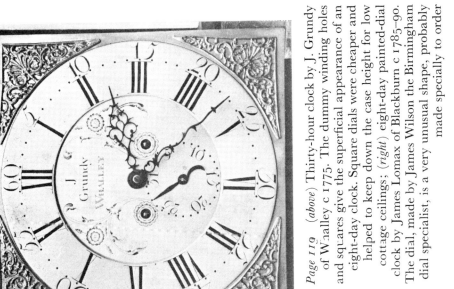

*Page 110* (*above*) Thirty-hour clock by J. Grundy of Whalley c 1775. The dummy winding holes and squares give the superficial appearance of an eight-day clock. Square dials were cheaper and helped to keep down the case height for low cottage ceilings; (*right*) eight-day painted-dial clock by James Lomax of Blackburn c 1785–90. The dial, made by James Wilson the Birmingham dial specialist, is a very unusual shape, probably made specially to order

*Page 120*    (*left*) Eight-day clock by Lomax of
Blackburn c 1785–90 in mahogany, height
7ft 8in. This demonstrates that some of the
finest cases were made for painted-dial clocks;
(*above*) hood and dial of eight-day clock by
G. Stones of Blackburn c 1800. The cut-out moon
dial shows the shape of the moon as well as the
lunar date—here the 21st

*Litherland, John.* Warrington. Watchmaker. Married Christian Robey, 1755.

*Litherland, Peter.* Liverpool. Patented watch improvements in 1791 and 1792. In 1793 advertised them at 20 Mount Pleasant. Died 1805. Watch No 971 hallmarked 1795.

*Litherland, Peter.* Liverpool. Salford museum have watch hallmarked 1831.

*Litherland, Richard.* Liverpool. Brownlow Hill, 1814–22—'inventor and patentee of the new chronometer'. One of this name at 33 Manchester St in 1848 could be same man.

*Lithgoe, Joseph.* Farnworth. Watchmaker. Married Mary Heyes, 1826.

*Livesey, John.* Bolton. Lantern clock recorded c 1700. Longcase clock noted c 1750.

*Liversay, George.* Prescot. Watchmaker. Application for freedom rejected 1666.

*Lloyd, Henry.* Farnworth. Watchmaker. Married Alice Lowe, 1834.

*Lloyd, James.* Prescot. Watchmaker at Rainhill. Son born to wife, Mary, 1824.

*Lloyd, Joseph.* Wigan. Millgate in 1811 (Hawkes).

*Lloyd, Thomas.* Farnworth. Watchmaker. Married Hannah Pool, 1798.

*Lloyd, William.* Manchester. Watchmaker. Married Ann Sidebotham, 1802.

*Loftus, John.* Liverpool. Watchmaker there 1734.

*Loftus, John.* Liverpool. Watchmaker. Married Ann Nelson, 1822.

*Lomas, Richard.* ? One-handed 30-hour clock dated 1717 signed without town—believed to be North Lancs.

*Lomas, Samuel.* Poulton. Clockmaker. Bond in 1744 to marry Elizabeth Johnson. See also Samuel Lomax.

*Lomax, James.* Blackburn. Clock and watchmaker. Born 1749, son of Samuel and Ann Lomax. Late 18th-century longcase clock noted. Preston museum have watch of 1798. Died 1814.

*Lomax, Joseph.* Prescot. Watchmaker. Married Jane Fillingham 1802. Son born 1819.

*Lomax, Samuel.* Blackburn. Clockmaker. Son, James, born 1749 to wife, Ann. Leased property at Astley Gate in 1778 for one year; later purchased it. In 1781 was paid for winding church clock and repairs.

*Lomax, William.* Prescot. Watchmaker. Children born 1795–7 by wife, Mary.

*Lomax, William.* Prescot. Watchmaker. Married Ann Forber 1795. Children born 1796–7.

*Longmore, William.* Manchester. 6 Dyers Court in 1834; 25 Lower Mosley St, 1848–51.

*Longsworth, Peter.* Liverpool. St John's Lane, 1822–34. Also made chronometers.

*Lord, Henry.* Liverpool. 233 Scotland Rd, 1848–51.

*Lowe, Edward.* Liverpool. Hanover St, 1761–90.
*Lowe, George Cliff.* Manchester. 26 St Ann St in 1851.
*Low, James.* Prescot. Movement-maker (watch). Married Ann Wright, 1767.
*Lowe, James.* Darwen. 1 Bridge St in 1858. Salford museum have watch.
*Lowe, Jesse William.* Darwen. Market St in 1848.
*Lowe, John.* Darwen. Market St in 1851.
*Lowe, Robert.* Preston. 8 Fishergate in 1834; 148 Church St, 1848–58.
*Lunt, Samuel.* St Helens. Tontine St in 1851.
*Lyon, Edward.* Prescot. Watch-maker. Son, Edward, born 1796 to wife, Mary.
*Lyon, Edward.* Prescot. Watch-maker. Married Margaret Appleton, 1819.
*Lyon, Edward.* Prescot. Watch-maker. Married Elizabeth Taylor, 1816.
*Lyon, George.* Liverpool. Watch-maker. Children born 1691–1700. Lived at Castle St.
*Lyon, Henry.* Farnworth. Watch-maker. Married Margaret Atkinson, 1819.
*Lyon, John.* Warrington. Supplied church clock 1666. Worked on it 1669–72 (Hawkes).
*Lyon, John.* Prescot. Watchmaker. Son born to wife, Nancy, in 1796.
*Lyon, Joseph.* Prescot. Watchmaker. Married Mary Heap, 1797.
*Lyon, William.* Farnworth. Watch-maker. Married Mary Hall, 1804.

*Lythgoe, John.* St Helens. Tontine St in 1851.

*M'Convill, Edward.* Liverpool. German clocks at 25 Carpenters Row in 1848.
*McCune, Henry.* Liverpool. 300 Scotland Rd in 1851.
*McDonald, Joseph.* Liverpool. 21 Cheapside in 1790; 9 Pownal Square in 1814.
*McFerran, William.* Manchester. 8 Victoria St, Market Place in 1851.
*McGregor, Anthony.* Manchester. Clockmaker. Married Frances Wright, 1792.
*McMillan, Richard.* Manchester. Clockmaker. Married Nancy Travis, 1801.
*McMinn, John M.* Manchester. 8 Oxford St in 1848; 11 Ducie St, Exchange in 1851.
*McMurray, Thomas.* Liverpool. Watchmaker in 1800 directory.
*Maddox, Charles.* Liverpool. Watch-maker. Son born to wife, Mary, in 1824. At 9 Webster St in 1828.
*Malley, John.* Lancaster. Watch-maker and jeweller. Born there 1823. At 23 Market St, 1848–51. Married Elizabeth Wyvill, who came from Nottingham. Children born 1849–51.
*Manchester, Thomas.* Bolton. Clock cleaner at Howell Croft in 1834. Clock and watchmaker at Ridgway Gates, 1848–51.
*Mancor, James.* See Mencor.
*Marcer, William.* Liverpool. Watch-maker. Married Grace Wakefield, 1726.

*Margon, Thomas.* Manchester. 51 Stretford New Road, Hulme in 1848.

*Marks, Lyon/Leon.* Liverpool. Paradise St, 1848–51.

*Marr, William.* Ulverston. Watchmaker there in 1837 (Hobbs).

*Marrow, Richard.* Liverpool. Lost watch advertised 1796.

*Marsden, James.* Prescot. Watchmaker. Child born 1824 to wife, Mary.

*Marsh, Edward.* Prescot. Watchmaker. Married Margaret Hewit in Farnworth 1768.

*Marsh, Henry.* Huyton, Liverpool. Painted-dial longcase clock by him, said to be late 18th century.

*Marsh, J. T.* St Helens. Church St in 1858.

*Marsh, James.* Farnworth. Watchmaker. Married Mary Dennet, 1800.

*Marsh, Samuel.* Liverpool. Watchmaker in 1754 list.

*Marsh, Thomas.* Prescot. Married Nanny Pickton 1790, by whom children born 1790–5.

*Martin, John.* Liverpool. Longcase clock c 1790, signed Great Crosby.

*Martin(e), Thomas.* Wigan. Free 1675. Burgess 1686. Mayor 1706. Died 1716, leaving will (Hawkes).

*Martin, Thomas* (II). Wigan. Born 1688, son of Thomas (I). Still working 1744 (Hawkes).

*Martin, William.* Liverpool. 41 Castle St in 1795. Liverpool museum have watch.

*Mason, Alexander.* Liverpool. Lost watch advertised in 1792 (No 6452).

*Mason, Thomas.* Blackburn. 6 New Market St in 1858. Blackburn museum have watch.

*Mason, Thomas.* Preston. Bamber Bridge, Walton-le Dale, 1848–51.

*Mason, William.* Prescot. Watchmaker. Died 1769.

*Massie, Edward.* Liverpool. Lost watch advertised in 1785.

*Massey, Edward John.* Liverpool. Chronometer maker at 41 Russell St in 1848.

*Massey, Francis.* Liverpool. 8 Warren St in 1824.

*Mather, Nathan.* Liverpool. Watchmaker. Married Rachel Willaser, 1707.

*Mathew, J.* Rochdale. Whitworth Rd, Spotland in 1858.

*Mawdsley, Hargreaves.* Southport. Lord St, 1848–58. Also jeweller and optician.

*Mawdsley, John.* Manchester. 15 Princess St in 1851.

*May, David.* Prescot. Watchmaker. Married Mary Tarbuck 1792. Daughter born 1794.

*Mayer, Joseph.* Liverpool. 70 Lord St in 1848. Also dealer in electroplate goods.

*Mayer, Saul.* Manchester. 62 Market St, 1848–51, in which latter year also had shop at 45 Swan St.

*Mayo, William & Son.* Manchester. Market St, 1834–51. In 1848 had second shop at 15 Corporation St.

*Mayo, William.* Rochdale. 9 Yorkshire St in 1851. Also jeweller.

123

*Mayor, John.* Manchester. German and Dutch clocks at 54 Port St in 1834.

*Mears, H.* Wigan. 67 Scholes in 1858.

*Mecanley, William.* Liverpool. 3 Whitechapel in 1848.

*Medcalf, William.* Liverpool. Watchmaker at Circus St in 1795.

*Medley, Robert.* Colne. Children born by wife, Ellen, 1791–9. Lived at Crawshaw. Was a weaver and labourer until 1799 when became clockmaker. Wife died 1802 aged 46.

*Melling & Co.* Liverpool. 39 South Castle St, 1848–51. Also chronometers.

*Mellor, John.* Liverpool. 13 Byrom St, 1822–5. Liverpool museum have watch 1821.

*Mellor, John.* Manchester. Clockmaker. Married Mary Mellor (*sic*) 1790. 98 Market St in 1824 —patent lever watches.

*Mencor, James.* Bolton. Bridge St, 1834–58.

*Mendelson, Henry.* Manchester. 38 King St, 1834–51.

*Mentha, Fritz.* Manchester. 51 Princess St in 1848.

*Mercer, John.* Farnworth. Watchmaker. Married Ann Green, 1830.

*Mercer, John.* Liverpool. Sir Thomas's Buildings, 1814–24; 2 Dickston St in 1824.

*Mercer, John.* Manchester. Watchmaker. Died 1759.

*Mercer, William.* Liverpool. Watchmaker. Died 1754.

*Mercer, William.* Prescot. Watch-

maker. Married Mary Woods 1803. Still there 1826.

*Merton & Co.* Liverpool. Liverpool museum have watch c 1785.

*Metcalf, Augustine.* Liverpool. Ranelagh St in 1761. Watchmaker.

*Metcalf, John.* Liverpool. Watchmaker. 36 Sparling St in 1790; 5 Upper Dawson St in 1824.

*Metcalf, William.* Preston/Kendal. Watchmaker. Born 1833 at Preston where he worked till c 1863, when moved with wife and children to Kendal.

*Michaloritz, T. Z.* Manchester. 12 Princess St in 1851.

*Miles, John.* Liverpool. Watchmaker in 1800 directory.

*Miller, Hugh.* Farnworth. Clockmaker. Married Alice Mutch, 1793.

*Miller, John.* Walton-le-Dale. Clockmaker. To marry by bond Ann Charnley in 1741. In 1747 took Nathaniel Abbot apprentice watchmaker for £10. May be same man as below.

*Miller, John.* Preston. Brass-dial 30-hour longcase clock recorded. Watch signed 'Miller—Preston' stolen in 1798 from shop of William Anderson of Lancaster. See previous entry.

*Miller, John.* Prescot. Clockmaker at Whiston. Children born to wife, Sarah, 1823–6.

*Miller, Robert.* Prescot. Watchmaker. Took John Ashcroft apprentice in 1752 for £14.

*Miller, William.* Farnworth. Watchmaker. Married Sarah Sixsmith, 1824.

*Mills, Edward.* Liverpool. Watchmaker in 1800 directory.
*Mills, John.* Prescot/Oldham. Watchmaker. Born 1745. Married Mary Wilkinson 1773. Children born Prescot, 1775–80. A man of this name died at Oldham, a clockmaker, in 1790, leaving will—presumably same man.
*Milner, R.* Wigan. 46 Market Place in 1858.
*Milner, Thomas.* Wigan. Queen St in 1848; Millgate in 1851; 1 St Thomas St in 1858. Wall clock in Wigan museum.
*Minshull (Minchull), John.* Ashton-under-Lyne. Old Street, 1825–9.
*Mitchall, William.* Liverpool. Liverpool museum have watch made 1805, the name Joseph Wilson replacing the numbers.
*Molyneaux, John.* Liverpool. Watchmaker. Daughter born 1699.
*Molyneux, William.* Liverpool. Liverpool museum have watch movement c 1780.
*Moncas, John.* Liverpool. Castle St, 1822–9.
*Moncas, Thomas.* Liverpool. Richmond Row in 1834. Also chronometers.
*Monk, John.* Bolton. 162 Deansgate, 1848–58.
*Monk, Samuel.* Bolton. Deansgate in 1834.
*Monk(e)s, George.* Prescot. Market Place in 1824. Liverpool museum have longcase clock c 1810.
*Moore, I. T.* Blackburn. Blackburn museum have watch.
*Moorfield, James.* Farnworth. Watch-

movement maker. Married Jane Mills, 1785. Apparently had remarried by 1795.
*Moorhouse, Robert.* Burnley. Watchmaker at Padiham, 1848–58.
*Moorhouse, W.* Preston. 35 Lord St, 1851–8.
*Moorhouse, William.* Liverpool. Painted-dial longcase clocks reported c 1820–30.
*Morath, Fedele & Bros.* Liverpool. German clocks at 63 Dale St, 1848–51.
*Morgan, John Varley.* Liverpool. 73 Sir Thomas's Buildings, 1848–51.
*Morrey, John.* Manchester. Clockmaker. Married Ellen Radcliffe, 1801.
*Morris, George.* Liverpool. 24 Cropper St in 1824.
*Morris, Mary.* Bolton. 83 Deansgate, 1824–9.
*Morris, William.* Liverpool. Liverpool museum have watch c 1810.
*Morrow, John.* Liverpool. Watchmaker. Son born to wife, Ann, in 1823.
*Morton, Thomas.* St Helens. Watchmaker. Market St, 1822–9; Church St, 1834–48. Married Hannah Simcock 1805. See next entry.
*Morton, Thomas.* Manchester. St Mary's Gate, 1848–51. From St Helens?
*Moseley, Morris Lewin.* Liverpool. 26 Castle St, 1795–1800. Liverpool museum have watch of 1800.
*Moss, Charles.* Liverpool. 29 Old Haymarket in 1848.
*Moss, James.* Liverpool. 32 Old Haymarket in 1834.

*Moss, James Dennett.* Liverpool. 100 Brownlow Hill in 1834.

*Moss, John.* Rochdale. King St, 1822–34.

*Moss, Michael.* Preston. 116 Church St in 1848.

*Moss, Richard.* Ulverston. Died 1776. Watchmaker.

*Moss, William Selby.* Manchester. Great Ancoats St, 1824–34; Oldham St, 1848–51.

*Mowcar, James.* Bolton. Bridge St in 1828.

*Mozley, M. L.* Liverpool. See Moseley.

*Muncaster, John.* Manchester/Dalton. Watchmaker from Manchester married Francis Gibson at Dalton in 1809.

*Muncaster, John.* Lancaster/Ulverston. Watchmaker. Free at Lancaster in 1806, then of Liverpool. Son of William Muncaster of Broughton. Still worked at Lancaster in 1816, when son born. Moved to Market Place, Ulverston where worked 1824–6.

*Murphy, Thomas.* Lancaster. Clockmaker. Born Dublin, 1809. In 1851 was a bachelor visitor at widow Ellen Addlinson's lodging house in Sugar House Alley.

*Musket, John.* Prescot. Watchmaker. Married Jane Hunt, 1766.

*Nathan, David.* Liverpool. 53 Paradise St, 1848–51.

*Nathan, Jacob (& Lemon).* Manchester. Jacob was watchmaker and silversmith there by 1808. In 1824 Jacob and Lemon were

together at 144 Long Millgate; in 1834 together at 8 King St.

*Nathan, John.* Liverpool. Castle St in 1822; Upper Newington, 1824–8.

*Nathan, Mosley.* Liverpool. 42 Seel St in 1851.

*Nathan, Philip.* Liverpool. 25 Castle St, 1824–34.

*Nathan, Rosina.* Liverpool. 13 Lord St in 1848; 56 Bold St in 1851.

*Naylor, Charles.* Liverpool. Watchmaker at Ray St in 1790; Pall Mall in 1796.

*Naylor, Thomas.* Childwall. Watchmaker. Married Ann Appleton, 1763.

*Naylor, William.* Liverpool. Watchmaker. Married 1697.

*Nelson, Bernard.* Liverpool. Waterloo Rd in 1848.

*Nelson, Gerard.* Liverpool. 6 Sidney Place in 1824.

*Nelson, John.* Bury. Watchmaker at 4 Haymarket in 1858. Liverpool museum have watch movement c 1840.

*Nelson, Robert.* Prescot. Watchmaker. Son, Thomas, born 1796 to wife, Ann.

*Nelson, Stephen.* Wigan. Clockmaker at Millgate. Died 1807 aged 78 (Hawkes).

*Nelson, Thomas.* Manchester. Clockmaker. Married Elizabeth Schofield, 1790.

*Nelson, Thomas.* Liverpool. Watchmaker. Son born to wife, Mary, 1823. At 3 Bevington Bush, 1824–34.

*Nelson, William.* Liverpool. Watchmaker at Cable St in 1795. A

*Nelson, William.* cont. man at Paradise St in 1781 may be same one, though listed as watch wheel finisher then.

*Newall, John.* Wigan. Watchmaker. Freedom application rejected 1666 (Hawkes).

*Newsham, Richard.* Liverpool. Watchmaker in 1790. In 1796 listed as watch engraver at Plumb St.

*Newton, George.* Manchester. Imported clocks at 132 London Rd in 1848.

*Newton, Isaac.* Manchester. 146 London Rd in 1851.

*Newton, Joseph.* Liverpool. Edmund St in 1781; Bath St, 1790–1834.

*Nicholls, Henry.* Liverpool. Watchmaker and dealer in watch materials at 170 Dale St, 1848–51.

*Nicklin, William.* Liverpool. Watchmaker at Moor St in 1773.

*Nield, Daniel.* Rochdale. Clock dealer at George St North in 1834.

*Nixon, George.* Farnworth. Watchmaker. Married Margaret Houghton, 1832.

*Noblatt, Edward.* Preston. Late 18th century musical longcase clock noted.

*Noble, James.* Lancaster. Watchmaker. Free 1733. Died before 1784. Watch No 4677 reported, not dated.

*Norman, John.* Warrington. Watchmaker. Married Jane Hodgkinson, 1773.

*Norman, R.* Prescot. Watchmaker at Atherton St in 1858.

*Norris and Campbell.* Liverpool.

Chronometer makers 1848–51 in South Castle St.

*Norris, Francis.* Liverpool. 108 Mount Pleasant in 1834.

*Norris, Henry.* Liverpool. 55 Warren St in 1824.

*Norris, Mary.* Liverpool. 28 Mount Pleasant in 1848. Chronometers.

*Norris, Patrick.* Liverpool. 32 Trueman St, 1796–1800.

*Norris, William.* Liverpool. Watchmaker at Ray St, 1790–1800.

*Nuttall, C.* Manchester. Bridleway, Newchurch in 1858.

*Nuttall, James.* Ormskirk. Aughton St in 1854.

*Oakes, John.* Oldham. High St, 1822–34.

*Oakes, William.* Oldham. Yorkshire St in 1834; High St, 1848–51.

*Oclee, Frederick A.* Oldham. West St in 1848; Mumps in 1851.

*Ogden, T.* Oldham. 50 Royton St in 1858.

*Ogden, William.* Oldham. Rochdale Rd in 1848–51.

*Ogden, William.* Bacup. Temple Court in 1851.

*O'Hara, James.* Liverpool. Watchmaker. Son born 1824 to wife, Mary Ann.

*Oldfield, John.* Manchester. Watchmaker. Married Ann Nicklin, 1799. Listed there in 1800.

*Oldham, Joseph.* Prescot. Atherton St, 1834–48.

*Oldham, Joseph.* Liverpool. 72 Highfield St in 1824.

*Oldham, Richard.* Chorley. Market St in 1840.

*Oliver, John.* Manchester. One of this name married Elizabeth Rydings, 1712. In 1744 took John Braddock from Hayfield, Derbyshire, as apprentice clockmaker for £20. In 1749 sale of stock seems to indicate his retirement. Died 27 June 1766 aged 83. Various clocks noted.

*Oliver, John.* Manchester. Must be another later maker of this name, by whom painted-dial longcase clocks of late 18th century noted.

*Oliver, Samuel.* Manchester. Clockmaker. Married Hannah Singleton, 1804.

*Ollivant, John & Son.* Manchester. Watchmakers in 1788–1800 directories.

*Ollivant, Thomas & John.* Manchester. At 2 Exchange St and 1 St Mary's Gate (two shops?), 1828–51.

*Onion, John.* Manchester. Watchmaker in directories 1794–1800.

*Orford, John.* Prescot. Watchmaker. Children born to wife, Sarah, 1819–25.

*Orford, William.* Prescot. Watchmaker. Son born to wife, Alice, 1819.

*Orme, John.* Preston. Watchmaker. Free at Lancaster in 1712.

*Orme(s), Thomas.* Manchester/Oldham. Clockmaker. Married Mary Firth 1794 at Manchester. Listed at Manchester St, Oldham, 1824 –8.

*Orrell, John.* Preston. 28 Friargate, 1822–34; 29 Lune St in 1848. Preston museum have watch.

*Orton, John.* Manchester. 1 Rigby St, Salford in 1824.

*Osborne, Thomas.* Bolton. Clockmaker. 'Slayne' and buried there 1665.

*Outhwaite, Thomas & Co.* Liverpool. 2 South End Dry Dock in 1814.

*Over, Thomas.* Liverpool. 12 Prussia St and 12 Basnett St in 1848; 33 Basnett St in 1851.

*Overton, William.* Manchester. Imported clocks at 11 Cornwall St, Oldham Rd in 1848.

*Owens, Owen.* Liverpool. 4 South Castle St in 1851.

*Palethorp, William.* Liverpool. 26 Hill St, Park in 1834.

*Park(e), James.* Preston. 12 Fishergate, 1822–48. Also silversmith. At 32 Avenham Lane in 1858.

*Park, Joseph.* Liverpool. Clockmaker. Working there by 1734. Died 1776. Liverpool museum have two clocks.

*Parker, George.* Ulverston. Born 1800 at Kirby Ireleth. Married Frances Jane Hanley, 1824. At Market Place, 1825–58. Married Jane Briggs secondly in 1847. Watches and longcase clocks recorded.

*Parker, John.* Prescot. Watchmaker. Married Alice Hill, 1781.

*Parker, John.* Liverpool. Watchmaker in Fleet St in 1763, later Edmund St. Died 1795.

*Parkin, Bartholomew.* Manchester. Clockmaker. Married Susanna Blase, 1792.

*Parkinson & Frodsham.* Liverpool. Chronometer makers at 38 Castle St in 1834.

*Parkinson, J.* Bacup. Queen St in 1858.

*Parkinson, Joseph.* West Derby. Watchmaker. Daughter born 1818 by wife, Hannah.

*Parkinson, Nathaniel.* Preston. 37 Lord St in 1848; St John St in 1851.

*Parkinson, Robert.* Lancaster. Clockmaker. Free there 1732. Married Ellen Davies there 1739. Died 11 April 1759, leaving will. Various longcase clocks noted, including some which bore the name of Joshua Harrocks inside movement, one of which was dated 1746. Harrocks evidently worked as his journeyman. Succeeded by son, William (qv).

*Parkinson, Thomas.* Bury. Millgate, 1822-8; Bolton St in 1834.

*Parkinson, William* (I). Lancaster. Clocksmith. Free there 1758. Son of Robert Parkinson (qv). Mentioned in father's will of 1760 with his wife, Ellen. Had son, William (II) (qv). Clock noted c 1760, signed, as many of theirs were, 'Parkinson—Lancaster', with Joshua Harrocks's name inside the movement, apparently as journeyman. Died 1800.

*Parkinson, William* (II). Prescot/Lancaster. Watchmaker. Free at Lancaster in 1789. Son of William (I). Lancaster museum have clock by him. Worked at Lancaster later, where he died 1804, leaving will.

*Parks, John.* Prescot. Watchmaker. Children born to wife, Mary, 1819-24.

*Parr, Henry.* Prescot. Watchmaker. Children born to wife, Margaret, 1823-5.

*Parr, John.* Farnworth. Watchmaker. Married Ellen Chandler, 1828.

*Parr, John.* Liverpool. 30 Haymarket in 1814; Whitechapel, 1822-34.

*Parr, John.* Prescot. Movementmaker (watch?). Married Elizabeth Conneys, 1768.

*Parr, Peter.* Liverpool. 19 Dickinson St in 1834.

*Parr, Robert.* Prescot. Clockmaker. Daughter born 1795 by wife, Margaret.

*Parr, W.* Manchester. Clockmaker. Married Mary Smith, 1798.

*Parr, William.* Farnworth. Watchmaker. Married Mary Lyon, 1798.

*Parr, William.* Liverpool. Clockmaker at 62 Dale St, 1781-1800.

*Parr, William.* Liverpool. Liver Crescent, Bootle Lane in 1848.

*Parr, William.* Prescot. Movementmaker (watch?). Married Martha Lightfoot, 1779.

*Parr, William.* Prescot. Watchmaker. Married Ann Read, 1795.

*Parr, William.* St Helens. Clockmaker at Eccleston in 1784, when married Elizabeth Foster there.

*Parry, William J.* Liverpool. 58 Tithebarn St in 1848; 3 Whitechapel in 1851.

*Patten, James.* Prescot. Watch-maker. Married Margaret Hosker, 1765. Children born 1770–80.

*Patten, Robert.* Liverpool. 22 Great Crosshall St in 1824. Watch No 1171 hallmarked 1829.

*Patterson, James.* Liverpool. 49 Sir Thomas's Buildings in 1848.

*Patterson, Robert.* Liverpool. 16 Bath St in 1851.

*Pearce, George.* Liverpool. 53 Copperas Hill in 1851.

*Pearson, William.* Blackburn. 2 Astley Gate, 1822–8; Holme St in 1834.

*Pedrone, Louis.* Liverpool. 57 Lord St, 1848–51.

*Pendlebury & Son.* Todmorden. Supposedly working there 1840.

*Pendleton, Peter.* Prescot. Watch-maker. Married Martha Barrow, 1803. Children born 1818–23.

*Pendleton, Samuel.* Prescot. Watch-maker. Married Betty Sankey at Farnworth 1768. Died 1778, leaving will.

*Penlington, John.* Liverpool. 2 Parker St, 1822–4; 65 Church St in 1828. Also chronometers.

*Penlington, Joseph.* Liverpool. 39 Church St, 1828–34; 3 St George's Crescent North, 1848–51. Also chronometers.

*Penlington, Samuel & Thomas.* Liverpool. 22 Tarlton St in 1851. Chronometers too.

*Pennington, James.* Prescot. Eccleston St in 1851. Also chronometers.

*Pennington, John.* Ince. Clockmaker. Died 1764.

*Pennington, John.* Liverpool. 17

Hart St in 1824. One such also at 83 London Rd in 1824. Same man?

*Percy, William.* Liverpool. Watch-maker. Married Catherine Travis, 1834.

*Peugh.* See Pugh.

*Philipson, Henry* (I). Winster/Ulverston. Clockmaker. Worked as journeyman for Jonas Barber of Winster. Born 1754. Worked alone after Barber's death in 1802 till 1804 at Winster. Moved to Ulverston by 1805. Died there 1834. Succeeded by son, Henry.

*Philipson, Henry* (II). Ulverston. Clockmaker. Born 1793, son of Henry senior. Married Elizabeth Askew, 1820. Succeeded his father in 1834 at Soutergate. Still working there 1865. After his death the business passed to the Hird family.

*Phythian, John.* Prescot. Watch-maker. Married 1718. Son, John, born 1723.

*Phythian, John.* Prescot. Watch-maker. Had several children by wife, Rachel, between 1754 and 1771.

*Phythian, John.* Prescot. Watch-maker. Married Ellen Wedgewood, 1760.

*Phythian, John.* Prescot. Watch-maker. Child born 1795 to wife, Mary.

*Phythian, John.* Prescot. Watch-maker. Died 1785, leaving will. Known as John senior.

*Phithian, Joseph.* Liverpool (West Derby). Watchmaker. Died 1767.

*Pickavance, Samuel.* St Helens. Watchmaker. Married Elizabeth Taylor, 1822, by whom several children born till 1830.

*Pickford, John.* Liverpool. 20 Mersey St, 1822–34; 39 Mersey St, 1848–51.

*Pickford, Joseph.* Stockport. Clockmaker. Died there 16 November 1844 aged 74. Believed from Lancashire.

*Pickford, Richard.* Liverpool. 1 Manchester St in 1848; 270 Scotland Rd in 1851.

*Pickford, William.* Stalybridge. Grosvenor St in 1848.

*Pierpoint, John.* Liverpool. Watchmaker. Children born to wife, Elizabeth, in 1822. At 54 Great Crosshall St in 1824.

*Pierpoint, Thomas.* Liverpool. Watchmaker at 12 St Paul's Square in 1781.

*Piers, Charles.* Liverpool. Chronometer maker at 34 Strand St in 1848.

*Pilkington, Hugh Joseph.* Chorley. Market St, 1834–58.

*Pilkington, James.* St Helens. Watchmaker at Parr. Married Mary Travers, 1771, to whom several children born till 1783.

*Pilling, John.* Boothfold. Longcase clock recorded c 1840 (erroneously as c 1800).

*Pinnington, James.* Prescot. Watchmaker. Married Alice Shele, 1779.

*Pinnington, Thomas.* Liverpool. 1 Leigh St in 1814; 20 Coopers Row in 1822; 10 Standish St in

1824; 66 Great Crosshall St in 1834; Paisley St in 1848.

*Pipe, Isaac.* Manchester. 29 Market St in 1834.

*Place, James.* Preston. 18 St John's St, 1824–8. Preston museum have watch dated 1787.

*Plant, Thomas.* Manchester. Clockmaker. Married Martha Waine, 1802.

*Plant, William.* Manchester. 39 Portland St, 1848–51.

*Platt, James.* Prescot. Watchmaker. Daughter born to wife, Ellen, in 1795.

*Platt, John.* St Helens. 126 Westfield St, 1848–51; Cross St in 1858.

*Platt, Oliver.* Wigan. Watchmaker. Free 1674. Formerly apprenticed to Roger Darbyshire (Hawkes).

*Platt, Thomas.* Prescot. Watchmaker. Son born to wife, Margaret, in 1825.

*Plowman, Thomas.* Lancaster. Bensons Court in 1824; Market St, 1834–51. Also jeweller.

*Plumb, John.* Wavertree. Watchmaker. Died 1729, leaving will.

*Plumb, Matthew.* Liverpool. Clockmaker at Tythe Barn St in 1767.

*Plumb, William.* Liverpool. Watchmaker at 33 Tythe Barn St, 1790–6.

*Plumpton, John.* Liverpool. Watchmaker at 17 Shawhill St, 1781–90.

*Pomfret, Horatio.* Manchester. Imported clocks at Blossom St, Ancoats, 1848–51.

*Poole, James.* Liverpool. Clock and watchmaker and jeweller in 1828 directory.

*Porter, James.* Farnworth. Watchmaker. Married Elizabeth Johnson, 1809.
*Porter, Peter.* Prescot. Watchmaker.
Married Ellen Mercer, 1808, by
whom several children up to 1824.
*Porter, Robert.* Prescot. Watchmaker. Daughter born to wife,
Catherine, in 1794.
*Porter, Thomas.* Prescot. Watchmaker. Married Mary Bromilow, 1773.
*Porter, Thomas.* Prescot. Watchmaker. Married Thomasin Sephton, 1774.
*Porter, Thomas.* Childwall. Watchmaker. Married Mary Harper,
1813.
*Porter, William.* Prescot. Watchmaker. Married Jane Birchall,
1783, to whom children born till
1796.
*Porter, William.* Prescot. Watchmaker. Married Sarah Windle,
1800.
*Porter, William.* Prescot. Watchmaker. Married Mary Holihead,
1831.
*Portland, ——.* Liverpool. Liverpool
museum have watch c 1805.
*Poston & Woldnough.* Liverpool.
Dial enamellers at 21 Peter St in
1828.
*Poston, Robert.* Liverpool. Watch
dial maker. Daughter born to
wife, Ellen, in 1824. In 1834
listed as clock and watch dial
enamellers at 21 Peter St. See
also above entry.
*Potter, John.* St Helens. 2 Duke St in
1851.
*Potter, Richard.* Manchester. 22

Oxford St, Chorlton-on-Med-
lock, 1848–51.
*Potter, William.* Farnworth. Watch-
maker. Married Margaret Much,
1825.
*Potter, William.* St Helens. 2 Duke
St, 1848–51.
*Powell, John.* Liverpool. 29 Lime St
and also imported clocks at 19
Peter St in 1851.
*Powlton, William.* Lancaster. Clockmaker. Born 1791 at Kendal.
Working at Lancaster with wife
Betty by 1820 as journeyman for
Russell. Began own business in
1832 at Gage St. Then at Moor
Lane, 1848–51; then Friar St by
1858. Longcase clocks, wall
clocks and skelton clock reported.
Label inside clock case reads:
W.P. 'Respectfully informs his
friends and the public that he has
commenced the above business
and from his practical knowledge
in all its branches (having been
21 years in the employ of the late
and present Mr. Russell) trusts
he shall be able to give satisfaction
to all those who favour him with
their commands. 5th Sept. 1832.'
*Poynter, William.* Farnworth.
Watchmaker. Married Mary
Massey, 1828.
*Pratt, John.* Preston. 12 Friargate in
1858.
*Prescot, John.* St Helens. Watchmaker. Married Elizabeth Holland, 1827, to whom several
children born till 1834.
*Prescot, Thomas.* Prescot. Watchmaker. Children born to wife.
Ellen, 1818–26.

*Preston, Job.* Prescot. Watchmaker. Children born to wife, Ann, 1818–26.

*Preston, Job.* St Helens. Watchmaker. Children born to wife, Catherine, 1770–88.

*Preston, John.* Prescot. Watchmaker. Married Ann Baldwin, 1799. Second marriage 1808 to Ann Platt? Children born 1818–26.

*Preston, Robert.* Liverpool. Watchmaker at Dale St advertising 1782. Bankrupt 1793.

*Preston, William.* Lancaster. Watchmaker at Market St, 1822–34. Longcase clock recorded. Lancaster museum have watch. A watchmaker of this name married in 1828 at Farnworth to Mary Beesley—presumably same man.

*Price, Edward.* Liverpool. Watchmaker at 2 Ormond St in 1777.

*Price, Thomas.* Farnworth. Clockmaker. Married Mary Bromilow, 1818.

*Priest, John.* Liverpool. 7 Harford St in 1834.

*Prince, John.* Manchester. Watchmaker. Son born 1821.

*Pritchard, Griffith.* Liverpool. Watchmaker. Married Elizabeth Rose, 1834.

*Probert, James.* Wigan. Standishgate in 1816.

*Pryor, Joseph.* Liverpool. Watchmaker. Children born by wife, Grace, 1676–88. Wife died 1709. He died 1719. Inventory of his goods survives.

*Pugh, Richard Dyke.* Liverpool. Scotland Rd, 1848–51.

*Pye, James.* Farnworth. Watch maker. Married Alice Hurst, 1799.

*Pye, John.* St Helens. Watchmaker. Daughter born 1785.

*Pye, John.* Manchester. Clockmaker. Married Susanna Ward, 1791.

*Pye, Robert.* Manchester. Clockmaker. Married Mary Calvert, 1792.

*Quilliam, Samuel.* Liverpool. 28 Elliott St, 1848–51.

*Radcliffe, Charles.* Liverpool. Watchmaker. Children born 1693–99. Died 1700.

*Radcliff, Charles.* Liverpool. 41 Duke St, 1848–51.

*Ramsbotham, Richard.* Bury. Clockmaker. Died there 1734. Inventory of his goods survives. Probate to widow, Martha.

*Ramsey, William.* Liverpool. Watchmaker. Listed in 1780.

*Ratcliffe, John.* Manchester. 4 Old Bridge St in 1834.

*Rawson & Royle.* Wigan. There in 1858.

*Rawsthorne, John.* Ormskirk. Moor St in 1834.

*Rawsthorne, John.* Clitheroe. Castle St, 1848–58.

*Read, Thomas.* Manchester. Clockmaker in directories 1797–1800. Married Sarah Walsh, 1801.

*Reed, James.* Liverpool. 27 Basnett St in 1851.

*Renk, A. & C.* Salford. Salford museum have regulator by him c 1840, and watches.

133

*Renshall, John.* Farnworth. Watchmaker. Married Mary Anderton, 1800.

*Renshaw, James.* Prescot. Watchmaker. Daughter born 1819 to wife, Ann.

*Reynoldson, John.* Ulverston. Watchmaker. Son, William, died there 1786 (Hobbs).

*Rhind, Thomas.* Manchester. 15 Oxford St, Chorlton in 1834; 126 Clarendon St, Hulme in 1851 (foreign clocks).

*Rhodes, John.* Manchester. 76 Rochdale Rd, 1848–51.

*Rice, John.* Prescot. Watchmaker. Died 1765.

*Ricee (Ricce), John.* Ulverston. Clockmaker, 1786–7 (Hobbs).

*Richards, J.* Lancaster. Watch by him stolen in 1798 from shop of William Anderson of Lancaster.

*Richardson, Henry.* Southport. Lord St in 1848.

*Richardson, John.* St Helens. Watchmaker. Son born 1770.

*Richardson, John.* Manchester. 5 St George's Rd, 1828–34; 5 Rochdale Rd, 1848–51.

*Richardson, Richard.* Lancaster. Casemaker? Label inside clock case states 'cabinet maker, Lancaster', c 1840.

*Richardson, Richard.* Liverpool. Watchmaker at 29 Highfield St in 1795.

*Richardson, Thomas.* Manchester. Swan St, 1822–51.

*Richmond, Robert.* Lancaster. Watchmaker. Free 1817. Son of John Richmond, gardener.

*Rider, Tryall.* Manchester. Arched dial 8-day longcase clock with moon in arch noted, c 1750–60.

*Rider, William.* Farnworth. Watchmaker. Married Hannah Pennington, 1790.

*Rigby, Henry.* Liverpool. Watchmaker at Cable St, later John St. Lost watch advertised 1775. Liverpool museum have watch dated 1781. Longcase clock noted. Died 1787.

*Rigby, J.* Warrington. Watchmaker at Ashton-in-Makerfield in 1858.

*Rigby, James,* Liverpool. 30 Richmond Row, 1822–34.

*Rigby, Joseph.* Prescot. Watchmaker. Daughter born to wife, Margaret, 1797.

*Rigby. Nicholas.* Ormskirk. Watchmaker. Died 1754.

*Rigby, Thomas.* Prescot. Hillock St in 1834.

*Rigby, W.* Leigh. King St in 1858.

*Rigby, William.* Newton. Watchmaker there 1848.

*Rigby, William.* Prescot. Watchmaker at Rainhill, 1818–26, when children born to wife, Ann.

*Riley, Gillingham.* Todmorden. Apprentice to Ely Stott of Wakefield in 1773. Then at Todmorden till 1822.

*Rimmer, Henry.* Cronton. Watchmaker. Married Ellen Blundell, 1794.

*Rimmer, Robert.* Liverpool. Working there 1828.

*Rimmer, William.* Liverpool. Liverpool museum have watch hallmarked 1771. Lost watch advertised 1785.

*Riordan, Matthew.* Ulverston. Market St in 1869. Also jeweller.
*Roach, Patrick.* Manchester. Imported clocks at 5 Sidney St, Salford in 1848.
*Roberts, George.* Liverpool. 54 Pitt St in 1848.
*Roberts, John.* Burnley. Market St in 1822; St James St, 1824–34.
*Roberts, Michael.* Bury. Butcher Lane in 1848; Stanley St in 1851; Spring St in 1858.
*Roberts (alias Johnson), William.* Flixton, Manchester. Clockmaker. Died there 1755 of a bad fever aged 80.
*Robertshaw, John.* Manchester. Imported clocks at 47 Bridgewater St, 1848–51. In 1848 also had second shop at 62 Gaythorn St.
*Robertson, John.* Liverpool. Watchmaker. Children born 1689–97.
*Robinson, Benjamin.* Manchester. Working by 1800. At Chapel St, Salford, 1822–34; then Deal St, Salford, 1848–51.
*Robinson, Charles.* Warrington. Watchmaker. Married Grace Cheatham, 1775.
*Robinson, George.* Liverpool. 26 John St in 1828.
*Robinson, Henry.* Liverpool. 83 Church St, 1848–51.
*Robinson, Isiah.* Rochdale. 12 Toad Lane in 1851.
*Robinson, James.* Warrington. Scotland Rd, 1824–34. Also turret clocks.
*Robinson, John.* Lancaster. Watchmaker. Free 1783. Died before 1812.

*Robinson, John.* Dalton/Barrow. 7 Devonshire Terrace, Dalton in 1866. Also made nautical instruments. At Barrow in 1869.
*Robinson, Thomas B.* Liverpool. Watchmaker in 1790. 13 Webster St, 1822–4.
*Robinson, William (& Co).* Liverpool. Liverpool museum have two watches, earliest c 1780. At 26 Highfield St, 1795–1800. At 47 Pool Lane in 1814. William Robinson & Co at 6 Union St in 1848, may be a different man.
*Roche, Richard.* Liverpool. 79 Park Lane in 1848.
*Roe & Jacob.* Liverpool. 56 Church St in 1851.
*Rogan, Edward.* Liverpool. 35 Springfield Rd in 1851.
*Rogers, William.* Liverpool. Watch of c 1840 reported.
*Roscow, Robert.* Liverpool. 28 Lionel St in 1824.
*Rose, Henry.* Wigan. Watchmaker at Millgate, 1811–25; when he died aged 66 (Hawkes).
*Rose, John.* Farnworth. Watchmaker. Married Martha Woods, 1792.
*Rose, Joseph.* Liverpool. Watchmaker. Son born 1822 to wife, Dorothy.
*Rose, Thomas* (senior). Wigan. Millgate in 1824.
*Rose, Thomas* (junior). Wigan. Market Place, 1824–34. Married Alice Simkin, 1811 (Hawkes).
*Rose, William.* Liverpool. Liverpool museum have watch hallmarked 1790.

*Roskell, John* (junior). Liverpool. 21 Church St, 1848–51. Chronometers.

*Roskell, John & Robert.* Liverpool. 11 Church St, 1814–22. Liverpool museum have watch by John alone c 1815.

*Roskell, Joseph.* St Helens. Watchmaker at Hardshaigh in 1818 when daughter born to wife, Phebe.

*Roskell, Robert* (& *Son*). Liverpool. Working by 1800. Numerous watches recorded dating between 1805 and 1865. '& Son' from 1828–34. Bracket clocks, regulators and semi-regulators recorded. Also chronometers.

*Rostance, James.* Manchester. Clockmaker. Married Mary Fogg, 1791.

*Rothwell, James.* Bolton. Clockmaker. Died 1796, leaving will.

*Rothwell, John.* Ormskirk. Clockmaker. Son born to wife, Elizabeth, in 1824. Working in Church St, 1824–34.

*Roughley, Henry.* Burtonwood/St Helens. Watchmaker of Parr. Married Elizabeth Parr (*sic*), 1784, who died 1785. Son born to (second) wife, Ellen, in 1793.

*Rowland, Henry.* Liverpool. 2 Hatton Gardens in 1824.

*Rowland, John.* Manchester. Watchmaker in *Manchester Mercury* in 1792. Married Mary Blaky, 1796.

*Rowley, Henry.* Liverpool. 71 Rose Place in 1834.

*Rowley, William.* Liverpool. Currie St in 1848.

*Rowson, Christopher.* Liverpool. 52 Sir Thomas's Buildings, 1848–51. Also at 30 Pembroke St in 1851.

*Royland, John.* Liverpool. Lost watch reported 1785.

*Royle, John.* Bolton. Square brass-dial clock noted with four season spandrels c 1750–60.

*Royle, Ralph.* Manchester. Watchmaker. Died 1760, leaving will.

*Royle & Rawson.* Wigan. Watchmakers 'between the two railway stations' at 76 Wallgate in 1858. Watch in Wigan museum.

*Royle, Thomas.* Liverpool. Watchmaker in 1754 lists.

*Rubottom, William.* Liverpool. 20 Redcross St, 1790–6.

*Ruff & Tritchler.* Bolton. Bradshawgate in 1848.

*Runchorne, Richard.* Liverpool. 7 Brooks St in 1777.

*Runcorn, Richard & Robert.* Manchester. *Manchester Mercury*, 1782–95.

*Rushton, James.* Colne. Walton Lane Bottom, Great Marsden in 1848.

*Russell, Thomas.* Lancaster. Watchmaker. Supposedly served apprenticeship at Broughton, then came to Lancaster as assistant to William Wakefield. Married Mary Ellis at Ingleton, 1808. Had William Powlton as journeyman from 1811 to 1832, by which time his son had taken over. Shop was in Market St. Watches at Preston and Lancaster museums.

*Russell, Thomas & Son.* Liverpool. 22 Slater St, 1848–51. Watch in

*Russell, Thomas & Son.* cont. Lancaster museum. Others in Liverpool museum hallmarked 1897–1902.

*Russell, William.* Liverpool. Pitt St, 1834–51.

*Russells Ltd.* Liverpool. Liverpool museum have watch hallmarked 1903.

*Ryall, Thomas.* Manchester. Oldham Rd, 1848–51.

*Rycroft, Timothy.* Liverpool. Died in 1704, in which year his son was born.

*Ryland, James.* Ormskirk. Watchmaker there 1786.

*Ryland, John.* Ormskirk. Aughton St, 1822–8.

*Saber, Wolff & Lewis.* Liverpool. 109 Whitechapel in 1848. In 1851 Wolff Saber alone at same address.

*Sackerson, William.* Manchester. Watchmaker. Married Esther Cheetham, 1802.

*Sagar, James.* Blackburn. Watchmaker in Northgate, 1838–51.

*Sagar, John.* Blackburn. Church St, 1834–51.

*Sagar, Robert Holgate.* Blackburn. Astley Gate in 1822; Church St, 1825–51. Also jeweller and silversmith.

*Sager, R. & J.* Blackburn. Church St in 1858.

*Salter, William.* Manchester. 1 Rosamond St, Salford in 1828.

*Salusbury, William.* Ormskirk. Aughton St in 1834.

*Sampson, Thomas,* Liverpool. 33 Moorfields in 1851.

*Samuel, Edwin L.* Liverpool. Wholesaler at 9 South Castle St in 1848.

*Samuel, Eliza.* Liverpool. 82 Paradise St in 1834. See Nathan Samuel.

*Samuel, F. & Co.* Liverpool. Patent lever watches at 36 Castle St, 1822–4.

*Samuel, Flora & Co.* Liverpool. 54 Bold St in 1828; 4 St George's Crescent North in 1834.

*Samuel, George & Israel.* Liverpool. 20 Basnett St, 1848–51.

*Samuel, Henry.* Liverpool. 18 Vauxhall Rd in 1848; 24 Manchester St and 91 St James St in 1851.

*Samuel, Lewis & Co.* Liverpool. Castle St, 1814–28; Lord St, 1834–48. Also Paradise St in 1834.

*Samuel, Lewis Henry & Co.* Liverpool. 60 South Castle St, 1848–51.

*Samuel, Moses.* Liverpool. 15 Cornwallis St in 1824.

*Samuel, Nathan.* Liverpool. Paradise St in 1828.

*Samuel, Samuel J.* Liverpool. 60 Pool Lane in 1834.

*Samuel, Saul.* Liverpool. 8 Mount Pleasant in 1851.

*Samuel, Sylvester L.* Liverpool. 48 Lord St in 1848; 2 Lord St in 1851.

*Samuel, Simpson (Brothers) & Co.* Liverpool. 31 Castle St, Brothers & Co in 1822; Simpson & Co in 1824.

*Sanders, Nathaniel.* Manchester. Clockmaker. Married Mary Braddock, 1768. Working there till 1800. Buried at Bowden, Cheshire, 26 April 1828 aged 86.

I

*Sanderson,* ——. Liverpool. Lost watches reported 1771 and 1772.

*Sandiford, James.* Manchester. Clockmaker. Married Ann Tongue, 1762. Buried there 12 April 1775 aged 50. Brass-dial 8-day clock noted.

*Sankey, James.* Warrington. Movement-maker (watches). Daughter born 1767 to wife, Mary.

*Sater, Joseph & Co.* Oldham. 8 West St in 1851.

*Saul, Matthias.* Lancaster. Joiner by trade, Longcase clock recorded with his name round dial in place of figures. May be a clock made for him? Died 1860 aged 73. Designed his own tombstone.

*Scales, Edward.* Manchester. Half St, Cathedral Yard, 1848–51.

*Scamble, Peter.* Liverpool. 3 Dean St in 1851.

*Scarisbrick, Anthony.* Prescot. Watchmaker. Married Sarah Worsley, 1795.

*Scaresbrick, James.* Liverpool. Clockmaker. Married Anne Hayes, 1663.

*Scarron, James.* Wigan. Working 1797.

*Schlesinger, Casper Wolff.* Liverpool. 44 Pleasant St in 1834.

*Scholfield, Edmund.* Rochdale. clockmaker. Son of Major Scholfield, clockmaker. Born 1730. Died 15 April 1792 aged 62, leaving will.

*Scholefield, Jonathan.* Ogden. Clockmaker. Died 1747.

*Scholfield, Josiah.* Manchester. Clockmaker. Married Mary Fletcher, 1803.

*Scho(l)field, Major* (senior). Rochdale/Manchester. Clockmaker. Born 1707. One clock recorded dated 1730, signed Rochdale. Apparently worked in Manchester. Wife, Elizabeth, died Rochdale in 1755. He died there 24 March 1783 aged 76. Father of Edmund and Major (junior).

*Scho(l)field, Major* (junior). Salford/Manchester. Clockmaker. Born 1749, son of Major Scho(l)field (senior). Married Ann Heywood, 1784. Lived at the Flying Horse, Huntbank, where he died 23 September 1813 aged 64. Clock in Salford museum.

*Scholfield, Robert.* Rochdale. Clockmaker. Died 17 February 1736. His daughter, Hannah, died there 1741, and son, John, in 1747.

*Scholefield, Robert.* Rochdale. Clockmaker. Took Joseph Batty of Halifax as apprentice in 1752 at £5 5s. In 1753 owed money to John Stancliffe, clockmaker of Halifax. Died 1759 leaving will, which mentions wife, Esther, three daughters and son, James. Clock noted c 1750 in carved oak case. Lived at Hundersfield, in Rochdale parish.

*Scholefield, Robert.* Rochdale. Brass-dial clock recorded dated 1794.

*Schwersensky, Isaac.* Liverpool. 6 Whitechapel, 1848–51.

*Scotson, Isaac (Joseph).* Liverpool. Clockmaker at Old Shambles, 1767–77. Listed as Joseph Scotson in 1784. Clock in Liverpool museum.

*Scott, John Hargreaves.* Burnley. 16 Market St, 1848–51. Also silversmith.

*Seager, John.* Liverpool. Simpson St, 1824–34.

*Sealey, William.* Preston. Mainspit Wynd in 1848.

*Sedden, Henry.* Farnworth. Watchmaker. Married Elizabeth Wainwright, 1806.

*Seddon, James.* Farnworth. Watchmaker. Married Betty Tunstall, 1800.

*Seddon, John.* Wigan. Wigan museum have 19th-century watch.

*Seddon, Josiah.* Manchester. Watchmaker. Married Ann Holland, 1764.

*Seddon, Samuel.* Liverpool. Watchmaker. Plumb St, 1767–77, when he died.

*Seddon, William.* Manchester. Imported clocks at 4 Chester Rd, Hulme, 1834–51.

*Seed, John.* Liverpool. Wavertree in 1828.

*Sephton, Edward.* Prescot. Watchmaker at Eccleston in 1826 when daughter born to wife, Ellin.

*Sephton, John.* St Helens. Watchmaker at Sutton. Married Ellen Denton, 1768.

*Sephton, Kenwright/Henwright.* Prescot. Watchmaker at Rainhill. Children born to wife, Sarah, 1795–8.

*Sephton, Kendrick.* St Helens. Watchmaker at Windle, Children born to wife, Ellen, 1826–34.

*Sephton, Luke.* Prescot. Watch

maker. Son, Edward, born 1796 to wife, Ellen.

*Sephton, Peter.* Prescot. Watchmaker at Rainhill. Children born to wife, Prudence, 1796–7.

*Sewill, Joseph.* Liverpool. 61 South Castle St, 1848–51. Chronometers.

*Shakeshaft, Lawrence.* Preston. Clockmaker. Painted-dial clock noted c 1800. At 10 Stony Gate, 1824–8; 29 Shambles, 1834–48.

*Sharples, James.* Liverpool. Movement maker (watch?). Married Elizabeth Woodward, 1785. At 34 Brownlow Hill in 1814.

*Sharrocks, Henry.* Wigan. Clockmaker at Millgate in 1822 when daughter born to wife, Elizabeth.

*Shaw, John.* Lancaster. Watchmaker. Son of Thomas Shaw, clockmaker. Free there 1801.

*Shaw, Richard.* St Helens. Watchmaker. Son born 1781.

*Shaw, Robert.* Lancaster. Clockmaker at Dolphinholme. Free 1789. Son of Robert Shaw, deceased. Still alive in 1825.

*Shaw, Thomas.* Lancaster. Clocksmith. Free 1766. Died before 1801 when son, John, was free as a watchmaker.

*Shaw, William.* Liverpool. Watchmaker at 59 Old Hall St in 1790.

*Shenfield, John.* Manchester. Imported clocks at 71 Thomas St, Shude Hill, 1848–51.

*Shepherd, Thomas.* Liverpool. Basnett St, 1790–5.

*Shepherd, William.* Liverpool. Castle St, 1763–81. Watch in Liverpool museum.

*Shepherd, William.* Liverpool. 13 Bath St, 1848–51. Chronometers.

*Shepley, Edward.* Manchester. Clockmaker. Married Elizabeth Burton, 1788.

*Sherratt, Isaac.* Manchester. Clockmaker in 1800.

*Sherratt, J.* Wigan. Watchmaker at Hindley in 1858.

*Sherring, John K. & Co.* Manchester. 40 Downing St, Chorlton-on-Medlock in 1848; 15 Canal St, Ancoats in 1851.

*Sherwood, Thomas.* Prescot. Watchmaker. Wife, Ann, had children 1796–8.

*Sheward, Thomas.* Prescot. Watchmaker. Wife, Alice, had child 1826.

*Shierwater & Lloyd.* Liverpool. Liverpool museum have turret clock of 1912 from Central Station.

*Sim, Charles.* Farnworth. Watchmaker. Married Elizabeth Critchley, 1799.

*Sim, George.* Farnworth. Watchmaker. Married Margaret Wright, 1799.

*Sim, George.* Prescot. Watchmaker. Wife, Lydia, had child 1795.

*Simm, Joseph.* Farnworth. Watchmaker. Married Elizabeth Stanley, 1828.

*Sim, Joshua.* Prescot. Watchmaker. Married Sarah Lyon, 1815, by whom children born till 1826.

*Sim, Thomas.* Prescot. Watchmaker. Married Ann Runshaw, 1809. At Hillock St in 1822.

*Simcock, Thomas* (senior). Warrington. Watchmaker. Married Alice Bennet, 1809, at Farnworth. At Bridge St, 1822–34.

*Simcock, Thomas* (junior). Warrington. At Sankey St in 1834; then Buttermarket St, 1848–51.

*Simcock, William.* Warrington. 115–117 Bridge St, 1848–58.

*Simmons, Isaac.* Manchester. 9 St Ann's Square, 1834–51.

*Simner, James.* Liverpool. 19 Mersey St in 1814.

*Simpson, Stephen* (senior). Greta Bridge/Caton/Preston. Clockmaker. Born 1752, son of William Simpson of Gisburn. Became a Quaker in 1779. Married Elizabeth Porter, 1788 at Lancaster. Worked at Greta Bridge. Made sundial for Melling churchyard. In 1801 moved to Caton, then in 1804 to Preston, where he set up shop at 109 Church St. His shop was known by the sign of the 'Tup's Clock' and had a model ram over the door which used to strike the hours on a bell with its horns. Made clock for Chipping church in 1814 for £60; it lasted till 1909. Wife, Elizabeth, died in 1814, and he re-married in 1817 to Mary Gibbs, through which re-marriage he ceased to be a Quaker. Died 23 November 1821 aged 69 at Preston. Took Robert Summersgill as apprentice in 1813. Children included the following who became clockmakers too: 1781 William; 1791 Stephen; 1794 Edmund; 1800 Isaac. Various clocks noted with brass and painted dials, one with

*Simpson, Stephen* (senior). cont. 'R. Buterfield' in place of hour numerals.

*Simpson, William.* Preston/Bingley. Clockmaker. Born 1781 at Gretna Bridge, eldest son of Stephen Simpson, clockmaker. Apprenticed to his father. Married twice, second being Elizabeth Wilkinson in 1804 at Preston, by whom he had ten children. Soon after 1804 moved to Bingley, Yorks. Wife died and he re-married in 1829 to Hannah Longbottom. Also made factory tower clocks and textile machinery. Died 22 February 1846.

*Simpson, John.* Liverpool. Chronometer maker with Thomas Roberts at the Strand. Eldest son of William Simpson of Preston and Bingley. Married twice but left no issue.

*Simpson, Stephen* (junior). Preston/ Mansfield. Born 1791 son of Stephen Simpson senior. Was a clockmaker at Preston for a time, then in 1823 moved to Mansfield, Notts, where he became a gas engineer and made various types of meters. Ran the Church St, Preston shop in 1822. Died at Mansfield in 1840.

*Simpson, Edmund.* Preston. Born 1794, son of Stephen Simpson senior. Married in 1812 when only 17, to Ann Leeming, who was pregnant at the time, on account of which he was disowned by the Quakers. Ann died in 1817. He died in 1820.

Can have made very few clocks in this short working life. May well have worked for his father.

*Simpson, Isaac.* Chorley/Preston. Clock and watchmaker. Son of Stephen Simpson senior. Born 1800. Apprenticed to father as a clockmaker. In 1820 married Mary Ann, eldest daughter of Robert Hargraves, clockmaker, of Skipton, Yorks. Set up business in Chorley Market St. Took as apprentices John, son of William Fell, and John, son of his brother, William Simpson. Left the Quaker faith he was born in. Wrote a book on watchmaking and another on calculations for clockmakers—both survive in manuscript only with a descendant. In 1831 he moved to Fox St, Preston. He later set up a gold thread business there and in 1853 patented a machine for making this. He died at Preston in 1859, his widow in 1871. Sold a 30-hour clock to William Fell in 1822 for £2 16s. Wall clock noted bearing Chorley address.

*Simpson, Edmund.* Preston. Son of Isaac Simpson, clockmaker. Was initially a watchmaker and later in the gold thread making business. In 1857 he patented a safety apparatus for pit shaft cages.

*Simpson, John.* Lancaster. Clockmaker. Born c 1744, son of William of Greta Bridge. Brother of Stephen Simpson senior. Was initially a clockmaker at Lancaster but by 1776

*Simpson, John.* cont.
became a soldier and left the trade.

*Simpson, Jonathan Wortley.* Preston. Clockmaker. Grandson of John Simpson above and great nephew of Stephen Simpson senior. Married Ann Ianson, 1820, shortly after which he came to live in Preston. At 151 Friargate, 1820–5; 20 Lune St, 1834–58.

Simpsons—the following not known to be related to the above:

*Simpson, John.* Garstang. Chapel St, 1822–8.

*Simpson, Joseph.* Preston. 151 Friargate in 1828. See also Jonathan at this address.

*Simpson, R.* Lancaster. White dial longcase clock reported, mid-19 century.

*Simpson, Robert.* Garstang. There in 1834.

*Simpson, Robert.* Poulton-le-Fylde. Market St, 1822–48.

*Simpson, Robert.* Liverpool. Watchmaker in 1800 directory.

*Simpson, Samuel.* Colne. Mason by trade. Born 1774. After 1797 learned to make and dress clocks. Gave evidence in deposition of 1833 concerning John Spencer (III). No clocks known to survive by him.

*Simpson, Samuel.* Liverpool. 9 Temple Court in 1834.

*Singleton, John Arthur.* Manchester. Watchmaker. Married Ann Holden, 1798. Son entered school there in 1811.

*Singleton, John.* London/Lancaster. Watchmaker. Free at Lancaster in 1806, said to be then of London. Not known if he ever worked at Lancaster.

*Skeene, John.* Liverpool. 89 Pitt St in 1834.

*Skellorn, John.* Liverpool. 13 Moon St in 1851.

*Skirrow, James.* Wigan. Clockmaker and barometer maker in Chapel Lane from 1797 to 1834. Wife, Betty, died 1799 aged 43 (Hawkes).

*Slater, George.* Liverpool. 31 Prescot St in 1848.

*Slater, James.* Ormskirk. Aughton St in 1848; Moor St, 1851–4; Church St in 1858.

*Slowe, William.* Manchester. 10 William St in 1848.

*Smailes, Richard.* Rochdale. Cheetham St, 1848–51.

*Smalley, John.* Lancaster/Blackburn. Clockmaker of Blackburn when free at Lancaster in 1721. Died 1725, leaving will. Grandmother clock reported c 1720.

*Smethurst, Henry.* Farnworth. Watchmaker. Married Maria Rigby, 1786.

*Smith, George.* Liverpool. Watchmaker, 1784–90.

*Smith, George.* Manchester. Watchmaker. Married Elizabeth Mitchell, 1803.

*Smith, John.* Ashton-under-Lyne. 110 Stamford St, 1828–34.

*Smith, John.* Manchester. Water St, 1834–51.

*Smith, John S.* Manchester. 1 Sandon St, Salford in 1848.

*Smith, Robert.* Farnworth. Watchmaker. Child born 1818 to wife, Lucy.

*Smith, Thomas.* Wigan. Clockmaker. Free 1755 (Hawkes).

*Smith, T.* Lancaster. Brass arched dial longcase clock reported c 1760.

*Smith, Thomas.* Liverpool. Watchmaker from London. Son born there 1724.

*Smoult, James.* Lancaster/Newcastle-on-Tyne. Born 1723, son of Thomas Smoult of Lancaster. Still there 1749 when father died, but by 1753 had moved to Newcastle-on-Tyne, where in that year he took Thomas Phillipson as apprentice.

*Smoult, Thomas.* Lancaster. Married Margaret Atkinson there 1712, by whom he had ten children. Was a watchmaker and 'gentleman'. Free there 1739. Took James Backhouse as apprentice in 1749 at £15. Died 1749.

*Smythe, I.* Fleetwood. Blackburn museum have watch.

*Snead, J.* Lancaster. Cheapside in 1858.

*Somervell, James.* Great B(r)oughton. Clockmaker. Died 1746.

*Southern, Daniel.* St Helens. Watchmaker. Wife, Mary, had children 1822-8.

*Spalding, William.* Liverpool. Liverpool museum have watch hallmarked 1784.

*Speakman, T.* Warrington. 50 Horse Market in 1858.

*Spears, Frederick.* Liverpool. Tenterden St in 1834.

*Spedding, Richard.* Blackburn. Penny St in 1834.

*Speers, Charles.* Liverpool. 52 Upper Frederick St in 1828; 10 Lower Sparling St in 1834.

*Spencer, Charles.* Liverpool. Watchmaker there 1734.

*Spencer, Eli.* Bolton. 189B Deansgate, 1824-8; Chancery Lane in 1834.

*Spencer, James.* Stalybridge. Ramsbottom St in 1848.

*Spencer, John* (I). Colne. Clockmaker. Born 1711, son of Henry Spencer, farmer. Married Sarah Ramsden, 1738. Children born 1739-57, include John (qv). Sundial by him dated 1750 and carved doorstone bearing a clock and the date 1760 survive with a descendant. Lived at Birchenlee Farm, Great Marsden, where he died in 1794 aged 83.

*Spencer, John* (II). Colne. Clockmaker, born 1739, son of John (I). Married Mary Hartley, 1785. Children born 1791-1806 include John (III) (qv). Lived at the Parkers Arms till 1804, then at the 'house opposite the King's Head' till c 1807, when moved to the Masons Arms till 1809. Died at Birchenlee Farm at Christmas 1809 'of an inward complaint' aged 71. Various clocks exist including one with masonic symbols on dial and also a world time dial clock exists.

*Spencer, John* (III). Colne. Clockmaker and farmer, son of John (II), born 1791. Lived at Bir-

143

*Spencer, John* (III). cont. chenlee Farm with wife, Barbara, till he took up innkeeping. Trained as clockmaker with father, and after his death with John Battinson. Sold Birchenlee, later claiming (in 1833) that he had been cheated.

*Spencer, Thomas.* Manchester. 8 East St in 1824.

*Speth, Andrew.* Liverpool. German clocks at 170 Dale St in 1848.

*Spreat & Co.* Manchester. 1 Ducie St, Exchange, 1848–51.

*Spurr, James.* Liverpool. Clock and watch dial enamellers at 2 Temple St in 1834.

*Stafford, George.* Liverpool. 1 Church St in 1851.

*Stancliffe, John.* Burnley. Watchmaker. 6 Croft St in 1824; Howe St 1828. Son born there 1835 to wife, Mary.

*Standish, John.* Warrington. Watchmaker. Married Mary Dyson, 1769.

*Standish, John.* Prescot. Watchmaker. Son buried 1795.

*Standish, John.* St Helens. Watchmaker at Hardshaw in 1827 when son born to wife, Elizabeth.

*Standring, J(eremiah).* Bolton. Clockmaker. Three train ting-tang longcase clock noted c 1760. Thirty-hour clock noted c 1770.

*Stanley, Charles.* Liverpool. Watch of c 1780 in Liverpool museum.

*Stanley, John.* Manchester. 10 City Rd, Hulme in 1851.

*Stanley, John.* Prescot. Watchmaker. Married Sarah Marsh, 1822. Children born 1823–5.

*Stanley, Richard.* Liverpool. Watchmaker at Dale St in 1773.

*Stanley, Thomas.* Liverpool. Watchmaker. Ranelagh St in 1769; Castle St in 1774.

*Stanley, Thomas.* Prescot. Watchmaker. Children born to wife, Alice, 1819–25.

*Starkie, Edward.* Liverpool. Watchmaker. Children born 1683–8 to wife, Martha, who died 1689.

*Steedman, William.* Milnthorpe. Longcase clock recorded c 1820.

*Stell, G.* Todmorden. Clock and watch cleaner at Millwood in 1858.

*Sternberg, John & Brothers.* Manchester. 113 Oldham St in 1851.

*Stewart, Joseph.* Liverpool. 5 Harford St in 1848; 16 Lord St in 1851.

*Stewart & McFerran.* Manchester. 10 Victoria St in 1848. Also chronometers.

*Stockton, Peter.* Liverpool. Watchmaker at Blackberry Lane, 1734–61.

*Stockwell, Joseph.* Manchester. 72 Bridge St in 1851.

*Stone, Charles.* Liverpool. Liverpool museum have two watches hallmarked 1797 and c 1800.

*Stones, George.* Blackburn. Church St in 1822. Longcase clock noted c 1820.

*Stone, Robert.* Manchester. 278 Oldham Rd in 1848; 79 Oldham St in 1851.

*Storey, Edward.* Ulverston/Cartmel. At Ulverston: Soutergate in 1842; Fountain St, 1846–51. At Cartmel Town, 1849–69.

*Storey, John.* Liverpool. Watchmaker. Daughter born 1678 to wife, Ann, who died 1699. He died at Harrington St in 1721.

*Story, Joseph.* Liverpool. Watchmaker at Fenwick St. Children born 1703–15 by wife, Mary, who died 1717.

*Story, William.* Barrow-in-Furness. Worked there and also at Halifax and Dewsbury. Died 1912 aged aged 74 (Hobbs).

*Storey, William.* Manchester. Clockmaker. Married Mary Evans, 1803.

*Stott, Ormerod.* Newchurch. Clock dealer at Mill End in 1851.

*Strickland, James.* Ulverston. Duke St, 1849–51.

*Stringfellow, John.* Rochdale. Clockmaker. Came from Rochdale to marry at Halifax in 1694, where he is believed to have worked till his death in 1718.

*Stringfellow, Richard.* Liverpool. 50 Circus St in 1814. Son born to wife, Frances, in 1823.

*Stuart, Henry.* Liverpool. At Park Lane, 1834–51. Also at Henry St in 1851.

*Stubler, Joseph.* Wigan. Clockmaker in Quarter Sessions Roll for 1799 (Hawkes).

*Stubley, Benjamin.* Liverpool Vauxhall Rd, 1834–51.

*Stubley, John (& Abraham).* Liverpool. 9 Vauxhall Rd alone in 1834; 127 Tithebarn St with Abraham in 1848; 160 Vauxhall Rd alone in 1851.

*Stubs, Peter.* Warrington. Famous toolmaker and supplier, espec-

ially of files, but ultimately of all manner of clock and watch making materials. Very large catalogue published c 1800 listed almost 300 items. Only a few copies survive.

*Stump, Richard.* Oldham. Market Place in 1824. Also jeweller.

*Summersgill, Robert.* Preston. Watchmaker. Apprenticed in 1813 to Stephen Simpson of Preston. At Fishergate, 1824–58. Still alive in 1881. Watches at Preston and Salford museums.

*Sumner, James.* Liverpool. Working there 1800.

*Surman & Kaltenback.* Manchester. German and Dutch and musical clocks at 226 Chapel St, Salford in 1834.

*Sutcliffe, James.* Oldham. Lees Brook, 1834–58.

*Sutlow, Thomas.* Manchester. Clockmaker. Married Sidney (*sic*) Williams, 1803.

*Sutton, William.* Liverpool. 14 Frederick St in 1795. One of this name at 26 Clement St in 1828, may be same man.

*Sykes, Benjamin.* Lancaster. 3 Common Garden St in 1869.

*Sykes, John.* Manchester. Clockmaker. Married Elizabeth Unsworth, 1793.

*Symm, Luke.* Prescot. Watchmaker. Married Alice Orme, 1780.

*Symonds, Joseph & Co.* Liverpool. Watchmaker at 29 Pool Lane in 1795.

*Tarbock, John.* Manchester. Watchmaker. Buried there 1732.

145

*Tarbuck, John.* Farnworth. Watchmaker. Married Mary Dennet, 1808.

*Tarbuck, John.* Prescot. Watchmaker. Married Ann Pilkington, 1765.

*Tarbuck, Joseph.* Prescot. Watchmaker. Daughter born 1823 to wife, Mary.

*Tarleton, Richard.* Liverpool. Watchmaker at 31 Church St in 1795. Liverpool museum have watch hallmarked 1814.

*Tarleton, Thomas.* Liverpool. 13 Highfield St, 1848–51.

*Tarleton, William.* Liverpool. 8 Church St, 1763–98, when moved to Lime St. Liverpool museum have watch of 1800 and bracket clock c 1795.

*Tarr, Thomas.* Manchester. Clockmaker. Son born 1755.

*Tate, James.* Liverpool. 26 Rupert St in 1828.

*Taylor, D.* Tunstead. Manchester. At Stackstead in 1858.

*Taylor, Edward.* Prescot. Watchmaker. Children born to wife, Ellen, 1819–25.

*Taylor, George.* Preston. Clockmaker. Died 1738.

*Taylor, George.* Liverpool. Watchmaker in Juggler St in 1712 when daughter born. He died at High St in 1722. Inventory of his goods survives. Gold watch reported lost in 1705. Liverpool museum have watch.

*Taylor, George.* Manchester. Clockmaker. Married Mary Smith, 1830. Son, Edward, born 1857 at 11 Bury St, Hulme.

*Taylor, Henry.* Manchester. Clockmaker. Son, John, admitted to school in 1760.

*Taylor, Henry.* Liverpool. 102 London Rd in 1828.

*Taylor, James.* Liverpool. 14 Tarleton St in 1822. Working by 1800.

*Taylor, James.* St Helens. Watchmaker at Hardshaw when son born 1786.

*Taylor, James.* Ashton-under-Lyne. Clockmaker. Died May 1813 aged 89. Wife, Mary, died 1780 aged 53. He had 15 children, 103 grandchildren and 61 greatgrandchildren when he died. Probably son of John Taylor, clockmaker, who died 1744 leaving tools to son, James.

*Taylor, John.* Ashton-under-Lyne. Clockmaker. Had children there between 1713 and 1718 including: 1714 Jonathan; 1715 John. Died 1744, leaving widow, Elizabeth. He left his tools and wheel-cutter to two sons, John and James.

*Taylor, John.* Farnworth. Watchmaker. Married Rachel Atherton, 1824.

*Taylor, John.* Liverpool. Lost watch reported in 1755.

*Taylor, John.* Manchester. Clockmaker. Son, John, admitted to school in 1745. *Manchester Mercury* in 1781.

*Taylor, John (Jonathan?).* Ormskirk. Year clock noted c 1720–30.

*Taylor, John.* Prescot. Watchmaker. Married Ann Elsby, 1804. Son born 1823.

*Taylor, John.* Wigan. Clockmaker from Wigan. Free at Lancaster in 1779.

*Taylor, John & Daniel.* Liverpool. North John St, 1834–51. In 1834 also at 47 Whitechapel.

*Taylor, John & Edmund.* Rochdale. 36 Drake St, 1848–58.

*Taylor, Jonathan.* Ashton-under-Lyne. Clockmaker. Buried 1 May 1808 aged 56. Wife, Martha, died 1822 aged 73.

*Taylor, Peter.* Prescot. Watchmaker. Children born to wife, Catherine, 1795–6.

*Taylor, S.* Liverpool. Liverpool museum have watch c 1785–90.

*Taylor, Samuel.* Liverpool. 88 Whitechapel in 1834.

*Taylor, Samuel.* Middleton (Manchester). Clockmaker. Buried there 12 May 1743.

*Taylor, Samuel (and D.).* Rochdale. Yorkshire St, 1834–48. Various longcase clocks reported. At Acker St in 1858 (with D. Taylor).

*Taylor, Thomas.* Manchester. 'Fancy' clocks including German and Dutch ones at Oldham Rd, 1824–8; then at 3 Mason St in 1834.

*Taylor, William.* Bold. Watchmaker. Died 1768, leaving will.

*Taylor, William.* Farnworth. Watchmaker. Married Elizabeth Rigby, 1816.

*Taylor, William.* Liverpool. At Crosshall St and 11 Clayton Square in 1822; 6 Redcross St in 1824; Much Woolton, 1848–51. Probably more than one man.

*Taylor, William Edward.* Liverpool. 41 Brownlow Hill, 1848–51.

*Taylor, William Thursfield.* Liverpool. Working there 1828.

*Terry, Thomas.* Manchester. Watchmaker. Married Jane Urquhart, 1822. At 12 Bridge St in 1834; 66 Stretford New Rd, Hulme, 1848–51.

*Thelwall, Charles John.* Manchester. 81 Oxford St, Chorlton-on-Medlock in 1851.

*Thelwell, Richard.* Manchester. 3 St Ann's Square, 1822–34. Son, Charles John, entered school in 1828 aged 10.

*Thom, Charles & Crump,* ——. Liverpool. Charles Thom continued alone after 1799, when Crump left the partnership, which existed 1790–5 (–9?). Sometimes erroniously listed as Thomas Crump.

*Thomas, William.* Liverpool. Watch finisher. Married Ellen Marshall, 1834.

*Thompson, J.* Blackburn. 1 Foundry Hill in 1858.

*Thompson, James.* Liverpool. Watchmaker in Dayle St. Sons born 1722–3. Still working 1734.

*Thompson, John.* Liverpool. Dale St, 1754–73. Liverpool museum have watch c 1770.

*Thompson, Joshua.* Fleetwood. Church St in 1848.

*Thompson, Thomas.* Lancaster/Liverpool. Watchmaker. Free at Lancaster in 1747. At Pool Lane, Liverpool, 1767–79.

*Tickle, Peter.* Farnworth. Watchmaker. Married Janet Hewit, 1819.

*Tickle, Richard.* Sutton. Watchmaker. Children born to wife, Elizabeth, 1809–23.

*Tickle, Robert.* Farnworth. Watchmaker. Married Sarah Baldwin, 1809. Preston museum have watch inscribed 'James Cowley 1806'.

*Tickle, William.* Prescot. Watchmaker. Married Elizabeth Renshaw, 1826.

*Tillingham, James.* St Helens. Watchmaker at Sutton in 1820 when son born to wife, Elizabeth.

*Tillinghast, Stephen.* Liverpool. Watchmaker. Took Percy Archer apprentice in 1742 for £15. At Castle St, 1763–90. Watch No 663 hallmarked 1781. Liverpool museum have watch.

*Tobias, M. J. & Co.* Liverpool. Name uncertain, appearing variously as Michael Isaac, Miah Isaac, Miel Isaac, and as initials M.J. At Lord St, 1814–34; then at Dorans Lane, 1848–51. Liverpool museum have watch c 1850 by M. L. Tobias.

*Todd, J.* North Meols. Watchmaker at Banks in 1858.

*Todd, R. I.* Liverpool. Watch No 12447 hallmarked 1857.

*Tom(b)linson, Timothy.* St Helens/Flixton. Watchmaker. Married (for second time?) in 1765 to Ellen Harrison. Died 7 March 1782.

*Tommison, John.* St Helens. Watchmaker at Eccleston. Son born 1768; another buried 1784.

*Tompion, Richard.* Liverpool. Liverpool museum have watch c 1790–1800. Other late 18th century watches recorded.

*Tooke, W. H.* Liverpool. Liverpool museum have watch c 1850 (late F. L. Hausberg).

*Tootell, John.* Eccles. Clockmaker at King St in 1828.

*Tootell, William.* Chorley. 51 Market St, 1822–8.

*Tootell, ——.* St Helens. Late 18th century longcase clock in St Helens library signed thus. May be William Tootell above?

*Topping, William.* Liverpool. Watch spring maker. Sons born 1640–1. He died 1717 at Cooke St. Very early example of specialisation.

*Torkington, William Henry.* Manchester. 10 Exchange St in 1834.

*Towers, John.* Farnworth. Clockmaker. Died 1747.

*Townley, John.* Liverpool. 37 Pleasant St in 1828; 16 Harford St in 1834.

*Townley & Quilliam.* Liverpool. 60 Renshaw St in 1834.

*Townley, Thomas.* Liverpool. 70 Hanover St in 1822; 10 Gerrard St, 1824–34; 176 London Rd in 1848.

*Townson, J.* Ulverston. Market St, 1858–60; Fountain St in 1862. Probably same man as below.

*Townson, John.* Barrow. Clockmaker at 4 Forshaw St in 1866. See also above entry.

*Travers, Adam.* Liverpool. Watchmaker at St Pauls Square, 1769–77.

*Travers/Travis, Henry.* Liverpool. Watchmaker at Key St when he died in 1723. Perhaps born there 1694.

*Travis, Edward.* Manchester. In 1788 directory.

*Travis, Joshua.* Manchester. Insolvent (*London Gazette*), 1748.

*Tritchler, John.* Bolton. Bradshawgate, 1851–8.

*Tunks, D.* Accrington. 36 Blackburn Rd in 1858. See Dunks.

*Tunstall, John.* Warrington. Watchmaker from Prescot. Married Elizabeth Rigby, 1775.

*Turner, Theophilus.* Middleton/Chadderton. Wife, Mary, died 1785 at Middleton; he died 1799 at Chadderton.

*Turton, Nathaniel.* Manchester. 86 Jersey St in 1824.

*Twist, Joseph.* Ormskirk. Burscough St, 1848–58.

*Twyford, John.* Manchester. Watchmaker in 1788 directory.

*Twyford, Josiah.* Manchester. Watchmaker. In *Manchester Mercury*, 1792. Son, John, entered school in 1808. At 252 Deansgate in 1822.

*Twyford, William.* Manchester. Listed in 1794 directory.

*Tyas, John.* Manchester. Clockmaker. Married Sarah Coppock, 1824.

*Tyrer, Edward.* Manchester. Watchmaker. Son baptised 1644.

*Tyrer, James.* Prescot. Watchmaker. Apprenticed to Thomas Jones in 1797.

*Tyson, Thomas.* Bolton. Derby St in 1848; 24 Weston St, 1851–8.

*Unsworth, Edward.* Farnworth.

Watchmaker. Daughter born to wife, Ellen, in 1818.

*Unsworth, James.* Chorley. Market St, 1834–51.

*Unsworth, John.* Farnworth. Watchmaker. Married Martha Ashton, 1768.

*Unsworth, Peter.* Liverpool. Leice St in 1795.

*Unsworth, Thomas.* Liverpool. Described variously as labourer, smith and watch spring maker. Worked in Lord St, 1715–24, perhaps later.

*Unsworth, Thomas.* Prescot. Watchmaker. Children born to wife, Jane, 1796–7.

*Unsworth, Thomas.* Prescot. Watchmaker. Child born 1826 to wife, Hannah.

*Upton, George.* Liverpool. 88 Bold St in 1851.

*Varnish, John.* Rochdale. Quoted by some authorities—error for John Barnish (qv).

*Verity, Henry.* Lancaster. 144 Market St in 1869. Also jeweller.

*Ver(i)ley, John Daniel.* Liverpool. 17 Parker St, 1834–48. Also musical boxes.

*Vernon, James.* Liverpool. Listed there in 1754.

*Vernon, Thomas.* Liverpool. Watchmaker. Working 1734. Died 1774, leaving will.

*Vernon & Eden.* Liverpool. Lost watch No 1385 reported in 1773.

*Vickers, Isaac.* Lancaster. Watchmaker. Born at Irton, Cumberland in 1820. Believed to have

149

*Vickers, Isaac.* cont. been apprenticed in Liverpool. At Market St, Lancaster by 1848, where still listed in 1869. Moved to new premises at Anchor Lane after a fire. Died at Salford in 1905 aged 73. Wife, Eleanor, was also from Cumberland. Longcase clocks recorded including one in Lancaster museum.

*Vose, John.* St Helens. Watchmaker at Hardshaigh in 1818, when son born to wife, Mary. At Green Bank in 1834.

*Wadeson, Richard.* Burton-and-Holme. Watchmaker there 1879.

*Wainwright, F.* Liverpool. Liverpool museum have watch hallmarked 1841.

*Wainwright, George.* Manchester. Clockmaker. Married Jane Hardman, 1795.

*Wainwright, John.* Ormskirk. Church St, 1834–58.

*Wainwright, John.* Liverpool. Listed as watchmaker in 1761.

*Wainwright, John.* Manchester. Watchmaker in directories of 1794–1800.

*Wainwright, Nathan.* Liverpool. Watchmaker. Died 1790.

*Wainwright, Thomas.* Prescot. Watchmaker. Married Elizabeth Chew, 1779.

*Wakefield, Timothy.* Lancaster. Watchmaker. Son of William Wakefield. Free 1811. Succeeded father at Market St, 1848–51.

*Wakefield, William.* Lancaster. Watchmaker, son of William

Wakefield. Free 1782. Market St, 1822–47, when he died. Believed to have had Thomas Russell as assistant. Longcase clocks recorded including one in Lancaster museum.

*Waldvogel, Matthew.* Bury. Stanley St, 1848–58.

*Walkden, James.* Blackburn. Bolton St, Over Darwen in 1834; 80 Darwen St in 1848.

*Walkden, John.* Blackburn. 6 Astley Gate in 1851; 13 Exchange Arcade in 1858.

*Walker, Benjamin.* Liverpool. 5 Rainford Rd in 1828; Great Crosby in 1834.

*Walker, James.* Wigan. At Scholes in 1844 (Hawkes).

*Walker, John.* Liverpool. Liverpool museum have watch hallmarked 1806. At 53 Hurst St in 1814.

*Walker, Joseph.* Prescot. Watchmaker. Son born 1826 to wife, Alice.

*Walker, Michael.* Bolton. Bradshawgate in 1822.

*Waller, John.* Preston. Brass-dial clock signed 'Johannes Waller de Preston'—early 18th century?

*Walley, Joseph.* Liverpool. 66 Castle St in 1781. Also goldsmith. Partnership with Robert Jones dissolved in 1788.

*W(h)alley, Richard.* Liverpool. Watchmaker. Children born 1716–25. Worked at Tithebarn St till 1721, after which at Chapel St. Married Ann Hodgkinson, 1712. In 1719 took William Bannister as apprentice at £10. Died 1743, leaving will.

*Walley, Robert.* Bolton. Clockmaker. Died 7 January 1675.

*W(h)alley, Samuel* (I). Manchester. Clockmaker. Married Mary Shallcross, 1733. Died 16 June 1744. Had son, Samuel, who was admitted to school in 1750.

*W(h)alley, Samuel* (II). Manchester. Watchmaker. Advertised in *Manchester Mercury* in 1768. Probably son of Samuel (I), and if so then it was he who entered school there in 1750. Samuel (II) also had a son named Samuel, who entered school in 1775.

*W(h)alley, Samuel* (III). Manchester. Watchmaker. Probably son of Samuel II and if so was admitted to school in 1775. Married Ann Postles, 1788.

*W(h)alley, Thomas.* Manchester. Clockmaker. Married Mary Barrow, 1759.

*Walmsley, Edward.* Manchester. Ducie Place in 1848.

*Walmesley, Mr.* Ormskirk. Watchmaker. Working 1711–12.

*Walton, James.* Lancaster. Watchmaker. Born there in 1832, son of a shoemaker. In 1851 lived at St Nicholas St with widowed mother, who came from Dorset.

*Warburton, Henry.* Liverpool. Clock and watchmaker listed there in 1734.

*Warburton, John.* Liverpool. St James St in 1824; 25 Upper Harrington St in 1848; St James St again in 1851.

*Ward, John.* Liverpool. 5 Spring Place in 1828.

*Ward, Richard.* Prescot. Watchmaker. Son born 1794 to wife, Catherine.

*Ward, Thomas.* Warrington. Watchmaker. Married Catherine Jackson, 1773.

*Ward, William Henry.* Liverpool. 4 Hanover St in 1824; 70 Whitechapel in 1828.

*Wardlaw, Henry.* Liverpool. 68 Dale St in 1814; 56 Lime St, 1822–34; 15 Pembroke Gardens in 1848. Liverpool museum have longcase clock.

*Wareing, James.* Liverpool. 56 Paradise St in 1814.

*Waring, Charles John.* Liverpool. 20 Lodge Lane, Windsor in 1848.

*Waring, George.* Liverpool. Watchmaker. Died 1783.

*Waring, Henry.* Warrington. Watchmaker. Married Hannah Knowles, 1776.

*Warmingham, Andrew.* Manchester. Clockmaker. Married Martha Harris, 1747.

*Warmisham, William.* Manchester. 152 Long Millgate in 1828; 5 Half St in 1834.

*Warren, S.* Liverpool. Lost watch recorded in 1772.

*Watkinson, H.* St Helens. Raglan St in 1858.

*Watmough, William.* Wigan. Robbing Lane End in 1851.

*Watson, H.(enry?).* Blackburn. Blackburn museum have clock by H. Watson. Clock c 1745 noted signed Henry Watson without town, perhaps by him. See also William Watson.

*Watson, James.* Haslingden. Wilkinson St in 1848; Dearden Gate in 1858.

*Watson, John.* Accrington. Abbey St in 1834.

*Watson, John.* Manchester. Market St, 1848–51.

*Watson, John.* Blackburn. Clockmaker, son of William Watson (qv). At 3 Darwen St, 1822–34 (next door but one to the Old Bull hotel).

*Watson, William.* Blackburn. Clockmaker. Father of John Watson. At Northgate in 1793. Blackburn museum have two clocks. Clock noted signed William Watson, without town could be by him (c 1770). See also Henry Watson.

*Waugh, William.* Liverpool. 73 Lord St in 1824.

*Weatherilt, Samuel.* Liverpool. Probably two of this name. Samuel senior at Brownlow Hill in 1795; 73 Highfield St in 1822. Samuel (junior?) at 16 Castle St in 1828; 23 Great Crosshall St in 1834.

*Webster, John.* Prescot. Watchmaker. Child born to wife, Ellen, 1795.

*Webster, John.* Liverpool. Watchmaker there in 1800—may be above man.

*Webster, William.* Prescot. Watchmaker. Children born 1819–26 to wife, Margaret.

*Wells, William & Charles.* Liverpool. 30 Paradise St in 1848; 106 Bold St in 1851.

*Welsby, Jonathan.* Prescot. Atherton St in 1851.

*Welsby, Peter.* Farnworth. Watchmaker. Married Elizabeth Cook, 1834.

*West, James.* Bolton. At Bradshawgate in 1824; Folds St, 1828–34; Bradshawgate again 1848–58.

*West, William.* Bolton. Fold St in 1828. See also James above.

*Westmore, Robert* (I). Fazakerly/Lancaster. Watchmaker. Free at Lancaster in 1761, though worked at Fazakerly. Still alive 1801. Son, Robert, was also a watchmaker.

*Westmore, Robert* (II). West Derby/Lancaster. Watchmaker. Son of Robert above. Free at Lancaster in 1785.

*Westmore, Robert.* Preston. Watchmaker. Son born at Dalton in Furness in 1811. Was at Preston in 1817 when his son, John, was made a freeman. At 179–181 Friargate, 1822–8. Also silversmith.

*Weston, William & Son.* Cartmel. Watchmaker in 1848.

*Whalley.* See Walley.

*Wheeldon, John A.* Barrow. Church St in 1866.

*Whipp, Thomas.* Rochdale. Yorkshire St, 1834–51; Tower Place in 1858. Longcase clock noted.

*Whipp, Thomas.* Bacup. Market St in 1851. No doubt the Rochdale man above.

*Whitehead, Joseph.* Liverpool. Vernon St in 1796.

*Whitehead, William.* Manchester. 253 Deansgate in 1828; St Mary's Gate in 1834.

*Whitehead, William.* Stalybridge. 22 Rasbottom St in 1834.

*Whiteside, James.* Ormskirk. Burscough St, 1824–8.

*Whiteside, Thomas.* Liverpool. 8 Pownall Square, 1777–86. Married 1786.

*Whiteway, Foliot.* Ulverston. Established 1864. King St in 1866.

*Whitfield, James.* Liverpool. Watchmaker. Died 1674.

*Whitfield, James.* Liverpool. Clockmaker. Lost watch reported 1745. Died 1756, leaving will. Liverpool museum have watch said to be c 1700–10. Could be son of Robert Whitfield.

*Whitfield, John.* Liverpool. Watchmaker. Daughter born 1677.

*Whitfield, Robert.* Liverpool. Watchmaker. Children born 1678–88 included James in 1682 (qv). Died 1726, leaving will.

*Whitfield, Thomas.* Farnworth. Watchmaker at Upton. Child born 1818 to wife, Sarah.

*Whitner, Thomas.* Manchester. Clockmaker in 1800 directory.

*Whitaker, George.* Rawtenstall. Watchmaker at Bank St, 1848–58.

*Whittaker, Isaac.* Stalybridge. Melbourne St in 1848.

*Whittaker, J.* Bury. Clock cleaner at 5 Cross St in 1858.

*Whittaker, James.* Middleton (Manchester). Clockmaker. Late 17th century clock noted signed without town. Died in 1720, leaving will in which he mentions brother, Samuel (qv). Inventory of his tools etc mentioned in the text section.

*Whittaker, Samuel.* Middleton (Man-

chester). Clockmaker. Presumably brother of James (qv). Died 1746, leaving will. Wife, Dorothy, and late brother, Gervase, mentioned.

*Whittington, Henry.* Manchester. 27 King St, 1848–51.

*Whittle, Edward.* Prescot. Watchmovement maker. Married Margaret Birchill, 1826.

*Whittle, John.* Liverpool. Liverpool museum have watch hallmarked 1861.

*Whittle, Peter.* Oldham. Clockmaker at Tydesley in 1848; at Shaw, 1851–8.

*Whitworth, Henry.* Rochdale. Clockmaker. James St in 1834.

*Whitworth, James.* Lussley. Clock noted c 1780 of distinct Lancs style. Two others noted in this area suggest this must be northern and not Lustleigh, Devon, as some authorities suggest, though I cannot locate this place. Both brass- and painted-dial clocks noted c 1770–90.

*Whitworth, Samuel.* Crankshaw. Listed by some authorities as a clockmaker dying in 1711. Examination of probate documents reveals that he was a clothmaker.

*Wickliff(e), William.* Liverpool. Watchmaker in Water St in 1724 when son died. Still working 1734.

*Widdop, W.* Burnley. 23 Market St in 1858.

*Wiggan, Robert.* Skipton/Colne. Clockmaker. Married Rebecca Holmes at Skipton, Yorks, 1806.

Working at Colne by 1807. Shop in Market Place. Died shortly before 1848, after which his widow succeeded him in the business till 1858. Numerous painted-dial longcase clocks noted.

*Wiggan, William.* Wigan. Made sundial in 1718 (Hawkes).

*Wignall, George.* Ormskirk. Aughton St in 1834.

*Wignall, Henry.* Burnley. 5 Market St, 1851–8.

*Wignall, John.* Ormskirk. Clockmaker. Working there by 1786. In 1804 charged £7 14s for 8-day clock with case, less allowance of £1 1s on old clock. In 1847 a turret clock by him was put in Trinity Church, Southport. At Moor St in 1848. Perhaps two men in succession with the same name.

*Wignall, M.* Ormskirk. At Aughton St in 1824. Also made gold balances.

*Wil(l)cock, John.* Sutton. Watchmaker. Took Thomas Leigh apprentice in 1752.

*Wilcockson, Henry.* Liverpool. Copperas Hill, 1834–48.

*Wilcox, William.* Liverpool. 11 Stafford St in 1848.

*Wildman, Richard.* Lancaster. Watchmaker. Free there 1757.

*Wildman, William.* Caton. Clockmaker. Came from Caton when married at Thornton-in-Lonsdale, Yorks, to Mary Titler in 1796.

*Wilkinson, John.* Cartmel/Ulverston. Working at Backbarrow by 1824. Married Eleanor Park at Ulverston in 1838.

*Wilkinson, Henry.* Ribchester. Repaired church clock in 1822 for 15s.

*Wilkinson, William.* Prescot. Watchmaker. Married Ann Oakley, 1818. See also next entry.

*Wilkinson, William.* St Helens. Watchmaker at Eccleston in 1824 when daughter born to wife, Ann.

*Wilks, Joseph.* Liverpool. 40 Sir Thomas's Buildings in 1834.

*Willacy, Edward.* Liverpool. 11 Spring Place in 1828. Gold dial maker.

*Williams, John.* Liverpool. Clockmaker at 3 Wykes Court in 1790.

*Williams, R.* Liverpool. Verge watch reported c 1820.

*Williams, T.* Newton-in-Mackerfield. At Earlstown in 1858.

*Williams, Thomas.* Liverpool. Liverpool museum have watch movement said to be c 1800. At 132 Upper Frederick St in 1834.

*Williams, Thomas.* Manchester. 6 Exchange St in 1834.

*Williams, Thomas.* Preston. Brass square dial 30-hour clock noted with mock winding squares as imitation 8-day, c 1750–60. Bought mahogany square dial case from Gillows of Lancaster in 1771 for £2 5s, and another at £2 15s.

*Williams, William.* Liverpool. Lost watch reported in 1775.

*Williams, William.* Liverpool. 108 Burlington St, 1848–51.

*Williamson*, ——. Ulverston. Watchmaker. Married Elizabeth Cotter, 1763 (Hobbs).

*Williamson, J.* Rochdale. 80 Yorkshire St in 1858.

*Williamson, John.* Bold. Watchmaker. Took John Abbott apprentice in 1757 for £21.

*Williamson, John.* Liverpool. Watch and watch-case maker. At Chapel St, 1710–16, when he died.

*Williamson, John.* Warrington. Buttermarket St, 1824–34.

*Williamson, Joseph.* Rochdale. 30 Yorkshire St, 1848–51.

*Williamson, Richard.* Liverpool. Watchmaker. Married Judith Newcombe, 1707. Free at Chester in 1732.

*Williamson, Samuel.* Wigan/Cronton. Free at Wigan in 1684, having been formerly apprenticed there to Thomas Martine. Probably went to Cronton where he died 1726, leaving will.

*Willis, Charles.* Liverpool. 51 Hunter St in 1834. Clock and watch-dial enamellers.

*Willis, Richard.* Liverpool. Tenterden St in 1834.

*Willis, Thomas.* Prescot. Watchmaker. Married Margaret Wainwright, 1803, by whom daughter born 1823.

*Wilmshust, Stephen.* Oldham. Clockmaker. Took Thomas Aldridge apprentice in 1752 for £10.

*Wilson, Becket.* Manchester. Mason St, Swan St in 1848.

*Wilson, George.* Prescot. At Huyton in 1851.

*Wilson, John.* Ulverston. Painted-

dial longcase clock recorded c 1770–90 (Hobbs). See also next entry.

*Wilson, John.* Broughton-in-Furness. Clockmaker. May be same man as at Ulverston. Believed married Mary Robinson, 1783, by whom children born 1783–88.

*Wilson, John.* Liverpool. Paddington, Edgehill in 1848.

*Wilson, Robert.* Manchester. Watchmaker. Died 1638.

*Wilson, Thomas.* Manchester. 234 Deansgate in 1828.

*Winder, Stephen.* Lancaster. Watchmaker. Son of Thomas Winder (I). Free there 1823.

*Winder, Thomas* (I). Lancaster. Watchmaker. Working in Penny St, 1823–34. Had three sons (qv), each in the same trade. Also jeweller.

*Winder, Thomas* (II). Lancaster. Watchmaker. Son of Thomas (I). Free 1825.

*Winder, William.* Lancaster. Watchmaker. Son of Thomas (I). Free 1830.

*Windle, Edward.* Prescot. Watchmaker. Child born 1798 to wife, Mary.

*Winstanley*, ——. Ormskirk. Marquetry longcase clock, c 1720, with rocking Father Time below XII numeral.

*Winstanley, Abraham.* Wigan. Clockmaker at Wallgate in 1811 (Hawkes).

*Winstanley, Alexander.* **Wigan.** Clockmaker. Working there by 1800. At Wallgate in 1822. Wife,

155

*Winstanley, Alexander.* cont. Margaret, died 1809 aged 63 (Hawkes).

*Winstanley, Edward.* Liverpool. In directories 1784–1800.

*Winstanley, Edward.* Preston. 15 Friargate in 1822.

*Winstanley, Edward.* Wigan. Working at Wallgate, 1809–28. Son died 1806 aged 3, another 1812 aged 16. Widow, Jane, died 1828 aged 68. His death not traced (Hawkes).

*Winstanley, James.* Liverpool (Wigan?). Watchsmith. A daughter born there 1675. A man of this name provided clock dial at Wigan in 1700, where he died in 1715 (Hawkes).

*Winstanley, John.* Manchester. 95 Chapel St, Salford in 1834.

*Winstanley, Joseph.* Liverpool. 8 Regent St, 1848–51.

*Winstanley, Michael.* Liverpool. 77 Great Crosshall St, 1848–51.

*Winstanley, Robert.* Ormskirk. Church St, 1822–8.

*Winstanley, William.* Liverpool. Watchsmith and watch-spring maker. Children born 1675–80.

*Winstanley, William.* Wigan. Clockmaker. Fined 1781 for practising clockmaking at Standishgate when not being free there (Hawkes).

*Winter, C.* Preston. Blackburn museum have watch.

*Winter, Thomas.* Liverpool. 9 Peter Lane in 1828; 51 Gerard St in 1834.

*Wollarm, J.* Liverpool. Lost watch recorded in 1785.

*Wood, A. Ramsbottom.* Stubbins Lane in 1858.

*Wood, J. & Son.* Darwen. Blackburn museum have watch.

*Woods, John.* Warrington. Watchmaker. Married Mary Blackburn, 1775.

*Woods, John.* Farnworth. Watchmaker. At Widnes in 1818 when child born to wife, Margaret.

*Wood, John.* Liverpool. 28 Wapping in 1814; 5–7 Church St, 1822–8. Liverpool museum have watch said to be c 1805.

*Woods, M.* Wigan. Hindley in 1858.

*Woods, Peter.* Liverpool. 20 Scotland Place in 1834.

*Wood, Robert.* Bolton. 20 Ashburner St, 1851–8.

*Wood, Samuel.* Ashton-under-Lyne. Clock and machine maker of Lees in parish of Ashton. Son, Samuel, baptised 1815 at Rochdale.

*Woods, Thomas.* Childwall. Watchmaker. Married Mary Robinson, 1765.

*Wood, William.* Bolton. 5 Oldhall St in 1851.

*Wood, William* (junior). Liverpool. 81 Hanover St in 1851.

*Wood, William.* Liverpool. 15 Torbock St in 1824.

*Woods, William.* Farnworth. Watchmaker. Married Jane Dennet, 1803.

*Woods, William.* Parr (St Helens). Watchmaker. His wife, Ellen, died 1787.

*Woodburn, Samuel.* Southport. 43 Lords St in 1851.

156

*Woodfine, Robert.* Liverpool. Liverpool museum have watch c 1810.

*Woodroofe, Richard (& Sons).* Liverpool. 81 Smithdown in 1848, alone. Liverpool museum have watch of 1873 signed '& Sons'.

*Woodward, John.* Farnworth. Watchmaker. Married Esther Halsall, 1834.

*Woodward, Thomas.* Liverpool. 5 Union St in 1851.

*Woolf, Lewis.* Liverpool. 10 Bold St in 1834; 35 South Castle St, 1848–51. Also chronometers.

*Woolfall, Richard.* Liverpool. 11 Claremont Terrace, Kirkdale in 1851.

*Woolfall, Richard* (junior). Liverpool. 1 Duke St, 1848–51.

*Woolfenden, John.* Rochdale (Manchester). Listed by some authorities as clockmaker at Toad Lane, Manchester in 1711. In fact he was a clothmaker who died at Toad Lane, Rochdale in 1711.

*Woolnough, Frederick.* Liverpool. 50 Crosshall St in 1834. Clock and watch dial enamellers.

*Woo(r)sey, William.* Prescot. Watchmaker. Children born 1824–6 by wife, Mary. Married (secondly?) 1833 to Ellen Porter.

*Wooton, John.* Manchester. Imported clocks at 4 Chapel St, Ardwick, 1828–51.

*Worrall, John.* Liverpool. Watchmaker. Married Eliza Wilson, 1708. Lived at Moore St, 1709–11, when children born.

*Worrall, John.* Liverpool. Brass dial clock noted c 1770–5. Liverpool museum also have one said to be late 18th century.

*Worsley, Thomas.* Liverpool. Watch finisher. In directory of 1790. Married Ellen Harding that year.

*Worswick, Thomas.* Lancaster. Watchmaker. From Singleton when free at Lancaster in 1753. In 1759 Gillows records mention that he had shipped a few watches to Petersberg value £40. Preston museum have watch dated 1768. Lancaster museum also have one. Listed as silversmith in 1787 when son, Robert, a banker, was free there. Believed to have succeeded Henry Bell in 1801.

*Worthington, James.* Liverpool. 41 Circus St in 1834.

*Wright, John.* Liverpool. Watchmaker of Common Garden. Died 1701.

*Wright, John.* Liverpool. Watchmaker. Died on the island of Nassau, New York province in 1771. From Liverpool.

*Wright, John.* Liverpool. 3 Park Rd in 1834.

*Wright, John.* Manchester. 56 London Rd in 1828.

*Wright, John.* Whalley. Clockmaker. Died 1755, leaving will and inventory. Apparently a bachelor without issue. Work tools mentioned in text section. Believed related to Grundy of Whalley (qv).

*Wright, R. T.* Manchester. 13 Downing St in 1824.

*Wright, Robert.* Bury. At Heywood, 1848–58.
*Wright, W. A.* Bolton. Deansgate in 1858.
*Wright, William.* St Helens. Watchmaker of Sutton. Died 1779.
*Wrigley, Isaac.* Manchester. Clockmaker. Buried 21 July 1742.
*Wulfson, Lewis.* Manchester. 21 Old Millgate in 1851.
*Wyke & Green.* Liverpool. Liverpool museum have longcase clock c 1790.
*Wyke, John.* Liverpool. Famous watch and clock toolmaker and supplier. Worked at Wykes Court, Dale St. Died 1787 aged 67. Produced very large catalogue of tools. Longcase clock noted bearing this name probably indicates that he also sold clocks—this one of the last quarter of the 18th century. Liverpool museum also have one c 1770.

*Yates, Henry.* Liverpool. Watch engraver and maker at Tarbock, 1755–7, when children born to wife, Lydia. At Dale St, 1769–73. Liverpool museum have watch c 1760–5.
*Yates, Henry.* Burtonwood. Watchmaker. Children born 1785–9 to wife, Mary.
*Yates & Hess.* Liverpool. Lord St, 1824–51.
*Yates, James.* St Helens. Watchmaker at Hardshaw, 1765–70, when children born.

*Yates, John.* Culcheth. Clockmaker. Died 1729 (probate).
*Yates, John.* Liverpool. Watchmaker at Rainhill. Took George Bowden apprentice 1747 for £35. At Bootle Mills in 1763; Church St in 1773.
*Yates, John.* Bootle. Watch engraver. Died 1796.
*Yates, Peter.* Haslingden. Deardengate in 1828.
*Yates, Samuel.* Liverpool. Watch recorded made at 9 Lord St in 1810.
*Yates, Thomas.* Prescot. Watchmaker. Married Alice Atherton, 1756.
*Yates, Thomas.* Prescot. Watchmaker. Married Ann Large, 1785.
*Yates, Thomas.* Preston. 159 Friargate, 1848–58. Patentee of new half second deadbeat watch. Watches in Preston and Blackburn museums.
*Yates, William.* Yatebank. Clockmaker. Took Nathan Andrews apprentice in 1724 at £30. Cannot trace this place.
*Yeomans, Edward.* Manchester. 194 Chapel St, Salford in 1851.
*Yeomans, James.* Manchester. Watchmaker. Married Hannah Jackson, 1836. At 13 Lever St in 1851.
*Young, Henry.* Liverpool. Liverpool museum have watch movement c 1800–10.
*Young, Isaac.* Prescot. Watchmaker. Married Mary Holyhead, 1811. Working at Eccleston, 1819, when child born.

*Young, Isaac.* Liverpool. Watch-maker. Died 1768.

*Young, James.* Liverpool. In directory of 1800.

*Young, John.* Liverpool. Watch finisher at Wykes Court in 1795.

*Young, William.* Huyton. Watch-movement maker. Married Mary Peak in 1760.

*Young, William.* St Helens. Watch-maker at Sutton when son born 1773.

*Zipfel, Anthony & Co.* Oldham. 73 Yorkshire St, 1848–51.

# CLOCKMAKERS BY TOWN

*Accrington*
Dunks, David
Greenhalgh, John
Jackson, James
Lees, William
Tunks, D.
Watson, John

*Ashton-in-Makerfield*
Aspinall, Peter

*Ashton-under-Lyne*
Booth, John R.
Brierley, Joseph
Broadbent, John
Broadbent, T.
Buchanan, John
Clark, Thomas
Farran/Farrow, S.
Fletcher, James
Fletcher, William F.
Gregory, John
Hughes, James
Iliffe, Henry T.
Jagger, Aaron
Lees, James
Lees, Samuel
Minshull, John
Smith, John
Taylor, James

Taylor, John
Taylor, Jonathan
Wood, Samuel

*Aughton*
Bamber, John

*Bacup*
Ashworth, John
Blakeborough, John
Butterworth, H.
Ogden, William
Parkinson, J.
Whipp, Thomas

*Barrowford*
Brown, Robert

*Barrow-in-Furness*
*(and Dalton)*
Atkinson, Elizabeth
Atkinson, Thomas
Davies, Edward
Gawne, Charles E.
Hird, Edward &
   William
Muncaster, John
Robinson, John
Story, William
Townson, John
Wheeldon, John

*Blackburn*
Bradley, John
Bradshaw, James
Bradshaw, William
Brewer, William
Collier, Robert
Comberbach, Edward
   S.
Farnworth, Thomas
Fell, John
Irving, James
Lomax, James
Lomax, Samuel
Mason, Thomas
Moore, I. T.
Pearson, William
Sagar, James
Sagar, John
Sagar, Robert H.
Sagar, R. & J.
Smalley, John
Spedding, Richard
Stones, George
Thompson, J.
Walkden, James
Walkden, John
Watson, H.
Watson, John
Watson, William

*Blackpool*
Bamber, S.
Bond, John T.

*Bold*
Abbot, John
Bold, Matthew
Bushell, Matthew
Garnett, John
Garnett, Richard
Garnett, Robert
Garnett, Thomas
Garnett, William
Garnett, William
Leigh, James
Taylor, William
Williamson, John

*Bolton*
Agar, W. & Co
Ashall, Charles
Ashall, John
Ashall, William
Aspinall, William
Bamber, Samuel
Barr, ——
Barry, John
Barry, Thomas
Baynes, R.
Berrington, James
Berrington, John J.
Bibby, Henry
Bradberry, Matthew
Bradshaw, T. & W.
Bradshaw, W.
Bridge, Thomas
Burghart, Augustin
Butler, Mrs
Catteral, Joseph
Chambers, R.
Herr, J.
Hoyle, William
Isherwood, J.

Johnson & Co
Kerr, Joseph
Kirkall, Thomas
Knowles, Andrew
Knowles, Thomas
Lee, J.
Livesey, John
Manchester, Thomas
Mencor, James
Monk, John
Monk, Samuel
Morris, Mary
Mowcar, James
Osborne, Thomas
Rothwell, James
Royle, John
Ruff & Tritchler
Spencer, Eli
Standring, Jeremiah
Tritchler, John
Tyson, Thomas
Walker, Michael
Walley, Robert
West, James
West, William
Wood, Robert
Wood, William
Wright, W. A.

*Boothfold*
Pilling, John

*Bootle*
Yates, John

*Broughton-in-Furness*
Bellman, Daniel
Bellman, William
Campbell, Thomas
Hird, Henry
Holme, John
Wilson, John

*Burnley*
Battinson, John
Bell, J.
Blakeborough, Henry
Blakeborough, John
  M.
Blakeburn, W.
Collinge, W.
Davis, Robert
Hargreaves, Thomas
Heap, John
Law, William
Moorhouse, Robert
Roberts, John
Scott, John H.
Stancliffe, John
Widdop, W.
Wignall, Henry

*Burtonwood*
Abbot, William
Ashton, Joseph
Houghton, James
Roughley, Henry
Yates, Henry

*Bury*
Agar, Thomas/Mary
Barber, E.
Croasdale, Thomas R.
Greenhalgh, J.
Henderson, Alexander
Ingham, S.
James, J.
Lee, Thomas
Lees, J. H.
Lees, Jonathan
Lees, Thomas
Nelson, John
Parkinson, Thomas
Ramsbotham, Richard
Roberts, Michael
Waldvogel, Matthew

161

*Bury*, cont.
Whittaker, J.
Wright, Robert

*Cark*
Lawrence, William

*Cartmel (& Cartmel Fell)*
Clark, Thomas
Dickinson, John
Knowles, Thomas
Storey, Edward
Weston, William
Wilkinson, John

*Caton*
Simpson, Stephen
Wildman, William

*Chadderton*
Turner, Theophilus

*Childwall*
Ellison, Henry
Houlgreave, Charles
Naylor, Thomas
Porter, Thomas
Woods, Thomas

*Chipping*
Carr, James

*Chorley*
Alker, James
Alker, Nicholas
Ashurst, James
Fell, John
Heald, T.
Hodson, Thomas
Leach, Henry
Oldham, Richard
Pilkington, Hugh J.
Simpson, Isaac
Tootell, William
Unsworth, James

*Chowbent*
Eckersley, Richard

*Clitheroe*
Brewer, Thomas
Dean, Joseph
Dewhurst, William B.
Hutchinson, John
Rawsthorne, John

*Colne*
Battinson, John
Inman, James
Medley, Robert
Rushton, James
Simpson, Samuel
Spencer, John, I, II
  & III
Wiggan, Robert

*Crankshaw*
Whitworth, Samuel

*Culcheth*
Yates, John

*Dalton*
See Barrow-in-Furness

*Darwen*
Lowe, James
Lowe, Jesse W.
Lowe, John
Wood, J.

*Ditton*
Alkerton, Henry

*Dutton*
Grounds, Gabriel

*Earlestown*
Cooper, T.

*Eccles*
Barlow, James

*Eccleston*
Barton, James
Brownbill, Thomas
Clitherow, Thomas
Johnson, Richard

*Farnworth (incl Cronton)*
Abbot & Garnett
Abbott, James
Abbott, Nathan
Abbott, Nathan
Abbot, Thomas
Alcock, Thomas
Appleton, Richard
Arnet/Arnold, Henry
Arrowsmith, John
Ball, William
Barrow, Robert
Barrow, Thomas
Beesley, James
Beesley, James
Beesley, John
Beesley, Joseph
Beesley, Thomas
Beesley, William
Beswick, William
Birch, John
Birch, Joseph
Bridge, Henry
Brown, George
Brown, Richard
Brown, William
Burrows, John
Burtonwood, William
Calderbanck, Richard
Clitheroe, John
Crookell, Richard
Cross, Richard
Cross, Robert
Davies, William
Doke, William

*Farnworth (incl Cronton)*, cont.
Doward, Henry
Doward, William
Dyson, Jacob
Fogg, William
Forster, Ralph
Gant, John
Garnett, Robert
Garnett, William
Gee, John
Gleave, Thomas
Glover, James
Glover, Thomas
Gore, James
Graham, Joseph
Hall, Thomas
Hall, William
Hardman, Gerrard
Harrison, James
Harrison, William
Helsby, James
Hesketh, Thomas & John
Hill, Thomas
Hill, William
Holliwell, Thomas
Howard, Thomas
Hunt, Edward
Hunt, Henry
Hunt, Henry
Hunt, Isaac
Hunt, James
Hunt, John
Hunt, Thomas
Hunt, W.
Hunter, John
Hurst, George
Hurstfield, John
Jackson, Thomas
Kerry, John
Knowles, John

Large, John
Lee, James
Lee, Thomas
Leigh, Thomas
Lightfoot, Roger
Lithgoe, Joseph
Lloyd, Henry
Lloyd, Thomas
Lyon, Henry
Lyon, William
Marsh, James
Mercer, John
Miller, Hugh
Miller, William
Moorfield, James
Nixon, George
Parr, John
Parr, William
Porter, James
Potter, William
Poynter, William
Price, Thomas
Pye, James
Renshall, John
Rider, William
Rimmer, Henry
Rose, John
Seddon, Henry
Seddon, James
Sim, Charles
Sim, George
Sim, Joseph
Smethurst, Henry
Smith, Robert
Tarbuck, John
Taylor, John
Taylor, William
Tickle, Peter
Tickle, Robert
Towers, John
Unsworth, Edward
Unsworth, John

Welsby, Peter
Whitfield, Thomas
Williamson, Samuel
Woods, John
Woods, William
Woodward, John

*Fazakerley*
Westmore, Robert

*Fleetwood*
Brownbill, R. S.
Smythe, I.
Thompson, Joshua

*Flixton*
Johnson alias Roberts, William
Tomblinson, Timothy

*Garstang*
Bell, J.
Bell, Peter
Carr, James
Simpson, John
Simpson, Robert

*Gloverstone*
Jones, Robert

*Great Broughton*
Somervell, James

*Greta Bridge*
Cawson, James
Simpson, Stephen

*Grindlestonethorne*
Layfield, Robert

*Halewood*
Alkerton, Henry
Barrow, William

*Haslingden*
Evans, W. T.
Holt, Robert

163

*Haslingden*, cont.
Lees, William
Watson, James
Yates, Peter

*Hawkshead*
Braithwaite, William

*Heywood*
Birch, Richard
Blakeborough,
  William R.

*Holme(s)*
Breckell, Richard
Wadeson, Richard

*Hulme*
Dumville, John
Dumville, Nathaniel
Gutteridge, Charles

*Huyton (& Roby)*
Fletcher, Robert
Hewit, Joshua

*Ince*
Pennington, John

*Kirkham*
Benson, Thomas
Cartmel, John
Costen, Adam
Costen, John
Costen, William
Cowburn, Henry
Daniel, Thomas
Houghton, Thomas
Jackson, John
Leech, John

*Lancaster*
Anderson &
  Robinson
Anderson, William
Armstrong, Thomas

Atkinson, Robert
Atkinson, Thomas
Backhouse, James,
  I & II
Bagot, John
Beesley, James
Bell, Henry
Bell, John
Bell, William
Bowness, George
Bradley, William
Brewer, Richard
Carruthers, John
Cawson, Edward
Cornah, James
Coward, William
Deveny, Thomas
Dickinson, John
Dickinson, Thomas
Fayrer, James
Fayrer, Thomas
Fell, James
Gardner, Edward
Garnett, Edmund
Gillow, Robert
Goad, Thomas
Gregson, John
Grice, Job
Halshey, Henry
Halton, G. C.
Harrocks, Joshua
Hatton, G. C.
Hodgson, Henry
Hodgson, John
Hodgson, William B.
Holme, John
Holt, Thomas
Holt, William
Horrocks, Joshua
Houseman, Jacob
Jackson, George
Jackson, John

Jackson, Samuel
Jefferys, William
Lawrence, John
Lawrence, William
Leighton, John
Malley, John
Muncaster, John
Murphy, Thomas
Noble, James
Parkinson, Robert
Parkinson, William,
  I & II
Plowman, Thomas
Powlton, William
Preston, William
Richards, J.
Richardson, Richard
Richmond, Robert
Robinson, John
Russell, Thomas
Saul, Matthias
Shaw, John
Shaw, Robert
Shaw, Thomas
Simpson, John
Simpson, R.
Singleton, John
Smalley, John
Smith, T.
Smoult, James
Smoult, Thomas
Snead, J.
Sykes, Benjamin
Thompson, Thomas
Verity, Henry
Vickers, Isaac
Wakefield, Timothy
Wakefield, William
Walton, James
Westmore, Robert
Westmore, Robert
Wildman, Richard

164

*Lancaster*, cont.
Winder, Stephen
Winder, Thomas,
  I & II
Winder, William
Worswick, Thomas

*Leigh*
Cheetham, J.
Dean, J.
Dean, Richard
Dean, Thomas
Hayes, Edward
Jameson, William
Rigby, W.

*Leyland*
Alker, John &
  Nicholas

*Liverpool*
Abbott, John
Abram, Thomas
Abrahamson, William
Adams, Nathaniel
Adamson, Henry
Ainsworth, Robert
Airey, Thomas
Allison, William
Anderson, Alexander
Anderson, George
Anderson, William
Anderton, J.
Angus, William
Archer, John
Archer, Percy
Arden, John
Ashburton, ——
Ashcroft, John
Ashley, Thos
Aspinall, Henry
Aspinall, James
Aspinall, John

Aspinall, Robert
Astley, Edward
Atherton, S.
Atkin, Francis
Atkin, Robert
Atkinson, Richard
Atkinson, Robert
Bailey, Joseph
Bailey, Thomas
Baker, William
Ball, John
Ball, William
Balmer, Thomas
Banner, Richard
Banister, Thomas
Banister, William
Barlow, Robert
Barned, Israel & Co
Barned, & Co
Barnes, Robert
Barrington, Isaac
Barron, Thomas
Barton, Joseph
Basnet, James
Beesley, George &
  Robert
Beesley, Thomas
Bell, Thomas
Bellion, Edward
Bellion, William
Bennett, William
Benton, William
Berrick, Bernard
Berry, Arthur
Bibby, Thomas
Bickerstaff, Peter
Bickerstaff, Robert
Bickerstaff, William
Billinge, James
Billinge, Topping
Binch, James
Birch, James

Birchall, John
Birchall, Joshua/Mary
Birchall, William
Bird, Charles
Birtles, Edward
Blackburn, John
Blackburn, Robert
Blackmore, Thomas
Blakely, John
Blore, William
Blundell, Thomas
Bold, John
Bold, William
Bolton, Henry
Bolton, T.
Bond, Samuel
Bond, William
Boore, John
Bosket, R.
Bott, Thomas & Co
Bowden, George
Bradford, J.
Bradley, James G.
Bradshaw, John
Bradshaw, William
Bramble, William
Brindle, Ralph
Broadhurst, James
Brown, ——
Brown, Henry
Brown, James
Brown, James
Brown, Jeremy
Brown, Joshua
Brown, Thomas
Brown, William
Brownbill, James
Brownbill, John
Brownbill, Robert
Brownbill, Thomas
Buckford, William
Bullman, John

165

*Liverpool*, cont.
Bullman, Thomas
Burgess, ——
Burgess, Bezaliel
Burgess, John
Burgess, & Langton
Burrows, Richard
Burrows, Thomas
Bushell, Robert
Bushell, Thomas
Byrne, ——
Caddick, Richard
Cairnz, John
Callwood, John/
  Susannah
Cameron, A.
Cameron, Alexander
Cameron, John R.
Cannin, Joseph &
  Co
Carnes, John
Catterall, John
Catterall, Peter
Cawson, James
Cawson, William
Chadwick, Benjamin
Chadwick, John
Chambers, James
Champion, Richard
Chapman, Ann
Chapman, Joseph
Chapman, Moses
Christian, John
Clark & Morris
Clarke, R.
Clark, William
Clay, Thomas
Clayton, Peter
Clements, Thomas
Clifton, John
Clitherow, Thomas
Clowes, B.

Clowes, D.
Clowes, John C.
Cobb, James
Cobham, Joshua
Cockshott, Ann
Cockshutt, Edmund
Cockshutt, John
Cockshutt, William
Cohan, Asher & Co
Cohan, John
Cohen, Simeon
Coigley, James
Coleman, Benjamin
  & Co
Coleman & Chapman
Condliff, James
Cooke, William
Coppell, ——
Coppell, Zallel
Corlett, James
Cornwall, James
Costala, Thomas
Cowell, Henry
Cragg, John
Cranage, John
Cranage, Joseph
Cranage, Thomas
  Stokes
Crichlow, Thomas
Critchley, Robert
Critchley, William
Cronage, Thomas
Cross, John
Crowe, John
Crowley, John
Crump, Thomas
Crumpsty, Thomas
Culverwell, Richard
  Major
Curran, Thomas
Dagnall, Henry
Daniels, Henry

Daniels, Henry
  & John
Davenport, ——
Davies, William
Davison, R.
Dawson, Stewart
  & Co
Dellesser, Ellis
Dickinson, Richard
Dismore, Thomas
Dodsworth, James
Doke, Richard/Sarah
Donkin, Gerard
Donkin, James
Donney, W. J.
Douglas, Robert & Co
Douglas, Samuel &
  Robert Jnr
Dowell, Daniel
Dowling, William
Downing, John
Downing, Samuel
Drielsma, Isaac Jones
Drielsma, Morris
Drinkwater, John
Drummond, Thomas
Duff, William & Co
Duggan, Thomas
Dumbell, John
Dumbell, Joseph
Duncan, R.
Dutton, John
Dutton, Samuel
Dyke, William
Eden, Ralph
Edmonds, B.
Edmonds, D.
Edmondson, John
Edwards, D.
Edwards, Francis
Edwards, Richard
Edwardson, John

*Liverpool*, cont.
Edwardson, William
Ellis, James E.
Ellison, John
Ellison, Samuel
Ensworth, Robert
Etches, John
Evans, Edward
Evans, George
Eyett, John
Fairclough, Edward
Fairclough, Henry
Fairclough, Richard
Fairhurst, John
Farnworth, John
Fawcet(te), ——
Fazackerly, John
Fewller, John
Fielding, Robert
Fietzen, Andrew
Finney, John
Finney, Joseph,
  I & II
Finney, Richard
Finney, Thomas
Fisher, Richard
Fitzer, William
Fleetwood, James
Fleetwood, Joseph
Fleetwood, Robert
Fleetwood, Thomas
Fleming, James
Fleming, Richard
Fletcher, James
Flower, Edward
Fogg, John
Forber, Edward
Forber, Joseph
Forbes, Joshua
Ford, Thomas
Foster, Henry
Fo(r)ster, John

Foster, John
Fox, William
Freeman, Charles
Frodsham, David
Frodsham, Henry
Furnival, Benjamin
Garner, James
Gatton, Edward
Gillis, Frederick
Gleave(s), John
Goldstein, Jacob
Gore, John
Gorsuch, Fleetwood
Gostage, Samuel
Gowland, George
Grace, William
Graham, John
Grayson, James
Green, E. (late
  Thomas)
Green, James
Green, Peter
Green, Robert
Green, Thomas
Green, Thomas
Green, William
Greener, C. & F.
Greener, F. & Co
Greenwood, Charles
Gregory, Thomas
Gregson, John
Griffiths, David
Grimshaw, John
Grimshaw, Thomas
Grocot, Thomas
Guy, John
Guy, Peter
Hadwen, Isaac
Hadwen, Hannah
Hadwen, Isaac
Hadwen, Joseph
Hall, Eaton

Hall, Thomas
Hall, William
Hallows, John
Hallows, Jonathan
Halsall, Edward
Hamlet, William
Hampson, Thomas
Hardman, Gerrard
Hardman, Henry
Harker, James
Harris, Charles
Harris, J. & A.
Harris, Lazarus
Harrison, John
Harrison, John
Harrison, Thomas
Hart, Moses
Hart, Napthali
Hatton, William
Haworth, Richard
Hawson, James
Hayes, William
Hayworth, Richard
Heckle, Alanson
Heckle, Henry H.
Heinekey, Robert
Helsby, James G.
Helsby, John
Hendrick, John
Hendrick, John
  & Peter
Heron, William
Hess, Ralph & Co
Hess, Rosetta
Hewitson, Richard
Heys, William
Hicks, Charles
Higginson &
  Fairclough
Higginson, Henry
Higham, Thomas
Highfield, Joseph

167

*Liverpool*, cont.
Highfield, Nathan
Highfield, William
Hill, Richard
Hilton, John
Hislop, Alexander
Hoffmayer, Alexander
Hoffmayer & Cley
Hoffmayer, Martin
Holden, Joseph
Holison, ——
Holland, Richard
Hollingsworth, George
Hollinson(e),
 Alexander
Hollison(e), William
Holliwell, William
Holme, Lawrence
Holme, Peter
Holme, Thomas
Hooten, Peter
Hope, Peter
Hornby, George
Hornby, George
Hornby, Gerrard
 (& Son)
Hornby, Henry
Hornby, James
Hornby, John
Hornby, John
Hornby, Richard
Hornby, Thomas
Hornby, William
Horridge, Robert
Houghton, Michael
Houghton, Richard
Houlbrook, Henry
Houlgrave, Edward
Howard, Henry
Howard, John
Howard, Thomas
Howard, Thomas W.

Hughes, Lewis
Huguenin, Aime/
 Sarah
Humphreys, Joseph
Hunter, James
Hunter, Thomas
Hurst, Stephen
Ingleby, ——
Inman, John
Inman, Sophia
Inman, William
Isaacs, Ralph
Isaacs, Soloman
Ivison, Henry
Jackson, Abraham
Jackson, Frederick
Jackson, John
Jackson, John
Jackson, Joseph
Jackson, William
James, John
Jefferys, Thomas
Jefferys, William
Jerome & Co
Johnson, Henry
Johnson, James
Johnson, James
Johnson, Joseph
Johnson, Rowland
Johnson, Samuel
Jones, Isaac Aaron
Jones, James
Jones, John
Jones, Peter
Jones, Robert & Son
Jones, Robert
Jones, Thomas
Jones & Wally
Joseph, Brothers
Joseph, B. L.
Joseph, Elias
Kane, Thomas

Kaye, John
Kaye, William
Kelly, John
Kendrick, John
Kenyon, ——
Kenyon, James
Kenyon, William
Kerfoot, Robert
Kerfoot, Robert
 junior
Kerfoot, Robert
Kind, John
King, Alexander
Kitchen, John
Knowles, Robert
Laithwaite, John
Laithwaite, Robert
Laithwaite, William
Lambie, Hugh
Lancaster, Francis
Lancaster, James
Langley, Thomas
Langton, Francis
Lassell, Thurston
Lassell, William
Lea, James
Leatherbarrow,
 Charles
Leders, John
Lee, Isaac
Lee, John
Leigh, Joshua
Leigh, William
Leigh, William
Levi, Barnet
Levy & Denziger
Lewis, Morris
Lewis, Peter
Lewis, Robert
Lewthwaite, William
Liddell, Adam
Linaker, Henry

*Liverpool*, cont.

Linton, John
Litherland, Ann
Litherland & Co
Litherland, Davies
  & Co
Litherland, John
Litherland, John
Litherland, Peter
Litherland, Peter
Litherland, Richard
Loftus, John
Loftus, John
Longsworth, Peter
Lord, Henry
Lowe, Edward
Lyon, George
M'Convill, Edward
McCune, Henry
McDonald, Joseph
McMurray, Thomas
Maddox, Charles
Marcer, William
Marks, Leon
Marrow, Richard
Marsh, Henry
Marsh, Samuel
Martin, John
Martin, William
Mason, Alexander
Massie, Edward
Massie, Francis
Mather, Nathan
Mayer, Joseph
Mecanley, William
Medcalf, William
Melling & Co
Mellor, John
Mercer, John
Mercer, William
Merton & Co
Metcalf, Augustine

Metcalf, John
Miles, John
Mills, Edward
Mitchall, William
Molyneux, John
Molyneux, William
Moncas, John
Moncas, Thomas
Moorhouse, William
Morath, Fedele
  & Bros
Morgan, John V.
Morris, George
Morris, William
Morrow, John
Moseley, Morris L.
Moss, Charles
Moss, James
Moss, James D.
Mozley, M. L.
Nathan, David
Nathan, John
Nathan, Mosley
Nathan, Philip
Nathan, Rosina
Naylor, Charles
Naylor, William
Nelson, Bernard
Nelson, Gerard
Nelson, Thomas
Nelson, William
Newsham, Richard
Newton, Joseph
Nicholls, Henry
Nicklin, William
Norris, & Campbell
Norris, Francis
Norris, Henry
Norris, Mary
Norris, Patrick
Norris, William
O'Hara, James

Oldham, Joseph
Outhwaite, Thomas
  & Co
Over, Thomas
Owens, Owen
Palethorp, William
Park, Joseph
Parker, John
Parkinson &
  Frodsham
Parr, John
Parr, Peter
Parr, William
Parr, William
Parry, William J.
Patten, Robert
Patterson, James
Patterson, Robert
Pearce, George
Pedrone, Louis
Penlington, Joseph
Penlington, Joseph
Penlington, Samuel
  & Thomas
Pennington, John
Percy, William
Phithian, Joseph
Pickford, John
Pickford, Richard
Pierpoint, John
Pierpoint, Thomas
Piers, Charles
Pinnington, Thomas
Plumb, John
Plumb, Matthew
Plumb, William
Plumpton, John
Poole, James
Portland, ——
Poston & Woldnough
Poston, Robert
Powell, John

L

*Liverpool*, cont.
Preston, Robert
Price, Edward
Priest, John
Pritchard, Griffith
Pryor, Joseph
Pugh, Richard Dyke
Quilliam, Samuel
Radcliffe, Charles
Radcliff, Charles
Ramsey, William
Reed, James
Richardson, Richard
Rigby, Henry
Rigby, James
Rimmer, Robert
Rimmer, William
Roberts, George
Robertson, John
Robinson, George
Robinson, Henry
Robinson, Thomas B.
Robinson, William
& Co
Roche, Richard
Roe & Jacob
Rogers, William
Rogan, Edward
Roscow, Robert
Rose, Joseph
Rose, William
Roskell, John junior
Roskell, John &
Robert
Roskell, Robert
& Son
Rowland, Henry
Rowley, Henry
Rowley, William
Rowson, Christopher
Royland, John
Royle, Thomas

Rubottom, William
Runchorne, Richard
Russells, Ltd
Russell, Thomas
& Son
Russell, William
Rycroft, Timothy
Saber, Wolff & Lewis
Sampson, Thomas
Samuel, Edwin L.
Samuel, Eliza
Samuel, F. & Co
Samuel, Flora & Co
Samuel, George
& Israel
Samuel, Henry
Samuel, Lewis & Co
Samuel, Lewis H.
& Co
Samuel, Moses
Samuel, Nathan
Samuel, Samuel J.
Samuel, Saul
Samuel, Sylvester L.
Samuel, Simpson
Bros & Co
Sanderson, ——
Scamble, Peter
Scaresbrick, James
Schlesinger,
Casper W.
Schwersensky, Isaac
Scotson, Isaac/Joseph
Seager, John
Seddon, Samuel
Seed, John
Sewill, Joseph
Sharples, James
Shaw, William
Shepherd, Thomas
Shepherd, William
Shepherd, William

Shierwater and Lloyd
Simner, James
Simpson, John
Simpson, Robert
Simpson, Samuel
Skeene, John
Skellorn, John
Slater, George
Smith, George
Smith, Thomas
Spalding, William
Spears, Frederick
Speers, Charles
Spencer, Charles
Speth, Andrew
Spurr, James
Stafford, George
Stanley, Charles
Stanley, Richard
Stanley, Thomas
Starkie, Edward
Stewart, Joseph
Stockton, Peter
Stone, Charles
Storey, John
Story, Joseph
Stringfellow, Richard
Stuart, Henry
Stubley, Benjamin
Stubley, John (&
Abraham)
Sumner, James
Sutton, William
Symonds, Joseph
& Co
Tarleton, Richard
Tarleton, Thomas
Tarleton, William
Tate, James
Taylor, George
Taylor, Henry
Taylor, James

*Liverpool*, cont.
Taylor, John
Taylor, John
& Daniel
Taylor, S.
Taylor, Samuel
Taylor, William T.
Taylor, William
Taylor, William E.
Thom, Charles
& Crump
Thomas, William
Thompson, James
Thompson, John
Thompson, Thomas
Tillinghast, Stephen
Travers, Adam
Travers, Henry
Tobias, M. J. & Co
Todd, R. I.
Tompion, Richard
Tooke, W. H.
Topping, William
Townley, John
Townley & Quilliam
Townley, Thomas
Unsworth, Peter
Unsworth, Thomas
Upton, George
Veriley, John D.
Vernon & Eden
Vernon, James
Vernon, Thomas
Wainwright, F.
Wainwright, John
Wainwright, Nathan
Walker, Benjamin
Walker, John
Walley, Joseph
W(h)alley, Richard
Warburton, Henry
Warburton, John

Ward, John
Ward, William H.
Wardlaw, Henry
Waring, Charles J.
Waring, George
Wareing, James
Warren, S.
Waugh, William
Weatherilt, Samuel
Webster, John
Wells, William
& Charles
Whitehead, Joseph
Whiteside, Thomas
Whitfield, James
Whitfield, James
Whitfield, John
Whitfield, Robert
Whittle, John
Wickliffe, William
Wilcockson, Henry
Wilcox, William
Wilks, Joseph
Willacy, Edward
Williams, John
Williams, R.
Williams, Thomas
Williams, William
Williams, William
Williamson, John
Williamson, Richard
Willis, Charles
Willis, Richard
Wilson, John
Winstanley, Edward
Winstanley, James
Winstanley, Joseph
Winstanley, Michael
Winstanley, William
Winter, Thomas
Wollarm, J.
Wood, John

Woods, Peter
Woods, William
junior
Woods, William
Woodfine, Robert
Woodroofe, Richard
& Son
Woodward, Thomas
Woolf, Lewis
Woolfall, Richard
Woolfall, Richard
junior
Woolnough,
Frederick
Worrall, John
Worrall, John
Worsley, Thomas
Worthington, James
Wright, John
Wright, John
Wright, John
Wyke & Green
Wyke, John
Yates, Henry
Yates & Hess
Yates, John
Yates, Samuel
Young, Henry
Young, Isaac
Young, James
Young, John
Young, William

*Lussley*
Whitworth, James

*Manchester (incl Salford,*
*Stretford & Eccles)*
Abbot, Francis
Agnew, Thos & Son
Allen, Thomas
Antrobus, John

*Manchester*, cont.
Antrobus, Philip,
  I & II
Appleby, Thomas
Armstrong, Alfred
Armstrong, Asnath
Armstrong, Edward
Armstrong, George B.
Armstrong, Joseph
Armstrong, Joseph B.
Armstrong, Robert
Armstrong, Thomas,
  I & II
Ashton, James
Ashton, Samuel
Aspinal, Thomas
Asworth, Richard
Atkinson, Jonathan
Barlow, Richard
Barnes, George
Barret, James
Barton, John W.
Barton, Thomas
Bayliff, John
Beaver, Louis
Beesley, James
Bell, John
Bennit, George
Berry, John
Berry, Joseph
Birckley, Frederick
Boardman, Samuel
Bolton, Thomas
Bond, ——
Booth, Charles
Booth, George
Booth, George
Booth, James B.
Booth, John
Bowker, Mrs
Bowler, Joseph
Bowler, Richard

Bowman, Richard
Braddock, John
Bradshaw, John
Bradshaw, John
Bradshaw, Thomas
Bridge, Thomas
Brown, Edward
Brown, John
Brown, Joseph
Brown, Nathaniel
Brown, Thomas
Brown, William
Bunyan & Gardner
Burb(r)idge, Joseph/
  Elizabeth
Burgess, John
Burgess, Richard
Burgess, Samuel
Burghart, Augustin
Burns, Richard
Burquhart, Augustin
Calbrook, James
Camb, T.
Cawley, John
Chadwick, John
Christian, J.
Clare, Peter, I & II
Clay, James
Clayton, Martin
Clegg, James
Clegg, William
Clegg, William F.
Clough, John
Cluley, William
Cohen, Max
Collier, David
Collier, Peter
Collier, Robert
Collier, Samuel
Collier, Thomas
Cooke, John
Cooper, J.

Cornah, James
Coughin, James
Cowel, David
Cowen, David
Cragg, James
Crighton, James
Critchley, Joseph
Crossley, Henry
Crowley, John
Dean(s), Thomas
Decachent, Stephen
Dewsbury, Samuel
Dickinson, John
Dickon, Mary Ann
Dillon, Jonathan
Done, William
Drescher, Simon
Duesbury, Samuel
Dyson, George
Dyson, Humphrey
Edwards, James
Eggleston, J.
Eld, Richard
Eldershaw, Thomas
Ellis, George
English, David/Mary
Etchells, Matthew
Falk, David & Co
Fallar, Theodore K.
Fallows, John B.
Fazakerly, Richard
Fletcher, John
Fogg, James
Foster, John
Foster, John
  & Thomas
Foster, William
Fothergill, William
Frame, John
Franklin, Abraham
Frodsham, Samuel
Gallimore, Joseph

*Manchester*, cont.
Ganter, Matthew
Garner, William
Gaskes, Samuel L.
Gee, James
Gervin, Thomas
Gibbons, John
Gilhooly, Ephraim
Gill, Isaac
Gill, John
Gillett, Charles E.
Glatz & Wunderley
Glatz, Joseph
Gledhill, Richard
Glover, Joseph
Godwin, William
Goldstone, Michael
Goodwin, Martin
Goodwin, William
Gray, James
Greaves, Thomas
Greenhalgh, Henry
Greenhalgh, John
Grener & Co
Hadfield, John
Hall, John
Halpern, Bros
Halton, John
Hammond, George
    & Thomas
Hampson, Robert
Hancock, Daniel
Hardie & Christie
Hardman, William
Harris, Frederick
Harris, Henry J.
Harris, L.
Hatfield & Hall
Haywood, David
Healey, John
Healey, Thomas
Hemingway, John

Heppet, James
Herman, James
Herman, Joseph
Heskey, Henry
Hibbert, Thomas
Higham, Robert
Holland, James
Holme, James
Holt, George
Hordern, Joseph
Howard, James
Howarth, William
Hughes, Thomas R.
Hulme, James
Hulme, Thomas
Hulse, Henry
Hunt, Richard
Hunt & Roskell
Imison, John
Inglish, David/Mary
Jagger, Richard
Jessop, George
Joel, Jacob
Johnson, John
Johnson, Owen
Jones, John
Jones, William
Jordan, John
Joy, Julius
Joyce, Thomas P.
Kaye, John
Kay, Samuel
Kay, William
Kemshead, Harvey
    & Son
Kemshead, Robert
    & Son
Kent, John
Kent, William
    Worsley
Kirk, William
Knight, Stephen W.

Knight, Thomas
Labrow, Thomas S.
Lacker, Michael
Large, John
Lawley, Theodore
Lawrence, William
Lawson, Robert
Leadbeater, Thomas
Lees, John
Levy, Henry & Co
Lewis, George
Lloyd, William
Longmore, William
Lowe, George C.
McFerran, William
McGregor, Anthony
McMillan, Richard
McMinn, John M.
Margon, Thomas
Mawdsley, John
Mayer, Saul
Mayo, William & Son
Mayor, John
Mellor, John
Mendelson, Henry
Mentha, Fritz
Mercer, John
Michaloritz, T. Z.
Morrey, John
Morton, Thomas
Moss, William S.
Muncaster, John
Nathan, Jacob &
    Lemon
Nelson, Thomas
Newton, George
Newton, Isaac
Nuttall, C.
Oldfield, John
Oliver, John
Oliver, John
Oliver, Samuel

173

*Manchester*, cont.
Ollivant, John & Son
Ollivant, Thomas
  & John
Onion, John
Orme, Thomas
Orton, John
Overton, William
Parkin, Bartholomew
Parr, W.
Pipe, Isaac
Plant, Thomas
Plant, William
Pomfret, Horatio
Potter, Richard
Prince, John
Pye, John
Pye, Robert
Ratcliffe, John
Read, Thomas
Renk, A. & C.
Rhind, Thomas
Rhodes, John
Richardson, John
Richardson, Thomas
Rider, Tryall
Roach, Patrick
Roberts (alias
  Johnson), William
Robertshaw, John
Robinson, Benjamin
Rostance, James
Rowland, John
Royle, Ralph
Runcorn, Richard
  & Robert
Ryall, Thomas
Sackerson, William
Salter, William
Sanders, Nathaniel
Sandiford, James
Scales, Edward

Scholfield, Josiah
Scholfield, Major,
  I & II
Seddon, Josiah
Seddon, William
Shenfield, John
Shepley, Edward
Sherratt, Isaac
Sherring, John K.
  & Co
Simmons, Isaac
Singleton, John A.
Slowe, William
Smith, George
Smith, John
Smith, John S.
Spencer, Thomas
Spreat & Co
Stanley, John
Sternberg, John
  & Bros
Stewart & McFerran
Stockwell, Joseph
Stone, Robert
Storey, William
Surman &
  Kaltenback
Sutlow, Thomas
Sykes, John
Tarbock, John
Tarr, Thomas
Taylor, D. T.
Taylor, George
Taylor, Henry
Taylor, John
Taylor, Thomas
Terry, Thomas
Thelwall, Charles J.
Thelwell, Richard
Torkington, William
  H.
Travis, Edward

Travis, Joshua
Turton, Nathaniel
Twyford, John
Twyford, Josiah
Twyford, William
Tyas, John
Tyrer, Edward
Wainwright, George
Wainwright, John
W(h)alley, Samuel,
  I, II & III
W(h)alley, Thomas
Walmsley, Edward
Warmingham,
  Andrew
Warmisham, William
Watson, John
Whitehead, William
Whitner, Thomas
Whittington, Henry
Williams, Thomas
Wilson, Becket
Wilson, Robert
Wilson, Thomas
Winstanley, John
Wooton, John
Wright, John
Wright, R. T.
Wrigley, Isaac
Wulfson, Lewis
Yeomans, Edward
Yeomans, James

*Middleton*
Cheetham, Samuel
Lees, James
Lees, James
Lees, John
Lees, John
Lees, Jonathan
Lees, Thomas
Taylor, Samuel

174

*Middleton*, cont.
Turner, Theophilus
Whittaker, James
Whittaker, Samuel

*Milnthorpe*
Armstrong, Thomas
Cragg, James
Steedman, William

*Newchurch*
Stott, Ormerod

*Newton-in-Makerfield*
Fletcher, J.
Williams, T.

*Newton-le-Willows*
Lawson, William
Leigh, William
Rigby, William

*North Meols*
Todd, J.

*Ogden*
Scholefield, Jonathan

*Oldham (incl Shaw)*
Aldridge, Thomas
Bankes, John
Barlow, Benjamin
Barlow, Edward
Barlow, James
Hayes, Christopher
Hayes, James H.
Hayes, W.
Heyes, Christopher
Hinchliff, J.
Hind, William
Jagger, Richard
Johnson, Richard
Kember, Joseph
Kenworthy, John
Kershaw, John

Ketterer & Co
Mills, John
Oakes, John
Oakes, William
Oclee, Frederick A.
Ogden, T.
Ogden, William
Orme, Thomas
Sater, Joseph
Stump, Richard
Sutcliffe, James
Whittle, Peter
Wilmshurst, Stephen
Zipfel, Anthony & Co

*Ormskirk*
Atkinson, Thomas
Banks, James
Barry, Thomas
Barton, James
Barton, James
Cammack, Robert
Garratt, Henry
Garratt, Hugh
Gregory, James
Grice, Job
Hall, Samuel
Halsall, Robert
Harrison, Richard
Helm, ——
Houghton, James
Houghton, Stephen
  & Son
Nuttall, James
Rawsthorne, John
Rigby, Nicholas
Rothwell, John
Ryland, James
Ryland, John
Salusbury, William
Slater, James
Taylor, John

Twist, Joseph
Wainwright, John
Walmesley, Mr
Whiteside, James
Wignall, George
Wignall, John
Wignall, M.
Winstanley, ——
Winstanley, Robert

*Poulton*
Abram, George
Brownbill, James
Lomas, Samuel
Simpson, Robert

*Prescot (incl Parr)*
Abbot, John
Abbott, William
Abbott, William
Abram, Thomas
Ackers, John
Ainsworth, James
Alcock, John
Alcock, Joseph
Appleton, John
Appleton, Thomas
Ashton, John
Ashton, Nicholas
Atherton, John
Atherton, John
Atherton, Thomas
Ball, Isaac
Ball, William
Balmer, William
Barr, Henry
Barron, James
Barrow, David
Barrow, John
Basnett, Thomas
Beesley, James
Beesley, John
Beesley, John

175

*Prescot (incl Parr)*, cont.
Beesley, William
Berry, James
Bibby, George
Bibby, Ralph
Birchall, George
Birchall, James
Birchall, John
Birchall, William
Birchall, William
Blackburn, James
Bold, John
Bradshaw, James
Bradshaw, Thomas
Brewer, Richard
Brimilow, Peter
Bromilow, George
Broom, Charles
Brown, J.
Brown, Richard
Brown, William
Brown, William
Brownbill, Edmond
Brownbill, John
Byron, John
Byron, Thomas
Case, Henry
Case, James
Catterall, James
Chesworth, Thomas
Chesworth, William
Chew, John
Chew, Thomas
Chorley, Matthew
Chorley, William
Claughton, Joseph
Clayton, John
Clitherow, William
Clitherow, William
Coppock, Thomas
Critchley, Lawrence
Cross, James

Cross, William
Crouchley, Thomas
Davies, Henry
Denton, George
Diverton, James
Dumbell, William
Eaton, Joseph
Entwistle, William
Fazakerley, Thomas
Fazakerley, William
Ferns, Richard
Fillingham, Robert
Finch, Jonathan
Finlow, Ralph
Finney, James
Fleetwood, Henry
Fleetwood, Thomas
Fogg, William
Ford, William
Foster, Henry
Foster, John
Friendly, Ralph
Gedman, Joshua
Gidman, Hugh
Glover, Alexander
Glover, James
Glover, John
Glover, Thomas
Goore, Giles
Goore, John
Gore, John
Gorsuch, Henry
Graham, Joseph
Green, William
Greenall, ——
Hall, James
Hall, Thomas
Hardman, Samuel
Harper, William
Helsby, Thomas
Henret, John
Hewit, George

Hewit, John
Hewit, Joseph
Hewit, Joshua
Hewit, Joshua
Hiatt, Henry
Higginson, Charles
Holcroft, John
Holme, Joseph
Holme, Thomas
Hornby, Thomas
Houghton, James
Houghton, John
Houghton, John
Houghton, Thomas
Howard, Edward
Howard, John
Hunt, Peter
Hunt, Thomas
Hunter, Henry
Hurst, James
Ireland, William
Jarvis, Henry
Johnson, James
Johnson, James
Johnson, Thomas
  & Isaac
Jones, John
Jones, Peter
Jones, Thomas
Jump, Thomas
Kilshaw, Nehemiah
Lancaster, John
Langshaw, Hugh
Lawrenson, James
Leadbetter, Thomas
Leaf, Leigh
Leather, Richard
Lee, Peter
Leech, Thomas
Leyland, Thomas
Liversay, George
Lloyd, James

*Prescot (incl Parr)*, cont.
Lomax, Joseph
Lomax, William
Lomax, William
Low, James
Lyon, Edward
Lyon, Edward
Lyon, Edward
Lyon, John
Lyon, Joseph
Marsden, James
Marsh, Edward
Marsh, Thomas
Mason, William
May, David
Mercer, William
Miller, John
Miller, Robert
Mills, John
Monk(e)s, George
Musket, John
Nelson, Robert
Norman, R.
Oldham, Joseph
Orford, John
Orford, William
Parks, John
Parker, John
Parkinson, William
Parr, Henry
Parr, John
Parr, Robert
Parr, William
Parr, William
Patten, James
Pendleton, Peter
Pendleton, Samuel
Pennington, James
Phythian, John
Phythian, John
Pinnington, James
Platt, James

Platt, Thomas
Porter, Peter
Porter, Robert
Porter, Thomas
Porter, Thomas
Porter, William
Porter, William
Porter, William
Prescot, Thomas
Preston, Job
Preston, John
Renshaw, James
Rice, John
Rigby, Joseph
Rigby, Thomas
Rigby, William
Scarisbrick, Anthony
Sephton, Edward
Sephton, Kenwright
Sephton, Luke
Sephton, Peter
Sherwood, Thomas
Sheward, Thomas
Sim, George
Sim, Joshua
Sim, Thomas
Standish, John
Stanley, John
Stanley, Thomas
Symm, Luke
Tarbuck, John
Tarbuck, Joseph
Taylor, Edward
Taylor, John
Taylor, Peter
Tickle, William
Tyrer, James
Unsworth, Thomas
Unsworth, Thomas
Wainwright, Thomas
Walker, Joseph
Ward, Richard

Webster, John
Webster, William
Welsby, Jonathan
Whittle, Edward
Wilkinson, William
Willis, Thomas
Wilson, George
Windle, Edward
Woorsey, William
Yates, Thomas
Yates, Thomas
Young, Isaac

*Preston*
Anderson, Richard
Bamber, Abraham
Banks, Ellen
Bond, John T.
Brewer, Thomas
Broderick, Thomas
Brown, William
Cowburn, J.
Fallows, Thomas
Fisher, Henry
Fisher, John
Frederick, Leonard
Hardy, John
Hatton, Thomas
Hayhurst, John
Hill, C.
Kells, R.
Leach, Henry
Leach, J.
Lowe, Robert
Mason, Thomas
Metcalf, William
Miller, John
Moorhouse, W.
Moss, Michael
Noblatt, Edward
Orme, John
Orrell, John

177

*Preston,* cont.
Parke, James
Parkinson, Nathaniel
Place, James
Pratt, John
Sealey, William
Shakeshaft, Lawrence
Simpson, Stephen,
   I & II
Simpson, William
Simpson, Edmund
Simpson, Isaac
Simpson, Edmund
Simpson, Jonathan W.
Simpson, Joseph
Sumersgill, Robert
Taylor, George
Waller, John
Westmore, Robert
Williams, Thomas
Winstanley, Edward
Winter, C.
Yates, Thomas

*Prestwich*
Guest, Ralph

*Rainford*
Fazakerley, James

*Rainhill*
Bowden, George
Clitherow, John
Garnett, Thomas
Glover, Alexander
Glover, Thomas
Houghton, James
Howard, Thomas

*Ramsbottom*
Howarth, Squire
Wood, A.

*Rawtenstall*
Burton, W.
Butterworth, H.
Whitaker, George

*Ribchester*
Dewhurst, William
Howarth, Peter
Wilkinson, Henry

*Rochdale*
Archer, George
Ashworth, J.
Barnish, John
Barnish, William
Barow, John
Birckley, Frederick
Brewer, John
Collier, James
Collingwood, Henry
Collingwood and
   Rainton
Collingwood, Robert
Dumbell Joseph
Dumbell, Thomas
Hill, Thomas
Holt, John
Holt, Valentine
Howe, George
Hoyle, William
Law, Samuel
Mathew, J.
Mayo, William
Moss, John
Nield, Daniel
Scholfield, Edmund
Scholfield, Major
Scholfield, Robert (3)
Smailes, Richard
Stringfellow, John
Taylor, John
   & Edmund

Taylor, Samuel
Taylor, Samuel & D.
Varnish, John
Whip, Thomas
Whitworth, Henry
Williamson, J.
Williamson, Joseph
Woolfenden, John

*St Helens*
Ackers, Edward
Ainsworth, John
Alcock, John
Ansdell, James
Ansdle, John
Arrowsmith, John
Berrington, James
Bradshaw, Peter
Bridge, Thomas
Bromilow, Thomas
Brown, Henry
Brown, Henry
Brown, William
Brown, William
Chadwick, James
Chadwick, Joseph
Charleston, John
Chethword, John
Cliff, John
Clitherow, Thomas
Cockshoot, William
Cotterell, Joshua
Critchley, Henry
Daniels, James
Dennett, James
Dennett, Thomas
Dixon, James
Dixon, William
Ellison, Robert
Fairclough, Jeffrey
Fairclough, John
Farrer, John

*St Helens*, cont.
Fazakerley, Henry
Fazakerley, James
Fazakerley, John
Fenny, James
Forster, James
Forster, John
Forster, Ralph
Forster, William
Gerrard, Edward
Glover, Henry
Glover, John
Glover, John
Graham, Thomas
Hardman, Thomas
Hatton, James
Hatton, William
Helsby, James
Helsby, John
Helsby, Richard
Helsby, William
Helsby, W.
Henderson, E.
Houghton, James
Houghton, John
Houghton, John
Houghton, Stephen
Houghton, William
Houghton, William
Jackson, J.
Johnson, Richard
Johnson, Thomas
Jones, Morres
Kerkham, Hugh
Lathom, George
Lea, Henry
Lever, Peter
Lightfoot, Roger
Lunt, Samuel
Lythgoe, John
Marsh, J. T.
Morton, Thomas

Parr, William
Pickavance, Samuel
Pilkington, James
Platt, John
Potter, John
Potter, William
Prescot, John
Pye, John
Roskell, Joseph
Roughley, Henry
Sephton, John
Sephton, Kendrick
Shaw, Richard
Southern, Daniel
Standish, John
Taylor, James
Tillingham, James
Tomblinson, Timothy
Tommison, John
Tootell, ——
Vose, John
Watkinson, H.
Wilkinson, Henry
Woods, William
Wright, William
Yates, James
Young, William

*Southport*
Kay, Thomas
Mawdsley, Hargreaves
Richardson, Henry
Woodburn, Samuel

*Stalybridge*
Brooks, Abel
Hoyle, Joseph
Leah, Henry
Whitehead, William
Whittaker, Isaac

*Sutton*
Ellam, William

Erlam, Job
Erlam, Percival
Garnett, Thomas
Glover, James
Willcock, John

*Todmorden*
Blakeborough, Charles
Bradley, John
Butterfield, John
Clewer, William H.
Davis, George
Hollinrake, James
Ingham, Henry
Ingham, William
Lawson, William
Pendlebury & Son
Riley, Gillingham
Stell, G.

*Ulverstone*
Addison, Thomas
Atkinson, Thomas
Bellman, Thomas
Burton, Isaac, I & II
Burton, Jonathan,
  I & II
Burton, Thomas
Clark, Thomas
Clark, T. C.
Cleminson, George
Cookson, Thomas
Coulton, John
Coulton, Thomas
Dawes, John
Fell, Abraham
Fell, Joseph
Fletcher, John
Gregson, John
Hird, Henry
Hird, Edward
  & William
Kilner, Samuel

*Ulverstone*, cont.
Marr, William
Moss, Richard
Muncaster, John
Parker, George
Philipson, Henry,
  I & II
Reynoldson, John
Ricee, John
Riordan, Matthew
Storey, Edward
Strickland, James
Townson, J.
Whiteway, Foliot
Wilkinson, John
Williamson, ——
Wilson, John

*Walton*
Barton, Richard
Dewhurst, Lawrence
Miller, John

*Warrington*
Abraham, John
Armitage, J. H.
Ball, Thomas
Barlow, Edward
Barrow, Edward
Bethell, John
Birchall, G.
Blackhurst, George
Booth, Edward
Carter, James, I & II
Carter, Joseph
Carter, Robert
Collier, Peter
Coward, J.
Denton, William
Dickinson, John
France, Richard
Garnett, Thomas

Gee, William
Halliwell, David
Halliwell, John
Hampson, Robert
Holliwell, John
Horrocks, Christopher
Key, John
Leighton, James
Litherland, John
Lyon, John
Norman, John
Rigby, J.
Robinson, Charles
Robinson, James
Sankey, James
Simcock, Thomas,
  I & II
Simcock, William
Speakman, T.
Standish, John
Stubs, Peter
Tunstall, John
Ward, Thomas
Waring, Henry
Williamson, John
Woods, John

*Warton*
Armstrong, T.
Jackson, Joseph

*Wavertree*
Hardman, John

*West Derby*
Gleave, Matthew
Parkinson, Joseph
Westmore, Robert

*Whalley*
Bell, A.
Grundy, John
Wright, John

*Widnes*
Doward, H.
Glover, John
Kent, R.

*Wigan (incl Hindley)*
Alker, James
Alker, John, I & II
Alker, Nicholas
Alker, Thomas
Ascroft, James
Aspinall, James
Ball, Thomas
Barker, Daye
Barker, Thomas
Barker, William
Barton & Esplin
Barton, William
Beaver, William
Billinge, John
Bolton, Robert
Bootle(s), Thomas
Bridge, Thomas
Burgess, John
Coates, Archibald,
  I & II
Coates, James
  & Robert
Darbyshire, Roger
Dennett, John
Doncaster, Thomas
Erling, Jonathan
Esplin, George
Fearnley, Peter
Green, Thomas
Green, William
Grounds, Johnson
Hampson, Robert
Harvie, William
Hatter, Thomas
Helsby, Edward
Hilton, Evan

*Wigan*, cont.
Hindley, Henry
Holgate, William
Holt, Matthew, I & II
Holt, William
Houghton, Richard
Houghton, S.
Houghton, T.
Howard, Henry
Johnson, Charles
Kennedy, Thomas
Kingsley, William
Latham, John
Lawson, Henry
Lawson, John
Lawson, Ramsay
Leadbetter, Charles
Leadbetter, William
  & Timothy
Leicester, Lawrence

Leigh, Peter
Lloyd, Joseph
Martin, Thomas,
  I & II
Mears, H.
Milner, R.
Milner, Thomas
Nelson, Stephen
Newall, John
Platt, Oliver
Probert, James
Rawson & Royle
Rose, Henry
Rose, Thomas, I & II
Royle & Rawson
Scarron, James
Seddon, John
Sharrocks, Henry
Sherratt, J.
Skirrow, James

Smith, Thomas
Stubler, Joseph
Taylor, John
Walker, James
Watmough, William
Wiggan, William
Williamson, Samuel
Winstanley, Abraham
Winstanley, Alexander
Winstanley, Edward
Winstanley, James
Winstanley, William
Woods, M.

*Windle*
Clark, Thomas

*Yatebank*
Andrews, Nathan
Yates, William

# FURTHER READING

Some of the following books may interest readers wishing to go further into horology. These are mostly modern books, which generally present a more correct interpretation of the subject than certain older ones.

Ashton, T. S. *An Eighteenth Century Industrialist* (Peter Stubs of Warrington, 1756–1806), Manchester, 1939 (reprinted 1961)

Beeson, C. F. C. *Clockmaking in Oxfordshire*, 1967

Bellchambers, J. K. *Somerset Clockmakers*, 1968

———. *Devonshire Clockmakers*, Torquay, 1962

Bird, A. *English House Clocks*, Newton Abbot, 1973

Bruton, E. *The Longcase Clock*, 1964

Edwardes, E. L. *The Grandfather Clock*, Altrincham, 1971

———. *Weight-driven Chamber Clocks of the Middle Ages*, Altrincham, 1965

Goodison, N. *Gillow's Clock Cases*, 1968

Loomes, B. *The White Dial Clock*, Newton Abbot, 1974

———. *Westmorland Clockmakers*, Newton Abbot, 1974

———. *Yorkshire Clockmakers*, Clapham, Yorks, 1972

Mason, B. *Clock and Watch Making in Colchester*, 1969

Miles-Brown, H. *Cornish Clocks and Clockmakers*, Newton Abbot, 1970

Roberts, K. D. *The Contribution of Joseph Ives to Connecticut Clock Technology*, Bristol, Conn., 1970

Simpson, Brevet-Col Stephen, *The Simpson Family*, 1922

Symonds, R. W. *Thomas Tompion*, 1969 reprint

Tyler, E. J. *European Clocks*, 1968

———. *The Craft of the Clockmaker*, 1973

# INDEX